BONZA VOYAGE

The Story of an Epic Gap Year Down Under

This edition, 2008

Copyright © John Watters, 2008
All rights reserved
The moral right of the author has been asserted

First published in Great Britain in 2008 by
Lulu Publishing Company
London

ISBN 9781409206309

First Edition

No part of this may be reproduced or transmitted in any form or by any other means without permission in writing from the author, except by a reviewer who wishes to quote brief passages in connection with a review written for insertion in a magazine, newspaper or broadcast.

For Mum, Dad and Kathryn. Your encouragement was endless and invaluable.
And Emma, who kept me laughing all the way.

I dedicate this book to you.

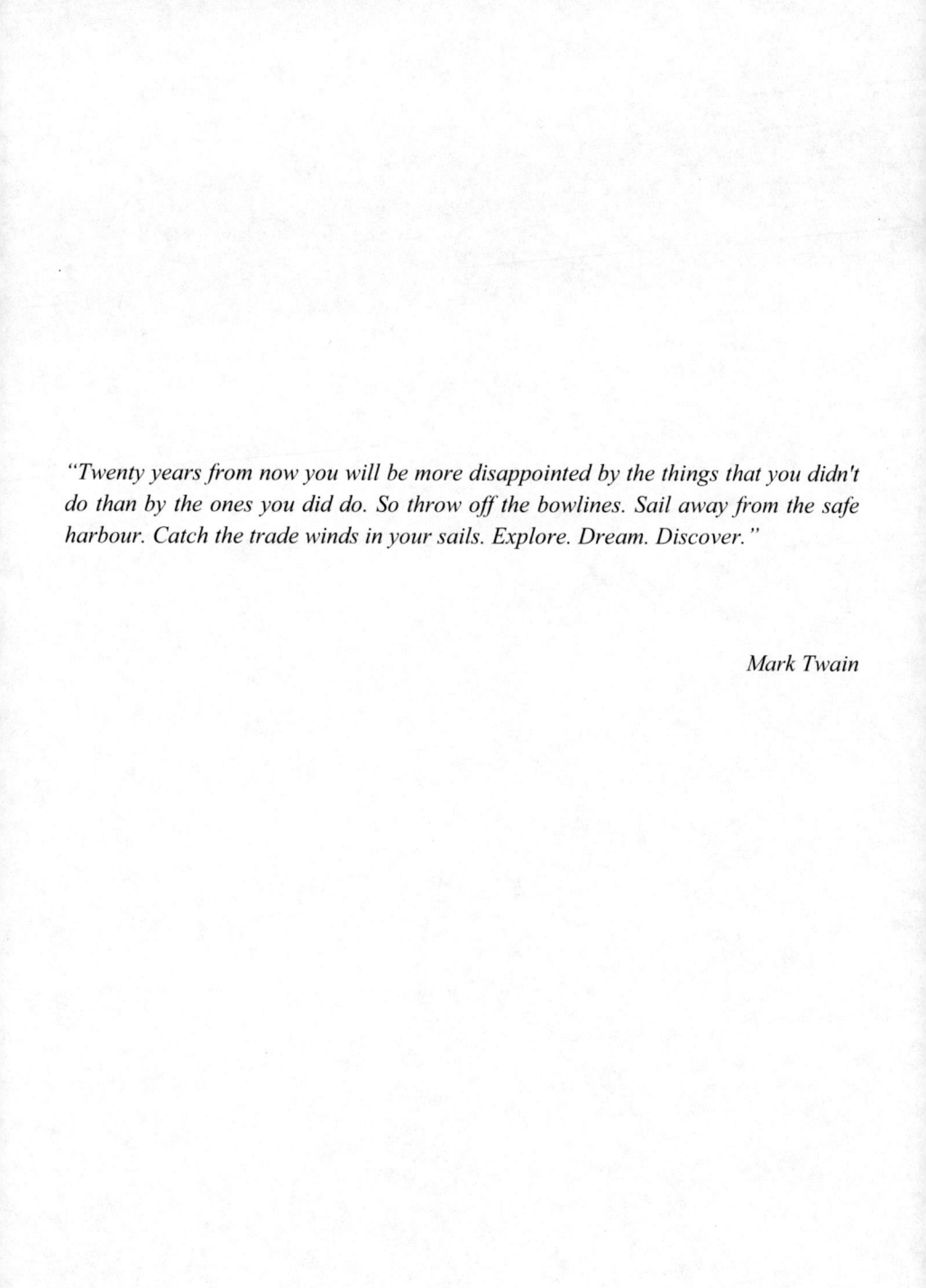

"Twenty years from now you will be more disappointed by the things that you didn't do than by the ones you did do. So throw off the bowlines. Sail away from the safe harbour. Catch the trade winds in your sails. Explore. Dream. Discover."

Mark Twain

www.bonzavoyage.blogspot.com

AUTHOR'S PREFACE

I have been reliably informed by my parents that back in *their* day there was no such thing as a 'gap year'. But then, back in their day there was no such thing as the internet, inflatable furniture or rotating washing lines. Do we really want to go back to such a primitive age? In fact, when they were growing up smoking was being promoted as 'good for your health' and doctors actively encouraged parents to feed their new-born children whiskey in order to help them sleep.

Of course though, the damage caused by this is laughable compared to the sinful delaying tactics used by gap year students in order to try and avoid the inevitable, harsh realities posed by the working world. Perhaps they are right - after all, as a very wise man once said *"the youth of today now love luxury; they have bad manners, contempt for authority; they allow disrespect for elders and love chatter in place of exercise. They now are tyrants."* And who was this wise man? The great Socrates in 400BC.

My point is that the youth generation have *always* been criticized for the changes they make to society and gap years are merely the latest victim. Unfortunately, the term is used so loosely that its merits will always be up for debate and I doubt whether a universal conclusion will ever be reached.

Are they a waste of time or do they provide an essential tool in young adult development? For me it was definitely the latter as I did not see it as an excuse to avoid work but instead a rare opportunity to experience a diverse culture, enjoy a proud heritage and search for acceptance. But I am not here to preach - I am here to tell you about my adventure and then hopefully you can make your own mind up. This is Bonza Voyage - the story of my gap year in Australia.

John Watters
May 2008

INTRODUCTION

Why do they call it 'culture shock'? You see, to me this seems to suggest that upon contracting it you will cower in the nearest corner, grab your ears for dear life and then rock uncontrollably back and forth. As I stood in the centre of Sydney on this first night though, nothing dramatic like that really happened. It was unfamiliar of course, but this was just a minor concern compared to my overpowering sense of excitement. I was a nineteen year old, as far away from my family and friends as is physically possible with the exception of New Zealand or The Moon. That thought alone should have been enough to shock me, but I suppose naivety has its advantages after all.

    Even at this early stage though, it hadn't been a completely easy ride. In fact, as the flight began its descent towards the antipodean tarmac, I positively hated the place. The reason for this was twofold: firstly, upon seeing the seatbelt sign illuminate, each of the air stewards on the flight suspiciously made their way to a room at the back of the aircraft. Not only was this slightly disconcerting, but they very rudely evaded my enquiry concerning the possibility of acquiring another glass of beer. To the shock of the passengers surrounding me, they then emerged wearing what can I only be described as primitive, fabric gas masks – but gas masks nonetheless –

and armed to the teeth with canisters of a somewhat sinister looking substance. Now, I am no flying expert but this twist was slightly unexpected to say the least. I mean, I knew I was a quite sweaty but taking industrial action against me seemed a little extreme. After all, I had been under the impression that the seatbelt sign was a safety measure designed for your own well-being, not a devilishly, sophisticated snare to restrict tourists' protests as they were disinfected against their will. The steward's claim that the gas was 'in no way dangerous' seemed ever so slightly ironic coming from a man wearing a highly cautious and protective mask. It's like a man in a space suit bearing a skull-and-crossbones badge dunking a uranium rod in your tea and telling you to drink up before it gets cold.

So I was angry at Australia for this and we hadn't even touched ground yet. Nevertheless, being a calm sort of person (and since the on-board entertainment had been turned off) I tried to distract my attention and duly reached into my bag for some light reading. Prior to departure my mother had collected a couple of newspaper cuttings concerning Australia she thought I might find interesting. Now, if you can, please try to imagine my expression when, coughing violently having just been sprayed by some kind of mystery potion my eyes see the headline 'Croc Shows Off Man's Body to Friends'. Basically I had flown twenty-six hours to a country where they clean you up like a salad before throwing you to a very cruel death. What a marvellous place.

Upon meeting the people though, my impression instantly changed, for not only did they smile continuously, but they seemed genuinely thrilled that you had chosen their country over all the others for your trip. With enviously brown skin and blindingly white teeth, everyone would greet you with an enthusiasm that could only be achieved by someone benefiting immensely from an incredibly healthy lifestyle. Either that or I had obliviously stumbled into a *Laboratoire Garnier* factory. These were but a few of many observations I made walking through the streets of Sydney on this first evening.

With the rest of the *World Challenge* group, I had just finished my first authentic Australian meal at a small Italian restaurant. It was bizarre to think that just forty hours ago I had been enjoying a relaxing final dinner with my family and an emotional farewell at Heathrow. Now, I was walking through a maze of skyscrapers with such an overpowering presence I felt scared to even peer skywards and attempt to gauge their size. They truly were a daunting sight and I still find it difficult to believe man can achieve such a sensational feat.

There were five of us in total, all too thrilled to sleep and determined to lap up the vibrant atmosphere surrounding the city. We had only known each other for a few hours, however there was still a strong sense of unity within the group. Thinking about it though, I suppose it had been relatively forced upon us. I don't say that in order to offend these people, more to stress that our friendships had not been developed through choice, but more through the lack of it. Nevertheless, a bond we had and this proved to be an essential tool in passing this initial and potentially overwhelming stage in my journey.

After about ten minutes of walking at a truly jetlagged pace I began to study the unfamiliar street signs- George Street, Pitt Street, Elizabeth Street. These names all seemed quite original now, but over the coming months I would soon realize how common they were in every Australian city, town, village or small inbred ranch. The creativity was so limited in fact, that whenever there were more than three streets that required naming, the town council would quite often resort to the highly inventive 'Little George Street' and, you guessed it 'Little Elizabeth Street'.

Fortunately for you readers, my attention was suddenly grabbed by something far more exciting – an oasis in the middle of the concrete city. In front of us stood Hyde Park - a huge area of beautiful green wilderness, exquisite walkways and marvellous fountains. Exploration seemed to be the theme for the evening and so a short detour seemed quite justified. Immediately I became fascinated as we studied (but kept our distance) the abundance of bright, tropical plant life and the reality that I was right in the middle of a major city soon faded. However, having selected a book entitled *'Australia's Dangerous Creatures'* as my pre-departure entertainment, I was only too aware of the dangers facing an unsuspecting tourist in the bushes and so kept myself on the footpath. The others seemed all together less concerned as they ventured through the undergrowth with me shouting red back spider warnings like an overprotective parent. This book seemed to have left me with some kind of psychological scarring as beads of sweat would drip uncontrollably down my forehead with every tiny noise from the bushes. Then right on cue, with the others mocking my over-cautious nature, the world's largest cockroach ran from the bushes, arrogantly through my legs and then scuttled off into a neighbouring shrub. Almost instantly we came to the unanimous decision that nature exploration should probably be left for another night.

Elizabeth Street, like many others in the city, is perfectly straight and easy to follow. We had been informed by our guide to 'just stick to that street for a few minutes and you'll get there eventually'. Obviously we had taken a slight detour into the park, but this surely couldn't have increased the journey length by thirty minutes could it? My first and probably most important lesson about this country had just been learnt - the phrase 'a few minutes' is applied so loosely it is relatively meaningless and can range from 'thirty minutes' to 'three days'. It never actually means a few minutes though.

We therefore had a lot more walking to do than was originally envisaged, but it gave us all a great opportunity to experience this fantastic city and bond with each other further (although not in the literal sense). From a personal perspective, it was difficult to explain how strange and alien this world seemed especially having come from a countryside village in rural Northamptonshire, but I got the impression this feeling was fairly mutual throughout the group. None of us had been in this situation before - while at home we had desired it, prepared for it and yet we were still overwhelmed now it had arrived. But with this, we indulged in a great sense of irrepressible excitement as we discussed just how surreal the situation seemed.

Soon, the retail outlets started to fade and were being replaced by bars, hotels and large entertainment squares full of luxurious fountains and benches. In truth, the number of water features was somewhat uncanny as I began to get worried I had landed in some kind of revolutionary fountain invasion. I had to hand it to the Aussies though as this place was certainly tranquil and the cleanliness unquestionable. Where was the litter and chewing gum that marred the streets of London? This was a new age city - a new age *clean* city. Of all the adjectives that exist, I didn't believe I would ever use 'clean' to describe a city, but it was. Don't get me wrong, I'm not saying that the floor was exactly attractive or lickable, I couldn't even see my reflection in it, but in comparison to other street floors it certainly rated very highly.

Conscious of time – after all I had been awake for the past two days thanks to the B.O ridden, fat German man sitting next to me on the plane – I started weaving my way through traffic in order to avoid the frustratingly slow walking pedestrians. To make matters worse a severe lack of roundabouts meant this skill had to be deployed far more frequently than one would care to imagine. Having arrived at our sixty-eighth pedestrian crossing, I was feeling more than confident about my traffic dodging capabilities and majestically swept between a Mercedes and white taxi without breaking sweat. On this occasion though, this feeling of success was short lived, for above my head I suddenly heard a loud 'whooshing' noise. I couldn't tell what exactly it was - but it was obviously moving towards me at very high speed as the ground beneath my feet began to vibrate. I tilted my head very cautiously, but at exactly the wrong moment and duly received a face full of ice cold, muddy water. This was my introduction to The Sydney Monorail - the flying car that explores the city at a leisurely pace and, when it's been raining, flushes gallons of water off its tracks onto unsuspecting victims. An event so hilariously unsubtle in its execution, it caused a homeless man to stop playing his recorder in order to have a quick chuckle at my misfortune. He soon realized however that we may be a good source of potential income so got straight back to playing his instrument in attempt to woo us with his charm. The wretched sound was simply awful. Next to him though there was a sign saying 'At least I'm giving it a go!'. That alone was worth fifty cents for its comedy value, although I would immediately regret the decision as it gave him a sudden burst of renewed enthusiasm and, as a result, volume.

We rounded another stone pillar, hopeful that it would prove to be our final obstruction. It was. I was now standing in a glorious postcard facing a remarkable scene that every human recognises, but very few have actually experienced in the flesh. Like meeting a famous person, I felt so strangely familiar with the situation yet curiously lost. Lost for words certainly, as I stood back and absorbed the immense magnitude of the view in front of my eyes. Is it the finest known to man? It is undoubtedly spectacular and truly ranks highly in the 'breathtaking' awards. The date was January 27th and it suddenly hit me that I was standing in the exact spot where Australian civilization began some 216 years and 1 day ago. Of course Port Jackson has changed a lot since then and it was hard to imagine how it would've looked for the seven hundred and fifty or so prisoners as they jumped off their lime-infested boat. I imagine if Britain were to send another ship full of convicts now, they would simply dance as they realized what fate had so kindly dished out to them. I was standing in Circular Quay surrounded by lively street bars and restaurants, looking at Sydney Opera House and The Harbour Bridge lighting up the night sky in all their angelic glory. With the exception of riding across the outback on a kangaroo whilst wearing a large cork hat and drinking a schooner of *'Fosters'*, is there anything that says 'I'm in Australia!' more? Not as far as I'm concerned and at that moment it hit me, I had done it, it had begun, I had made it to Australia.

PART 1

CHAPTER 1

I was once asked 'why do you want to take a gap year?'. It was a curious question so instead of providing an instantaneous answer, I decided to give it the careful consideration it deserved. Initially, I wanted to say 'look *mate*, I have been working six-hour days at school for the past fourteen years and with only twelve weeks annual leave, surely I deserve a year off to relax?' However, convinced that this would not be accepted as reason enough to merely desert my much defined academic path, I started thinking deeper for a more credible answer. I could lie and say that I came up with a spectacularly profound one, but the truth is that I didn't. Is this answer not sincere enough though? Like thousands of others, I just wanted to escape the standard routine of which I had found myself become a part and try to inject a little excitement into my life.

To be honest, I can't even remember the moment when I decided to take a year out, so I think it is just as accurate to say that the gap year chose me. In reality, most people don't necessarily make a conscious decision to have a year abroad – it is a self-selecting process in which those who possess a large degree of determination and ambition whilst thinking in an innovative, revolutionary way will inevitably embark on. Due to their unique way of thinking, those who enjoy these qualities in abundance will not simply settle for a life dominated by work, mortgages and children. They will seek something greater. Regrettably, this can prove rather difficult as the structure of the education system in Britain is designed to promote a philosophy that serves only to crush these creative aspirations.

I often remember sitting at school and being told if you try hard and succeed with your A-levels, then you're basically made for life. I was subjected to that talk so many times that my gap year just seemed like an inconsequential break before continuing along the expected academic route and leading a comfortable, normal life. However, during my final year, an old, wise saying continually made me reconsider my future dreams - *'life's a bitch and then you die'*. Obviously, this was always presented in a comical sense but I slowly began to realise there were elements of truth in it for a huge majority of society. The way humans can seemingly keep their spirits high through the torrid slog of life is to set themselves small, achievable targets. Poor, under-appreciated school children always think to themselves *'not to worry, things will get better when I get a job'*. Little do they know that in a cruel twist of fate, when a career is eventually embarked upon they will look back fondly on those memories of school with one thought in their mind *'not to worry, things will get better when I retire'*. The 'grass being greener' springs to mind as this vicious circle of dejection continues to revolve with no obvious end.

Does it not seem pointlessly depressing that the sole purpose of the education system is to prepare us for life in the workplace? As this truth slowly revealed itself to me, my desire to escape it did the same and I pledged not to squander my one chance at a more exciting life. Too often I had sat listening to the mundane mess of fundamentally worthless information being thrown at us during sociology class. You would've thought if they were going to make up a subject for the hell of it, they could've at least made it slightly interesting. I suggest they introduce a module on 'Dragon Slaying' or 'Leprechaun Hunting' as it would be far more entertaining and probably prove just as useful in later life. Not that I'm being overly negative you understand, I was merely frustrated to have wasted so much time on a subject which effectively serves no purpose whatsoever - in fact, if it ceased to exist the only noticeable difference to the world would be the increased number of students enrolling for politics and

English literature courses. Is this a slightly negative way to start a book? Oh well, things can only improve from this point forward.

So I had decided to break away from formal education and venture onto unknown pastures. The first logical step was actually deciding where I was going to go. Conscious not to fall into the tourist trap, I came to the conclusion that wherever I ended up going, I wanted to try and become a part of their society and sample the culture firsthand. This meant getting some sort of job, which in turn required me to have a reasonable understanding of the native language. Unfortunately for me, God had obviously been out drinking the night before constructing my brain and had quite clumsily forgotten to add the linguistics part. As I'm sure you can imagine, this was rather frustrating when taking my GCSE French but it did nonetheless allow me to narrow the search.

To further reduce my options I began reading literature concerning the main candidates on my list in order to establish which nation would best fit my needs. Of course they all had their advantages, but many had far more disadvantages than I could possibly cope with. For example, in America the legal drinking age is apparently twenty-one and although I wanted to experience another diverse culture, I sure as hell didn't want to do it sober. Plus I'd also heard that the size of the food portions could be awfully intimidating if you weren't under the influence of some type of sedative. I was a huge fan of food, but I was not too keen on the idea of obesity and the prospect of turning my internal organs into something resembling pâte was not an appealing one.

Thankfully, just as all hope was evaporating a country came to my rescue – a country whose social foundations had been built upon a love for sport, attractive women and lots of beer. Alas, I had not entered one of George Best's sordid dreams but had in fact found the land of Australia. Granted, there were a few setbacks with it harbouring the ten most lethal snakes on the planet, however this merely added to its enchanting, mysterious qualities. As quickly as that, my decision had been made and soon I would be packing my bags for the land Down Under.

First of all though, I felt it necessary to conduct a full historical, geographical and zoological assessment before committing my future. After all, you wouldn't move in with someone for a year without establishing whether or not they had a psychopathic past or a pet lion. Thankfully, what I found would only serve to heighten my curiosity and excitement.

Just through studying some basic facts, I immediately discovered that this wonderful country possesses an awesome array of statistics. For example, at 3700km long and 4000km wide it is the largest and most isolated island on Earth. If I can just put this in perspective for you, imagine travelling non-stop between Edinburgh and London six times, then add forty-degree heat along with a vast range of homicidal wildlife and you have just about crossed Australia.

As a consequence of this mammoth size, the country suffers from three major types of climate with tropics in the north, a desert in the middle and a relaxed maritime environment towards the south. The current population is estimated at about twenty million, which is around a third of Britain's. This however does not paint the whole story as, quite sensibly, a majority of these only reside in major cities, consequently leaving about 98% of the country essentially deserted. To put it bluntly, Australia is in essence very big but very empty, at least in terms of its human population. If you get lost, which is likely, then you truly are the most buggered anyone can ever be.

If of course you do manage to survive this barren desert and unbearable heat, the chances are your high spirits will become a somewhat lovely distant memory as the country's diverse collection of killer wildlife begins to nibble at your shoes. Believe me, there is not another place on Earth that boasts such a terrifying assortment of animals. For example, Australians have at their disposal, an abundant supply of great white sharks, crocodiles, funnel-web spiders, red-back spiders, the ten deadliest snakes in the world and the kangaroo (which I have heard on good authority can give you a nasty kick if you dare get too close). That, my friends, is quite an impressive arsenal I think you'll agree. And I haven't even mentioned the box jellyfish – otherwise known as the most poisonous creature on Earth - which lives in great quantity along the Queensland coast. In short, Australia is a country of enormous size packed full of creatures that actively seek human prey, but is depressingly void of any human assistance should you (God forbid) ever get a little 'nip' from a spider whilst out on a countryside walk. Essentially, Australia is a real-life *Jurassic Park* where humans are very much at the bottom of the food chain.

But why does Australia differ so greatly from the rest of the continents? Well, from the time it broke away from Pangaea, like an overeager dog, some 150 million years ago, the continent remained relatively untouched. Protected on all four sides by ferocious seas, the wildlife was left to simply flourish. Without any human interference, the country essentially became an extreme science experiment in which every animal was left to follow its own unique, evolutionary path. Evidently, this has produced some quite startling results.

Having been discovered in 1770, this garden of spectacular growth was finally revealed to the world, but the country didn't (as you may have expected) develop in a conventional fashion. In contrast, its short three hundred year history is somewhat colourful to say the least. However, I was first interested in how this colossal piece of earth had remained hidden for all these years. I mean come on guys, this isn't a question of finding a needle in a haystack - it's more like trying to find an elephant in your back garden. Some three hundred years prior to Captain Cook's famous voyage, scientists had predicted the country's existence purely on the basis that it made the continental distribution throughout the world seem slightly more even. So its existence had been theoretically predicted, yet it took an incredibly long time before this hunch was confirmed by Cook and his men.

This is not to say that other explorers did not come close, alas, many came a lot closer than they would ever know. A classic example of this was the Dutch explorer Abel Tasman, who in 1642 set off in his quest to discover the fabled 'South Land'. Unfortunately and quite unbelievably, he sailed right past Australia without even giving it a second glance before finally settling on a small island just 240km off its southern coast which he named Van Diemen's Land and that is now known as Tasmania. Without realising his beloved prize was located just across the horizon, Tasman dusted himself off, accepted defeat and sailed off into the east without ever noticing that the largest island in the world was so temptingly close. By definition, I believe this makes Tasman the unluckiest man in history. It's like travelling twelve-thousand miles in a quest to discover England, landing on the Isle of Wight, then simply giving up and going home.

Forget trying to find the elephant in your garden, this is like being struck in the face by its trunk and still not realising it's there. Even if he had given up but left in a vaguely northern direction, he would've certainly noticed (if not smashed into) the Victorian coastline and happily constructed his windmill. Sadly for him though, as is so often the case when you're the unluckiest man in the world, he simply sailed on by without a second glance as his passage into the history books slowly faded into a sea of missed opportunities.

Throughout the proceeding years many more explorers tried desperately to find Australia, but all failed in pretty spectacular fashion before Captain James Cook, the son of a farmer from Marton, North Yorkshire stepped in to save the day. Agreed, it is an unlikely source for such a formidable figure, but history seems to have a habit of producing the unexpected.

As part of a global science experiment, Cook, like many other explorers, had been sent across the world in order to gather important astronomical data from the transit of Venus. Conducting this from Tahiti, I doubt whether he was particularly enthralled by the prospect, but it did nonetheless allow him to explore the mysterious Southern Pacific oceans after.

In his ranks was an elite selection of fine scientists and sailors so any new discoveries could be analysed with expert precision. As a result, I imagine there was a great deal of excitement amongst the crew when they first spotted the south east corner of the Australian coast and built up speed towards its shores. And what a nice little bundle of joy they had waiting for them! Not only did every single animal try to kill them, the native Aboriginal people threw spears at their boats and although they were undoubtedly fascinated by the incredible array of diverse nature, the welcome wasn't exactly the warmest, so the boat set out for sea again.

Heading north, Cook and his crew then followed the shoreline which allowed them to map a quarter of the country and complete the first ever east coast tour. Little did they know that three hundred years later, young adults from around the globe would follow their pioneering foot-steps on a daily basis and although their adventures are filled with a certain sense of drunken inevitability, they are nevertheless still just as exciting. I mean no disrespect to Cook's amazing achievement by comparing it to an all-inclusive holiday in Ibiza, but would merely like to point out the irony that such an historic voyage is now idolised by a group of people who, all in all, are considered slightly less remarkable. I too would become one of these pilgrims, but not until later in this trip. Anyway, having established that Australia was indeed massive and narrowly escaping a close run-in with The Great Barrier Reef, the HMS Endeavour turned back cautiously and finally came to a halt at Botany Bay near Sydney.

So Cook had discovered the fabled South Land and on 21st August 1770 Australia officially joined the British Empire's vast collection of far away countries never to be spoken about again. The term 'discovered' should of course be used with caution in this instance - after all it seems slightly strange to suggest somewhere has just been discovered if there are already natives thriving on it, as the Aborigines were. In addition, there is some strong historic evidence suggesting that Dutch explorers used the northwest corner as a nautical service station some one hundred and fifty years prior to The Endeavour's famous voyage. Taking all this into consideration, it seems Cook didn't so much discover Australia (he wasn't even the first European to step foot on its shores), but was just the first to come home and shout about it.

  Surprisingly though, nobody really took much notice of him and the country was left to wilt like an unappreciated flower in the far corner of a greenhouse. To be perfectly honest though, this is quite understandable. After all, with such a huge empire at your disposal, why worry about some barren land which takes the best part of a year to get to? It had remained hidden from the world for the past few million years, so there was nothing to suggest it would have a sudden influx of tourists any time in the near future.

  However, following a gruelling defeat in America, Britain lost its colony and with it, the largest prison at its disposal. Since you could be arrested for just about anything in those days, the country soon became over-run with convicts and with nowhere left to send them, the government struggled to find a suitable solution. With all options seemingly running out, some bright spark suddenly remembered a distant land James Cook had mentioned seventeen years before.

  Finally, the forgotten country would be put to some use. Granted, it was as a prison but this decision marked a decisive moment in Australia's short, illustrious life. You have to hand it to the British leaders though - I mean, putting everyone from their '700 most wanted list' into a large boat and sending them as far away as is humanly possible to a relatively unknown, sterile land is a simply brilliant idea and one I would strongly encourage our government of today to consider.

As the British soon realised however, sending convicts to start a new colony can be somewhat of a tricky ordeal. For starters, the only real skill any of them actually possessed was stealing and, since they had all been caught, it appears they hadn't exactly perfected that either. With a severe lack of natural survival skills the new settlers immediately found the barren land to be even more hostile than the eight-month sea journey they had just faced. Indeed, the most dangerous creature any of them had previously encountered was the wasp, so they weren't really accustomed to working in an environment riddled with king brown snakes.

Since convicts aren't entirely famed for their agreeable nature either, I can't imagine the town planning meetings were particularly productive affairs. As a consequence, I think it's fair to say that the development of this new world got off to a somewhat stuttering start and after only one year the homestead was abandoned leaving western life in the southern hemisphere looking bleak. However, if I were to take you to that very spot today, we would be standing directly in the middle of one of the most prestigious and glorious cities this world has to offer. For these settlers were not just any settlers – they were the first residents of the marvellous miracle we now call Sydney.

It seems difficult to believe that the country could undergo such a rapid development in such a short space of time, but this achievement is made all the more impressive when you consider that Australia remained a prison for about one hundred years. Essentially, being sent there was seen as an undesirable lifetime infliction which everyone was desperate to avoid.

But then, on April 7th 1851 its fortunes (and those for most of its residents) changed forever. Now, people were no longer sent to Australia by a judge but came flooding willingly in their hoards as the country was transformed instantly from a disagreeable, snake-infested island to a land of wealthy opportunity. This was all thanks to Edward Hargraves who discovered that, not only did Australia have a little bit of gold scattered across its surface - it was pretty much bathing in the stuff. From that day forth, migrants stormed to the south pacific from all around the world with a pickaxe in one hand and a bucket for their cash in the other. Mining communities were being built on a daily basis as this once uninhabitable country began its swift transition into the civilised world.

Out of all the states, it was Victoria in particular that got the most attention with Melbourne's population rising from 75,000 to approximately 500,000 in the ten years proceeding 1851 in light of its somewhat healthy financial situation. Such was the interest in this emerging city, it attracted businessman and scientists alike with the Melbourne telescope being commissioned and completed as early as 1868. Unfortunately though, technology was not quite so advanced in Australia so the huge mirror had to be shipped from Europe only to discover on arrival that it had a large crack right down the centre. Not to be disgruntled by this minor mishap, another was sent out, but since the project was already running over budget, the commissioners decided to cut funding before the dome of the telescope could be completed. As any amateur astronomer will tell you, this effectively rendered the piece of equipment useless as any slight breeze larger than a mouse cough would severely distort the image of the celestial body being tracked. Still, although this may have proven to be a disaster (and an expensive one at that) it does nevertheless demonstrate that Australia was quickly rising from its swampy origins and developing into a society rich in wealth, spirit and academia.

This trend of intensive migration is still being followed today. For example, a poll during 2000 found that only 4.5 million (not quite a quarter) of the country's residents were actually Australian born. Far from annoy the inhabitants however, they are in fact incredibly proud of this fact as it represents the foundations on which their great nation was built. Without this influx of citizens, their country may not have survived the savage British regime, but is now prospering in its diverse, cosmopolitan and multi-cultural society.

CHAPTER 2

There is much more to discuss about the history of Australia, but I fear I am boring those of you who are not history buffs so I shall therefore continue with my story. After all, it's a far more exciting tale anyway. So, I now knew where I wanted to go and the next big decision was identifying whom I should travel with. For no other reason than I didn't particularly fancy turning myself insane (at least, not just yet) through severe isolation and loneliness, I decided that it was essential to find a travel companion. Surprisingly, none of my friends were very keen on the idea or simply lacked the confidence to escape society's dull expectations. Therefore, I was left with no choice but to find a company that specialised in gap year expeditions.

Having typed 'gap year company' into a search engine however, I was astonished by the sheer volume of websites offering their services. Ultimately, choosing one was an incredibly daunting prospect which I knew would shape the entire trip. Intimidated by the implications of such a decision, I did what every real man is famed for and simply ignored it for as long as possible before copying a friend of mine who was just returning from Tanzania. After all, it seemed reasonable to assume that *he* had done the research and I knew he wouldn't have chosen that company (*World*

Challenge) if they had been terrible. Their choice of Australian placements ranged from country stud-farm work to children's camp instructor and, since my only experience with a horse involved me being kicked in the head as a toddler, I opted for the camp placement. If offered a place, the total cost of the trip would be approximately £2000 which included return flights, a guaranteed work placement with food and accommodation for three months and the security of an in-country agent.

Although I was effectively paying to work, it provided me with a fantastic opportunity to interact and become part of an authentic Australian community, as well giving me the assurance that I was safe in a foreign land. Having completed my placement, my return ticket could be used anytime within the next year, leaving me free to conduct all the exploring possible. It all seemed ideal and as I filled out the application form on a cold December evening, I started getting a rush of excitement even though departure was still over a year away.

The following February I was asked to participate in a selection course weekend, but little did I realise the process was going to be far more rigorous than an SAS initiation. The last line of the letter should have provided a quite substantial warning: *'if you are driving home, please be aware that you will have limited sleep the night before'*, but I just thought they might be planning some sort of countryside rave for us all. Driving to Buxton in the Peak District though, I started looking through the material in detail and soon realised that a party was the last thing on their minds. This was a test of our abilities to perform in certain situations, usually demonstrated by completing some crazy, ridiculous tasks devised by old psychologists, with long white hair, hidden away in a dusty office full to the brim with books.

Upon arrival, I was pleasantly surprised to find the training centre positioned in beautiful settings overlooking a brilliantly sculpted, scenic valley. Like a patchwork quilt, the beautiful green fields were scattered with a few white sheep and divided by those tiny little walls that look as if they're on the verge of falling over, yet have survived for hundreds of years. On the opposite hill I noticed an odd grey-looking farmhouse with a broken tin roof and wondered whether or not is was derelict. Above all things, I think it is this modesty of the British countryside that makes it so appealing. It doesn't want fame or recognition, it simply just wants to be and it is that characteristic that makes me so very fond of it. I knew throughout the year I would see bigger and grander places, but would any be more humble and peaceful than this? The Peak District in particular is one of the most fabulous in England, mostly due to the crisp, fresh air that, upon sucking it in, seems to revitalise your pollution-filled lungs.

Walking into the centre, I was greeted warmly by the leaders and told to wait in the room next door as they made their final preparations for the course. Inside were fifty other people I had never seen before and who had congregated from all corners of the country. There was even one person who had travelled from an unidentified, small island by ferry, plane and car, making my journey seem a little amateurish in comparison.

The pre-course guidelines had specified that we should prepare a brief talk and after a few 'get to know you' games, we were asked to perform this to approximately ten others. It is understandable that many people do not posses enough self-confidence to stand up and talk for fifteen minutes, but to say the standard was low is somewhat of a generous understatement. I give credit to the organisers for having the confidence to let crazy teenagers conduct a talk on 'a subject of their choice' but couldn't help feel this extreme trust could well turn into a severe misjudgement. It did make the afternoon a tad more exciting though as I sat, eagerly anticipating a talk on 'techniques on getting rid of the infamous white-headed spot' and 'how to give your teacher a nervous breakdown'. The only thing I would get however was a case of brutal disappointment. I'm not sure how much time passed, but it certainly seemed like hours listening to talks entitled 'My Favourite Sport' and 'International Terrorism'

Thankfully, there was one guy who brought an end to this torrid case of abuse by providing a rather more exciting talk. The title was: 'Analysis of the Masterful and Ancient Art of Elastic Band Firing'. Contrary to the others, he actually entertained by demonstrating different firing techniques and rating them based on their accuracy, reliability and potential damage infliction. I actually found myself laughing so much that I couldn't breathe and almost let a surprisingly huge amount of dribble run down my chin, which had the potential to be very embarrassing. It would have been somewhat disheartening to get rejected from the course due to an inability to control my saliva. Anyway, his talk was marvellously enjoyable and, more importantly, original. I imagine he was on course for some very good marks until, just moments before the end, he announced that his planning for the talk had begun at 3am the previous morning having originally misread the criteria and thought it said *they* would provide us with a talk of *our* choice. As his marks for organisation slowly slipped away, we both agreed that this would have been a far better idea.

For the remainder of the day, we completed a series of tedious team building exercises in which the assessors found various ways of adjusting essentially the same task. It seems the dusty old psychologist believes blind-folding us and preventing us from speaking will improve our interpersonal skills. He's probably right – I mean if I ever find myself trying to cross a river whilst strapped to a one- legged, blind Frenchman, I'll know exactly what to do. Actually, thinking about it, if I were in that situation I would probably just toss myself into the flowing, lethal rapids.

The tasks were followed by an interview and, when complete, each group had to come up with a short sketch to perform before dinner. I suppose it was good practice for camp life, but I couldn't help feel I had gone back in time to my playschool days. Not to be defeated by humiliation, we decided to come up with the most random pile of rubbish we could and succeeded (even if I do say so myself) quite well. I won't go through the entire routine, but the climax involved one of our male members miraculously transforming into the domestic goddess Delia Smith. The voting was conducted by the leaders in such a way that we were made to feel like gymnasts or synchronized swimmers. Embarrassingly, we lost. Badly. Apparently the other groups were more inventive, but I ask you, what in the world is more inventive and original than turning an average man into Delia Smith and then cooking an invisible catfish?

I went to bed in a room occupied by around fifteen other guys. Evidently, my hope that the accommodation might be mixed was indeed very wishful. Most of the others were keen rugby players and, as a result I was concentrating on sleeping with one eye open. Only too aware of what their culture entailed, I didn't trust their antics, especially towards me – the vulnerable footballer.

Eventually though I heard their snores and knew it was safe to lose touch with realism and drift into a peaceful sleep. Then, suddenly I was rudely woken. BANG BANG BANG! What the hell?! Oh shit, it was one of the leaders. How he made so much noise with a frying pan and wooden spoon I don't know and at the time I didn't really care.

'GET DRESSED, OUTSIDE IN FIVE MINUTES' he shouted with unbelievable volume.

By the way, if anyone has recently lost their town crier, I have the perfect replacement. Looking at my watch, I noted that it was 1:30am. The temptation to take the frying pan and give him a bleeding nose was overwhelming, but I would have settled for simply poking him in the eye with the wooden spoon.

Half-asleep and yawning through exhaustion, we were subjected to a series of brutally mental, problem-solving tasks combined with a mile hike up what, during the day, looked like a relatively gentle sloping small hill, but at 2:30am had somehow transformed into the steepest mountain in Derbyshire. Stressed, tired and missing my lumpy bunk bed, the leaders put us through yet another series of mundane tasks which increased the challenge to stay awake ten-fold. Keeping my composure, I knew the judging wasn't over and so downed three litres of caffeine high energy drinks to try and increase my wilted spirits. Two hours later, having just completed a quiz and been told to go back to bed, the caffeine kicked in. Consequently, I lay awake staring wide-eyed at the ceiling and ready to take on the most challenging tasks they could throw at me.

Finally getting to sleep at about 5am, my relaxation was short lived as the town crier made yet another rousing appearance. Before we were allowed to tuck into breakfast however, we were required to solve Einstein's riddle – a problem which, in Einstein's own words *'98% of the population are unable to solve in their lifetime'*. Luckily, it had arrived in an e-mail addressed to me and I had completed it a month prior to this. Still, with eight people shouting out random, pointless and occasionally idiotic comments, it soon became more impossible than even Einstein could have imagined. The elastic band boy and I took charge and we eventually solved the problem after forty-five minutes of the most frustrating hell imaginable. When I saw breakfast, I soon began to wish that we had failed.

The military training eventually came to an end that afternoon following an hour long photo presentation from other student's gap programs. I suppose it was designed to 'whet our appetite' and I'm sure it would have if I hadn't slept for fifty-nine minutes of it.

A few days later I received my acceptance letter and free t-shirt in the morning post. The only sour point was that two days later, they sent me my first invoice. Nevertheless, I was invited back to Buxton for a skills-training course and so, five months later, found myself back on the road to The Peak District. This was rather relieving as, up until this point I had no idea where I was going or what exactly I would be doing when I arrived. Another relieving factor was that the general structure of the course gave it a far more relaxed atmosphere as our late night hike got replaced by a late night pub visit. Basically, it provided a great basis to get to know all the others with whom I'd be travelling and, since I didn't want to gouge anyone's eyes out, I considered this exercise to be relatively successful.

We were also given the opportunity to fire as many questions as is humanly possible at a young lady who had just returned from Australia. Up until this point, the *World Challenge* leaders had been somewhat vague with some of the specific details concerning our trip, but this girl was nice and honest. The keyword she used when describing our impending future was 'flexibility'. Of course, this is yet again another general term that can be used to describe fundamentally anything, so I enquired further.
'Remember guys – you are going there as an employee so you will be expected to work and work hard. Some jobs will be absolutely horrible in fact, but without putting in this hard graft you will never really appreciate where you are' she said fondly and although I couldn't really grasp exactly what she meant, I interpreted it as 'you won't fully appreciate Australia until you've cleaned out a toilet'. This seemed a little odd so I decided to listen on.
'When you get actively involved in all parts of camp life with the other leaders you will feel a really strong sense of community and this will make the experience far more rewarding. Go there with an open mind and so many possibilities will present themselves'.
I still wasn't sure if I was going to be asked to clean out a toilet, but things seemed a little more promising after this motivating (albeit slightly vague) speech.

We completed a basic first aid course the next day which was quite amusing not just because we were effectively kissing a rubber dummy, but because an incredibly annoying girl announced to the group that she believed humans could hold their breath for thirty minutes. I shall repeat that – thirty *minutes*, not seconds. She was subsequently quite bewildered as to why there was so much emphasis on unblocking an unconscious person's airway. Having suggested that I stick her head under water to test her theory, she soon backed down and we continued learning some more basic training. With the prospect of working with large groups of children, I saw this as quite an essential skill although they never did tell us how to cope with a snake bite or shark attack. Still, one can't complain and I was just grateful my first aid experience was no longer at the bottom of the scale.

Following a camp style lunch of burger and chips, the course came to an end as we exchanged e-mail addresses and then left. It was quite daunting to think the next time I would see these people would be at Heathrow. It had been quite a pleasant experience and having chatted to someone who had gone through the experience did calm my nerves slightly, but I still didn't even know where in Australia I was going. Should I be packing a raincoat or some flowery Caribbean shorts? A surfboard or a snowboard? These were all essential question and ones I still didn't have the answers to.

In fact, I didn't actually receive them until a month prior to departure. It was in the form of an e—mail from *World Challenge's* in-country agent Thea O'Sullivan. To my surprise, only six people had been given a placement in Victoria and thankfully I was one of them. This wasn't because I didn't want to be in New South Wales, but more because of Victoria's position in this huge country. You see, since it is at the extreme south this meant I could explore it fully during my days off then head north to Sydney and up the east coast for some relax time once my placement was finished. The camp name was 'Licola' and was located right on the edge of the 'Alpine National Park' in eastern Victoria. A mountainside community, it boasted that it had the beauty of the mountain regions but was conveniently located quite close to Melbourne. Maybe this was true in Australian terms, but 250kms in my view is not 'conveniently close', in fact, it's a 'bloody long way mate'. You would have thought that not being able to find Licola or any of the nearby towns on any maps would dampen my spirits and worry me, but in reality it just amplified the excitement of my adventure. The other challenger I had been placed with was a lad named Grant, whom I e-mailed immediately and was pleased to see we had quite a few things in common. It seemed that my Australian dream was slowly becoming a reality.

CHAPTER 3

I

All the way through the year finances were a huge issue, but not more so than the couple of months prior to departure. At this point in my life, money was going so quickly that I even resorted to putting my car into neutral while driving down hills in order to save fuel.

To cope with this, we had been encouraged on the selection course to write begging letters to various companies in an attempt to gain funds or potential sponsorship. That's all well and good for someone who is going to do a conservation project like 'save the rainforest' or teach young deprived children how to speak English goodly. But how do you send a letter to a company asking for them to pay so you can go and doss half way around the world on a youth, recreation camp? The answer is 'with no success at all'. In fact, out of the twelve letters I sent to adventure companies and climbing associations, only one had the decency to reply (even though it told to me to piss off and get my own bloody money, I still appreciated not being ignored) and so that line of scrounging seemed to be out.

The only solution I could come up with was conducting some sort of sponsorship event and, since I was full of youthful enthusiasm, this should have proved quite easy. Unfortunately, coming up with an idea proved far more difficult than I could have possibly imagined, so I turned to *World Challenge* for some inspiration.

I spoke to a very helpful lady on the phone who recalled an amazing story explaining how she solved the very same problem. I'm not entirely sure how this creation managed to manifest in her mind, but the idea is so inspirational I thought I would share it with you. Here goes nothing: Once-upon-a-time there was a 6th form student trying to raise money in order to fund a noble South American crusade. Her mission was to bring an end to deforestation, but if she was going to succeed in this quest, she was going to need financial help. Then, a crazy and potentially brilliant idea entered her mind. It was essentially the same as those 'buried treasure' grid games in which you place your name in a square and, if that is where the treasure is buried, you win yourself a packet of *'Fisherman Friends'* or something just as equally revolting and worthless. Searching for originality though, she eventually developed a very unique and somewhat unexpected twist. Having created a life- size grid across the school field, she ventured down to the local animal park for the piece-de-resistance. You see, she wasn't planning on burying any treasure as you might expect, but instead was looking for an animal that would urinate on her grid (so to speak). See, I told you there was an unexpected twist in store. Even more surprising however was her choice of animal – a camel. Now, this seemed like a curious decision to me as, in a game which relies not greatly but *completely* on an animal passing water, choosing one which by its very nature can go for simply weeks without doing so could present a big problem. In fact, the camel is specifically designed so that the thought of urination does not enter its mind for at least eighteen months after a drink. I didn't want this constructive criticism to be completely without reason and so I did some research on the internet (therefore it *must* be true) and it appears that camels can survive for up to ten days without drinking water and during this period, so as not to dehydrate, they do not sweat or urinate. There you have it, ten days is a very long time.

I don't know about you but I can envisage fifty or so enthusiastic kids standing gleefully, anticipating this marvellous act of nature and praying that they are victorious. Then, one and a half weeks later they are still sitting there, poised and ready, worried to blink in case they miss the event. When the camel eventually did its job, I wouldn't be surprised if it did it across two or three of the gird squares just to create a bit of controversy.

I tell you this story not as a humorous anecdote, but more to emphasise my incredible lack of creativity. You see, having failed to acquire a school field, a huge grid or a large exotic animal in the middle of rural Northamptonshire (I did set up a number of traps in nearby woods, but still to this day, success has eluded me) I settled on doing a sponsored run. Some of my friends had suggested I should take part in a 'sponsored leg wax' to which I replied 'okay' whilst giving them the finger.

Although the idea of a run was rather unoriginal to say the least, it would nonetheless allow me to shake off the mild case of obesity I had developed during 6th form and this could only be a positive. It also crossed my mind that being able to run fast would be a very handy skill in Australia, especially with the risk of stumbling upon a deadly, highly venomous and psychotic animal. Knowing my luck though, I would probably end up being mauled by the cutest little koala.

Conscious that my time would more than likely be incredibly slow, I didn't really fancy running a race against other competitors and so decided to plan my own course. Taking into account my fuel money situation as well, it seemed logical that the run should not only provide an interesting spectacle, but also be used as a means of transport. I therefore came to the conclusion that beginning at home and finishing at school would cover all these needs and, having measured the distance to be 9.6 miles, thought it was long enough to impress but was also quite achievable even for a novice such as myself.

So my training began and I started getting sponsors. Luckily for me, I was working in a local café at the time and one of our regulars was the editor of the local free newspaper - 'the only one man tabloid' I was told, although I haven't done enough research to back-up this claim. Thankfully, because of my excellent coffee pouring technique, he allowed me to do a small article in the paper advertising the run and accompanied by a photo of me looking sad, helpless and modelling my tatty running shoes. As a result, I think I was treated by the town as somewhat of a charity case but the money came flooding in nonetheless. Even my friends found it in their hearts to offer me money, though this was probably due to the fact that they couldn't envisage me making the finish line unaccompanied by a team of paramedics.

Determined not to be embarrassed in such a way, I got on my computer and planned a rigorous training regime for the six weeks leading to the actual event. Having printed it off and stuck it to my notice board, I stood back and admired my handy work before rewarding myself with a nice cool pint of lager and a double fingered *Twix*. This theme generally continued for the next three weeks as I realised sticking to the schedule would prove a lot more difficult than actually making it. Three weeks to go until the big day and I still hadn't managed to complete two miles without an hour long break in between.

Although the physical aspect was incredibly challenging, I found the mental side of things provided a much bigger hurdle. You see, my 1970s short shorts didn't have anywhere for me to store an MP3 player or miniature radio, so the training was effectively really boring. Therefore, pulling myself off the sofa for an event which was fundamentally painful and less interesting than Noel Edmonds choice of jumper design, required a huge amount of will power. To be honest, I simply didn't have any until I began to imagine the immense embarrassment I would feel if I didn't succeed, and this provided me with a slight motivational lift. With the pressure rising I began to make reasonable progress in my capabilities but, with the big day approaching, my school still seemed like a very distant mirage.

The night before, I suddenly realised a very basic flaw in my plan. You see, deciding to run to school is all well and good but I still had to be there for registration at 9am and consequently would have to leave my house ridiculously early. So, on the morning of the race I pulled myself out of bed at 6am ready for a breakfast of yoghurt and sugar.

Although the words of encouragement from my friends were overwhelming, my confidence had seemingly deserted me as I took those first tentative steps from my front door. I remember one message in particular from a friend of mine – it simply read 'good luck John, try not to die' which only went to increase my self-belief enormously.

With my elder brother accompanying as a support runner, we set off into the unknown, unwilling to speak for fear of using too much energy. After five miles, I passed the marker I had set two days before and had now run further than at any time previously in my life. I was nearly dead. I could hear my body screaming, trying to give up the information so the torture would stop, but it didn't.

After six miles I began coughing and spluttering and then a car emerged on the distant horizon as a group of my friends arrived to offer some much needed support. Between the coughing, I almost managed a gleeful smile as they followed me closely and subsequently caused a major traffic jam behind their vehicle. They were brilliant though, shouting amazing encouragement like 'come on John, only another mile to go......until you get to the end of the street' and 'God John, you're travelling so fast my speedometer is...not even registering a speed'. It was like being chased by the paparazzi and I loved every minute of it.

But then, after one hour and twenty-six minutes of hard out, celebrity status running, I turned into the home straight and a day of hard A-level lessons beckoned. To my pleasant surprise, all my peers had turned out collecting money for me and making a huge paper finish line, I only hoped I had enough energy to break through it. With all those people watching, I prayed not to fall over as, not only would it be embarrassing but, I was running down the centre of the road with my friends driving behind flashing their lights and sounding their horns. If I were to fall, the embarrassment would be somewhat insignificant compared to the full force of a Volkswagen Golf.

Luckily I didn't and as the finish line was breached, a feeling of pure bliss filled me as my exhausted legs gave way. I still find it difficult to express the incredible satisfaction that crossing the finish line gave me. At the start it seemed like mission impossible and even during the actual run I did not believe the end would ever come. But I managed to demonstrate that determination can take you a very long way in life (well about 9.6 miles to be exact).

To my surprise, people were incredibly impressed with my achievement and I was just as impressed by their generosity. With £300 in my pocket, the daunting task of raising the money for the trip was beginning to seem slightly more achievable. I am not going to give you the whole 'running can be fun – enjoy it!' speech because, to be frank, it wasn't. Au contraire, it was the worst kind of torture imaginable however, the question is not 'did you enjoy doing it?' the question is 'do you enjoy looking back on it, feeling like you achieved something?' and the answer to that is a resounding 'yes'.

II

The problem was that, although this money helped slightly, I still needed more. Thinking that people really wouldn't be too impressed by another sponsored run, I sat down to try and create a truly revolutionary money-making scheme. 'What do teenagers want to spend their money on?' I asked myself repeatedly and the only answer that came to me was 'sex, drugs and rock and roll'. What better way to achieve this than to organise one incredibly awesome and action packed night?

Of course, none of these things actually came to fruition, but my clever advertising would promise otherwise. With an easily accessible venue and an incredibly generous DJ friend named Matt who was willing to put the first few months of his degree on hold, a party seemed like the perfect solution to all my financial problems. With everything beginning to take shape, my mind began to run wild as I got visions of the night to come – a night that was going to shake the heavens.

As a team, Matt and I decided it should be a hard trance night and so it required an ultra-cool, catchy name. *'Revolution'* seemed as good as anything and for that reason, we chose it. The very same day I also ventured to possibly the most unhelpful town council in history and booked the town hall at a very uncompetitive rate indeed. Matt put me in touch with someone named Neil who apparently had a brilliant sound system that he would set up and supervise during the night. I spoke to him a few times on the phone and he seemed like a nice guy. Although more expensive than other companies, he was willing to run us through the equipment and show everyone how to use it so I decided to hire him. With a cigarette always hanging from his mouth and long blonde dreadlocks that made him look like a mop, I wouldn't say he was the most professional business man I had ever met, but his sound system certainly was impressive. In fact, when we arranged our first meeting so I could pay the deposit, we did so in a dark, disused car park which was rather surreal and made me feel like a gangster (be it, a rather soft one) of some description. Anyway, having made the exchange it was all finalised and I couldn't have felt happier.

With only four weeks to go however, I suddenly realised that nobody even knew that *Revolution* existed and began work on a vigorous and gruelling advertising campaign. Taking advantage of photocopying facilities in the office I was working in, I printed off hundreds of appealing posters and fliers. Although this may seem slightly dishonest, it did nonetheless provide a slight adrenaline rush to an otherwise unfulfilling job.

Unfortunately, by this point I had completed my time at school so a major source of advertising had slipped through my fingers. Not to be disheartened though, I ventured around the town and completely plastered the place in posters using shop windows, lamp posts and notice boards to capture everyone's attention. With my social life on hold, I even stood outside the pubs on Friday nights handing out fliers to my drunken potential market. Having simply littered the internet with adverts concerning *Revolution* as well, I was convinced this night was going to be full to the brim with dance, passion and (more importantly) money.

On the morning of the party, I was awoken rudely at 8am. Looking around I found myself lying on Matt's university dorm room floor, face to face with a beautifully stained carpet. My neck was really painful and as I looked around, I realised I'd been resting my head in a large hole all night. Student luxuries know no boundaries it seemed. My phone was ringing loudly on the other side of the room, so I stumbled across and hit the 'answer' button, slightly confused as to who could be ringing at this hour.
'Alright John mate, it's Neil here' he said.
'Hi mate, what's up? Are you all set for tonight?' I replied in between yawns.
'Well, that's the thing dude – I'm not sure if I've told you this but thought I better. It's about the sound system tonight - I haven't actually got any decks or a mixer so I hope you can get some by tonight. See you later' he said calmly and then abruptly hung up.
I was in pure shock and was even unable to speak as the consequences of the past twenty seconds began to sink in. There were eleven hours before the party began and the only thing I had was a big pair of speakers and a few flashy lights. SHIT! Following another thirty seconds of hyperventilation, I

grabbed my phone and tried to call him back. There was no answer and I was on my own. Rage was running through my body and I was angry at myself for using this guy. Matt tried to calm me down and after a few minutes we got cracking on how on earth we could get hold of this equipment at such short notice.

A few minor heart attacks later, I finally found the courage to get hold of my phone and start making some calls. As I made my calls, it appeared I hadn't been the only person to suffer from Neil's unreliability as people relayed stories of his arrogance. It seemed he had a certain knack of annoying those he had done business with like a virus of irritation and destruction. I only wish I had been warned about this before that infamous meeting in the car park.

Three difficult hours passed that afternoon as we made call after call to try and find the equipment. After much disappointment, another friend of mine finally came through. Apparently his brother was quite a keen DJ, but since he was away at boarding school, his mixer and decks were just lying around going to waste, so it seemed a shame not to use them. We didn't exactly have time to ask his permission, but sure he wouldn't really mind, we borrowed them anyway.

As I hadn't arranged ticket selling, I was just relying on word of mouth and hoping people would arrive. This was slightly disconcerting to say the least, as I had no indication on how many guests were expected. Apparently though, the youth these days like to be 'fashionably late' so my early evening worries were soon to be forgotten about as the queue grew dramatically. With the pubs closing, my market increased even further as I took advantage of their drunken generosity.

Soon, we were at full capacity as the tunes began to pump out of the hall and the ground beneath our feet shook. With my huge brother and four friends providing quite strict security, there was no trouble to be seen, only immense enjoyment as people gloriously kept on parting with their money.

With the heavens rocked, the punters satisfied and hall in a huge mess, the party slowly began to come to an end. My ears ringing from the music, I had a look around to asses if any damage had been done. Thankfully nothing had been broken, but there was a huge cleaning job to be conducted as I began collecting hundreds of glow sticks off the floor and threw them in the rubbish. As I left the bags of waste by the bins outside, I couldn't help but laugh as they glowed with a yellow fluorescence reminiscent of nuclear waste and wondered whether the refuse workers would be daring enough to handle them the next morning. As I began cleaning the toilets however, I soon stopped laughing. Three hours later and the hall couldn't have looked any better and as I stood back to admire my handy work, I collapsed through sheer exhaustion and a great feeling of relief.

After a very limited amount of sleep, I had time to sit down and reflect on the night properly. The guests had not exactly been hard trance fans, so the music was not fully appreciated to its highest level. They had also been a lot younger than I had initially hoped for with many only just passing the strict 'over 16s' policy and for this reason *Revolution* will probably not be remembered as the party of the century. However, in order to asses a project correctly you have to relate back to its main objective. In this instance, the point of the party was to make as much money as possible. Out of all my projects it was the one that took up the most time, took the most planning and created an incredibly incessant amount of stress. Yet, sitting in bed on Sunday morning surrounded by bundles of notes and coins I was in no doubt that *Revolution* had been an incredible success.

CHAPTER 4

By choosing to depart in September I had given myself a good six months to raise the remaining funds and, although my schemes were proving quite profitable, I wanted to maximize my potential spending money. Reluctantly, I therefore ventured into the unfamiliar world of temporary employment. I wouldn't normally mention this as it is rather mundane, yet I feel compelled to an issue a warning to those of you considering venturing along the same path. Trust me; if you are seeking responsibility, respect and any type of vaguely insightful conversation, you are going to be severely disappointed.

Of course, I wasn't exactly expecting to perform some type of advanced operation but I thought my talents would be put to slightly more use than removing staples. As I walked into the office on that first day as a scanning clerk however, I was to be bitterly disappointed.

Far from being a new exciting adventure, I found myself being patronised by an obese yank, with an exaggerated accent and a voice like a foghorn. With overconfidence more potent than his cheap aftershave, he was so stereotypically American I almost expected him to walk to the centre of the room and start bellowing out 'U-S-A' at the top of his voice. With an incredible ability to make the simplest tasks seem inordinately complex, he frustrated me so much I quit after only a couple of weeks and found myself unemployed yet again. It wasn't a decision I took lightly as I had already made quite a good friend who made me laugh as he talked about his pet rabbit named 'Bun Laden', but there are only so many terrorist-domestic pet references you can take before the depressing reality of your surroundings dampen your over-elated spirits.

Thankfully, I soon found a new job working as an administration assistant for a mortgage company. They had just relocated to some beautiful new offices, a converted barn in fact, located peacefully in a nearby village. On that first morning, I strolled across the newly-laid carpet and watched as people wandered around doing jobs I thought I would never understand. It seemed like the most complicated workplace in the world with the employees talking into headsets using a completely incomprehensible language. I caught a glimpse of some of the computer screens and stared at the mishmash of figures surrounded by extra-long words and felt like a primary school child who had inadvertently strolled into an A-level physics class.

So the work immediately seemed far more challenging, but as I was led across the office, people looked up from their desks and *smiled* at me. 'Well' I thought, 'this makes a pleasant change'. I was given a lovely new pine desk, an incredibly fast new computer and a splendid swivel chair which adjusted in every way thus alleviating the need to perform any strenuous physical movement at all. As they presented me with my first of many complementary drinks, I hit the recline button, looked out of the window at the wonderful surroundings and laughed at how my fortunes had changed so dramatically.

On the second day, I strolled in to the office and was greeted by a few smiling faces and even stopped to have a couple of conversations. This was incredible, I had only been there a day and already more people knew my name than at my last job. When I arrived at my desk, Ryan had already got me a drink and placed it on my beautifully clean desk. This was definitely the job for me.

As time passed, I gradually got to know the work inside out and, although it wasn't especially difficult, it was certainly a lot more fulfilling than removing staples. Sure, I didn't exactly look forward to going to work but I had developed a good relationship with my friends in the office and that made the days pass quickly and to some extent, enjoyably. Whenever I saw that the sales team were flat out and terribly busy, I would casually stroll past them reading a magazine and make a sly comment about them being 'the laziest people on Earth'. With this harmless banter in place, the days started to fly by much more quickly than I had anticipated as my departure date began drawing much closer.

Unfortunately though, the time had passed so quickly that my Australian research had been limited to reading the novel *'A Town Like Alice'* by Neville Shute. Although it is a fantastic novel and one that really captures the magical appeal of Australia, it was written in the 1950s and I couldn't help feel the cultural references would be somewhat irrelevant to my trip. It was then that I turned to my enlightened work colleagues for support. When it arrived however, I kind of wish I hadn't bothered.

Having researched a little bit of the history, I had come across a number of references to the diverse and dangerous wildlife lurking in the Australian wilderness, but until now I had generally put it to the back of my mind. As a result, when a work colleague of mine walked over to my desk one morning with a huge grin on her face, I knew exactly what was coming.
'I've got something for you to read' she declared trying to control her laughter as she handed over a huge book with the devastating title *'Dangerous Creatures of Australia'*.

I knew exactly what type of effect this would have on me and so was tempted not to read it, but as it sat there on my desk all day, intrigue finally got the better of me and I succumbed to that strange desire human's have to terrify themselves.

I can say that this book well and truly satisfied that urge. For example, the first page contained a photo of a harmless looking garden toad. Apparently though, apart from croaking in relatively the same tone, this toad was a world away from those we see hopping around in our UK gardens. In fact, by comparing the two you might as well be pairing Jack Dee with Jack the Ripper – both have a face you want to slap, but one is far more deadly than the other. You see, this Australian toad is capable of firing a highly toxic venom into the eyes of anyone unlucky enough to be standing within a metre of it. Still to this day, I have no idea *why* a big frog would need such a potent weapon, but it did nonetheless emphasise the point that nothing should be under-estimated. I continued to turn the pages in silent amazement, or maybe it was the sheer fear I felt looking down at words and photos in front of me. Ernest Hemingway once said that *'danger is a beautiful thing when it is purposely sought'*. This, I have decided, is completely untrue. Shame on you Ernest.

However, although this shocked me quite substantially, it was nothing compared to the trauma I would experience when reading the next few pages. It wasn't so much the terror this next creature could dish out that shocked me, but the fact that I had simply never heard of it before. How could such a dangerous fiend pass me by undetected for all these years? I was studying the *casvarius*, otherwise known as the cassowary. I don't think there is much way of describing this creature other than an exaggerated and glorified chicken on steroids, but as I flicked the pages the words seemed to describe a creature with a far more sinister personality. One sentence read *'wounds from the claws can be terrible, even if no vital organ is damaged there is the likelihood of massive bleeding'*. My attention was now certainly undivided. There is a *likelihood* of massive bleeding! The fact that a chicken could inflict wounds likely to cause *any* bleeding was news to me.

As if to stress their menace, the author then went on to tell quite a shocking story and, as a gesture of good will, I have decided to pass it on to you. Back in the early settlement years, cassowaries were a severely hunted species, to the extent that they are now endangered (from the point of view of someone not wanting to be devoured by a giant bird, I decided this was a positive thing). I suppose for the early inhabitants it would have been a keen sport in Australia, much like fox-hunting in the UK. Anyway, a young sixteen year old boy living in the northern territory decided to go out hunting one day. Walking for miles, he eventually cornered a cassowary and was just about to fire his weapon when the cassowary, suddenly aware of its superior power, decided enough was enough and ran full speed at the child. In a mad split second, the hunter had become the hunted. With lightening reactions, the bird caught up with the young lad, slashed him down the centre of the body with its dagger-like claws and left him for dead.

With such severe injuries from the deep wounds, the boy could only crawl and few yards before he eventually keeled over and bled to death. If nothing else, I suppose this story could be seen as a good warning to potential cassowary hunters or nosey tourists, so I took it as one and vowed never to chase anything no matter how humorous it looked. I was pretending to be doing work at my desk, but secretly my eyes were scanning through the pages of this book, searching desperately in vain for some survival tips.

Inevitably however, things got steadily worse as my eyes gazed across the terrible pages of potential death. And then, I moved onto a creature that has survived on the planet for over one hundred *million* years. Even compared to Margaret Thatcher this is a truly impressive feat. But the most impressive fact is that, not only has the crocodile *survived* all these years, it has actually flourished and thrived, unchallenged by anything even as remotely as imposing. It is their incredible design which has been perfected through years of evolution that helps them achieve this. For example, in order to pinpoint their prey they do not rely on sight or sound but instead use amazingly efficient vibration sensors to locate their exact position on the bank. With expert precision, they then move in with deadly accuracy, only revealing a small portion of their head above the water line. Even if their head is spotted, it is so brilliantly camouflaged like a log that the victim will just dismiss it as debris. Bang! They strike the victim with lightening speed, pull them back into the water with a sudden burst of power before performing the infamous 'death roll' and duly sinking back into the depths of the unknown never to be seen again. It is over so quickly that, by the time you've spun round to check out what the splash was behind you, your best friend will be missing and the only sign of him will be his cap floating across the ripples of the river.

Unfortunately for the victim, this will not be the end of their torture. You see, crocodiles are rarely large enough to finish a whole human corpse, so instead they drown their victims before storing the body and nibbling at the remains for the following few weeks. Unlike the cassowary however, crocodiles do not need to be provoked to attack and nor are they endangered. Far from it in fact, as with over one hundred thousand in the tropical north, the place is literally bursting with the things. It appeared that a run-in with one of these things was not just likely, but actually quite unavoidable which made me slightly concerned to say the least.

As if to reinforce the point, just days prior to my departure there was a stunning news story that shocked my mother along with the rest of the world. It was concerning three local friends who were quad biking along the

Finniss river in the Northern Territory. With bad flooding in the area, the mud had been deep which made an excellent biking environment but one which subsequently plastered them in mud. Approaching the water to clean themselves down, one of them fell and was swept away by the strong current. As the others swam to his rescue in the murky, brown water they spotted a set of devil like yellow eyes swimming towards them with malicious intent. If ever a 'swim for your life' situation had occurred, this was it. Shockingly, only two of them made it to the bank where they clambered up the nearest tree and watched as the thirteen-foot crocodile rose to the surface, opened its jaws and revealed their friend's mutilated body. With pure terror, the pair clung to the tree for another twenty-two traumatic hours as the crocodile stalked them from the river beneath, before they were winched to safety by a rescue helicopter team.

As I read this on the *BBC News* website, the article finished with the words *'saltwater crocodiles are the world's largest reptiles and are aggressive and dangerous'.* This, I decided, was the most unnecessary sentence ever written.

I still don't understand why humans wish to scare themselves into a mild sweat, yet we do it all the time. It's not as if it's a natural instinct either – after all, you never see wild rabbits sneaking up daringly behind a fox just for a cheap thrill do you? But for some explainable, bizarre and completely idiotic reason, I found it necessary to photocopy the goriest stories from the book and stash them in my journal for some light reading whilst away on my travels. Imagine tuning into the live camera on The International Space Station and seeing one of the astronauts shaking with nerves as he turns the pages of *'Apollo 13'*. With that thought in mind, I decided to end my research there.

My time at work had finished and departure was just a week away, so I thought I should probably concentrate on packing the rucksack I hadn't even purchased yet. Saying goodbye to my fellow colleagues was rather difficult on that last day, as although I hadn't exactly enjoyed my job, the camaraderie among the staff had created a brilliant atmosphere. I suppose it is the hardest thing a traveller must learn to cope with - saying farewell (that and living out of a tiny rucksack in which the one item you need is always at the bottom), but nevertheless it is a skill you learn to develop as it occurs on such a regular basis.

As I threw my brand new rucksack into the back of my parent's car one week later, I just prayed I would perfect it sooner rather than later.

PART 2

CHAPTER 5

It was 8am on my first morning in Australia and I had already been awake for hours. My body clock was like a drunken Irishman at closing time thanks to the awful flight. Not only had eleven hours just vanished from my life, but while they were being taken I had been forced to endure the ordeal sitting next to an obese, smelly German man who had a somewhat annoying habit of tying to talk to me just as I was beginning to doze. Through my smiling and nodding I thought he might have worked out that the language barrier was a hurdle neither of us was jumping, but he continued to chat the entire distance. At one point, I did try to bring the conversation to an abrupt halt by reciting a sentence from a survival travel book my friend had bought me
'You see here sir - it says if you are ever attacked by a male and wish to escape, you should grab and crush his testicles as if they were a bunch of grapes' but he merely looked at me blankly for a second before continuing with his German story.

Upon escaping the aircraft, my relief was shockingly short lived as I realised I had forgotten to bring my visa. I knew exactly where it was in my bedroom, however I wasn't sure if that would be good enough for the strict Australian customs. Thankfully, such is the marvel of technology, they had all my details stored on their computer system and I was allowed to pass through trouble free.

We had been met on the other side by our lovely in-country agent Thea who had organised a couple of days of administration and acclimatization. We were staying in a rather nice hostel called *'Y On The Park'* which overlooked Hyde Park right in the centre of Sydney. Before we could go exploring though, Thea had planned an early morning and rather memorable talk for us.

'You *will* come face to face with dangerous creatures' she warned us 'but you have to react properly so as not to worry the children'.

I didn't think this was particularly likely, in fact it seemed like the *least* likely to be followed set of instruction I had ever heard. She also told us a few horror stories of previous gap challengers who had unfortunately crashed into some kangaroos. Not that she was worried about the kangaroos at all

'If you hit them, make sure you kill the bastards' were her exact words.

It seems a bit harsh to be killing such a special and unique animal - an animal so exclusive to the country that it even appears on the national coat of arms. But if these were the wishes of a nation, who was I to stand in their way? She also spoke (not very fondly) of one particular girl who insisted on discussing her previous sexual experiences with some of the children on a camp. Needless to say she was deported pretty quickly along with her filthy little mind. Thea laughed as she told us these stories, although I suspected she was issuing some kind of warning to all of us. Still, it was pleasing to know that I would have to do something very extreme if I were to be thought of as the worst gap challenger ever.

The same day we were granted a few hours to explore the city at our own leisure. There were fifteen of us and collectively we decided that a visit to the aquarium would be a nice way to spend the afternoon. The *'Finding Nemo'* exhibition outside soon confirmed our decision to be a good one.

Grant took up tour guide status since he had already been before. He was joined up front by a girl named Sian. With long blonde hair and brown skin, the last thing I expected her be was Welsh, but that's exactly what she was. Having not been on the skills course (instead she had been travelling the world, helping with various conservation projects along the way) this was the first time any of us had met her and had the pleasure to experience her bubbly personality.

The sky was pure blue and the sun was beaming down heat like a furnace, creating a beautiful shine across Darling Harbour. Luxurious yachts sailed gracefully across the crystal water and families walked joyfully along the shore with ice lollies in hand. Even though I had never even heard of Darling Harbour, I couldn't help but feel mightily impressed by the place. The decorations from the Australia Day celebrations still lined the raised walkways from two days before. There was a relaxing, almost holiday-like atmosphere in the air which made it all seem so very detached from the commotion of city life. I adored it.

The aquarium was relatively quiet and without any queues to fight through, we walked straight up to the desk and happily handed over a large pile of unfamiliar, colourful notes. Then, only fifteen hours into my trip, I came face-to-face with the sinister glare of a five-metre long salt-water crocodile. With a look of utter annoyance, he stared at me from his tiny pen as if challenging any of us to make a move. Looking at his surroundings though, I quickly began to feel quite sorry for him and couldn't imagine his little enclosure was providing much crocodile style stimulation. I examined its stationary body through the glass and was impressed by the sheer power his armoured legs and tail portrayed. As if to reiterate this, there was a sign which read *'Do not lean over the side, if the fall does not kill you, the crocodile will'*.

Continuing to slightly more peaceful surroundings, we rounded a corner and were faced by a series of large aquariums. It was here that I spotted my first monotreme - a duckbilled platypus, which was quite simply the strangest and most awkward creature I have ever seen. It was as if God had got to the end of his designing stage and, in an attempt not to waste any materials, had simply thrown all his left-overs together and assembled them in the dark. The result was this thing that looked like the illegitimate child of a duck-otter lover affair. With a long silky body, sharp claws *and* a beak, it wriggled through the water making rhythmic body twirls as if dancing at a 1970s disco inferno. It is one of only two monotremes in the world and both are native to Australia – the other being an over-elaborate hedgehog named the echidna. The term originates from the fact that both only actually have one hole for everything, which is such a unique biological trait it baffled scientists for years. I could certainly see why.

Walking through underwater tunnels, I had a great view of one particular seal that was intent on performing tricks above my head. Although there was a layer of glass separating us, I still found myself ducking as he came shooting towards me at speed. As he swam away with me cowering on the floor behind, I swear I heard him let out a little laugh – the cheeky bastard. It goes without saying that this was indeed an enjoyable experience due mostly to the fact that we were finally seeing animals not confined to a tiny little tank.

But I was eager to see something slightly more exciting – something that had the potential to eat me basically. I was sweating with anticipation as I closed in on the shark tank and entered the immersed tunnel. In my head, the music from jaws was playing as I took those first timid steps into view. I wasn't disappointed. Surrounding me were hundreds of varieties of dangerous predators, and as they passed over my head I felt as though I could touch them - not that I particularly wanted to. The one sour note was the overcrowding of the tank. In fact, it was so densely packed, the animals seemed to be knocking into each other on occasions. It seemed a shame that such a wonderful spectacle was being ruined by a lack of traffic control procedures and with the wide open ocean only yards away, this was a slightly sombre view.

As a result, I wasn't really sure how I felt when I left the aquarium and rejoined the intense heat outside. On the one hand I liked it because it was quite pleasantly air-conditioned and had allowed me to experience most of the extreme Australian wildlife in a relatively controlled environment. But it had seemed rather faked and I couldn't help feel sorry for the creatures being kept in horrible captivity so close to their natural habit. Deciding this debate in my head was getting slightly too serious, I went and purchased an ice-cream which lightened the mood quite nicely.

We had been in Sydney now for almost a day and had not conducted any shopping whatsoever. The women decided that this was simply unacceptable so set of merrily to rectify it. Concluding that we would have plenty of time for this later in the trip, Grant and I made our way to the Skytower which is quite a defining part of the Sydney skyline.

We came to the entrance of a huge department store which was crowded by a large group of Japanese school children, each one of them holding a shopping bag larger than themselves. Eventually, we fought through them, made our way up the escalator and across a tunnel leading to the opposite side of the street. If they were trying to hide the entrance to this tower, they were doing a bloody good job. Through luck more than purpose, we came across a tiny kiosk and beside it there was a modest sign with the words 'Skytower Entrance' chiselled on. With a *Colgate* worthy smile, the woman behind the counter was incredibly friendly (if not a little nosey) and recommended lots of places to visit before my time in Sydney was up. This put me in a rather good mood and I didn't complain at all when handing over my $22 entrance fee which was unusual if nothing else.

The security had obviously been heightened considerably since 9/11 with a series of electronic detectors in place to search for any metallic object or explosive devices. I knew I didn't posses any (that I knew of), but was still strangely nervous when walking through and, for some reason, was strangely relieved when the sirens did not sound.

At 250 metres high, the tower is like a large version of an air traffic control centre with a long cylindrical body and a pod on top. Understandably, the lift took quite a while to reach the summit, eventually though we exited the doors and were standing directly in the centre of the lofty look-out. I walked cautiously towards the glass edge – it was a perfectly clear day and I could see the extensive city stretching out to the horizon in all directions. Even though they were so far away, the huge stature of The Harbour Bridge and Opera House dominated the view as my attention was immediately drawn to their majestic elegance. It is an unexplainable feeling – a phenomenon of Sydney life – that for some reason, if these two landmarks are in sight, your eyes are immediately drawn to them and your attention undivided. I imagine many road accidents have occurred in the city due to pedestrians casually strolling across the road under the influence of this mysterious trance. Even in the Skytower, the glass pane offering the best view of Circular Quay was surrounded by its obsessed fans trying to get that perfect photograph. Unfortunately, what they failed to realise was that no photo can ever do it justice. Not that Grant had noticed as he too started firing away with his new digital camera.

Trying to avoid the hoards of fans, I instead began circling the platform convinced that this city had far more to offer. Before I did this however, a little safety check was necessary just for peace of mind if nothing else.

'Exactly how thick is this glass?' I enquired turning to one of the tour guides wearing a bright red coat.

'Thick enough' she replied with a sympathetic chuckle.

Curiously, she didn't really answer the question and I wondered whether she actually knew the answer at all. Still, since she was standing closer to the edge than I was, I took belief from her faith and slowly edged my way towards the glass. Looking straight out at the horizon, it felt as though I was standing on the summit of a huge mountain, albeit one surrounded by large concrete buildings and neon signs. Even the fifteen story buildings below seemed tiny compared to me. Knowing that vertigo would set in, I decided to take a chance and look down at the streets 250m below my feet. Moving periodically, I could tell they were streaming with life but could not identify the individual entities below.

Subtly, I joined the back of a tour group and followed them round the circular viewing platform. It was full of people from all different nations, but the tour was entirely in English and everyone seemed to be enjoying it. It was conducted by a young and very confident lady, who had obviously done hundreds of these tours and was just rolling it off from memory. She showed us the famous suburbs of Manly and Bondi, gave us the history of Captain Cook's pioneering voyage and also pointed out one of Russell Crowe's old houses. It was mightily impressive to say the least and put me in a good mood as I toured the souvenir shops. Well, I say shops, but I should actually use the singular as I soon realised that it was merely the same shop twice and that walking round in a circle had obviously confused my senses much more than I should openly admit.

With Grant back under control from his photo tour we agreed to end this excursion and move on to pastures new. Like a drug addict craving for one final high, I ran back and took one more look at the harbour from this most spectacular platform before beginning the decent back down to Earth.

The Dymocks building on George street is truly massive and houses many different shops and information centres. Outside the entrance to the bookstore there is a large hallway with a number of hidden and seemingly pointless elevators. If you weren't looking for them, you wouldn't realise they were there. It seems a shame as this elegant entrance hides a truly important place for travellers – TCP or 'Travellers Contact Point'.

With free internet for all its customers, the expert employees also give a free advice seminar each day for novices of this travel malarkey and this is where Grant and I found ourselves now. Right on time, the talk began and guided us through things such as visa working restrictions and receiving a tax rebate. Unfortunately, it provided about as much entertainment as staring at a large, but mostly unremarkable cauliflower for an hour. Granted, I would have undoubtedly observed new things about said cauli, but the initial appeal would've worn off after seven minutes as it did here too. Nevertheless, I highly recommend this talk upon arrival in Sydney as it's free and provides you with important (if not mundane) information concerning job opportunities available during the trip. Okay, enough of this serious talk, it was time to experience the nightlife.

Seriously, what constitutes a 'genuine Irish pub'? One thing for sure is that it doesn't necessarily need to be located in Ireland. Alas, it doesn't really need any connections to Ireland at all, apart from a modestly illuminated *Guinness* sign on the wall. From a few trips to the French Alps, I had already learnt this all important worldly fact so I wasn't at all surprised to find one on Goulburn Street in the middle of Sydney.

One thing that did surprise me was that the barman seemed to be speaking with quite a strong Irish accent which was unprecedented to say the least. So unprecedented in fact that I even questioned him about it, only for his reply to come back with a strong Australian twang and look of extreme concern. I knew it was too good to be true. Perhaps the beer was taking its toll.

Earlier that evening we had gone for dinner in China town – a corner of the city that has been majestically transformed into the streets of Beijing, so much so that wherever you turn, you get a face-full of dead duck being turned ceremoniously on a spit. Apart from our group - the conspicuous tourists - the people were dressed in traditional silk clothing, decorated with wonderfully vibrant colours and patterns. Some even danced through the street in marvellously over-the top dragon outfits and the waiters ran round so quickly, it was like watching a video player that was stuck on fast-forward. In contrast, I ate the meal slowly, giving it the respect it deserved and savouring every last bite of its authenticity. As soon as we had finished, Thea stood up (with a little difficulty) and addressed our table.

'Australians work very hard' she said in a very serious voice, 'but we party even harder! So let's go and experience it shall we?'

Thank god, I was worried she was going to say something serious and meaningful for a second. As a result, we now found ourselves at *Scruffy Murphy's*. There was very little light in the pub, only that around the bar area and stage. I wondered whether this was an attempt to create a party atmosphere, or purely a preventative measure to hide the state of the furniture. Along the walls there were a number of TV screens showing various sporting events, gripping the attention of some Aussie men.

Tempted by the *Guinness*, I then recalled a god awful pint I sampled earlier in the year in France. Just like the English skin, it doesn't seem to travel without dire consequences. So instead, I went for a couple of bottles of *Carlton Extra Dry*, which is a completely misleading name as, whilst spilling it down my front, I discovered it was just as wet as any other beer. Despite this, my spirits were still amazingly high – too high for a man advertising to the world that, at the age of nineteen, he still requires a bib. The atmosphere was lovely though and everyone was simply enjoying themselves as we continued to bond. After a couple of hours of this, I felt as though I'd known them all for years, which would've been nice as they could probably accept my slurring, drunken conversation as being slightly amusing and not just peculiar. Thankfully though, it seemed everyone was in the same boat of confusion. During some stage in the night I bumped into Thea and spoke to her with that drunken confidence one so often possesses on nights such as these

'Why is there so much emphasis on drinking in Australia?' I asked her (although in reality I was probably shouting it).

'There is a saying in OZ' she said in a deadly serious voice.

'And what might that be?'.

'We say that alcohol is fun to drink, but better than that, it is the greatest social lubricant around'.

Well I couldn't help but laugh. She was right though, it was definitely true so I thought I better get myself another beer.

The next morning, I was surprisingly energetic as we dodged through the early traffic to the *Commonwealth Bank*. It was just before 9am, but the sun had already heated the air enough to make me sweat. There were twenty or so of us in the group, all making our way to open a current account as we had been advised to do. It made sense really – to carry around all that money in a bag would be stupid, not to mention dangerous. I'm sure the bank clerks weren't happy with our decision and most definitely cursed when they saw twenty of us wandering in first thing on a busy morning.

Being the gentleman I am, I went last in the queue, waited for a while and eventually got served. The lady behind the desk explained the details of the account to me – she knew them off by heart having already told ten people in the past thirty minutes. However, there was one thing she said that really shocked me, in fact I even asked her to repeat it in case I had misheard her. She repeated it again, but I hadn't misheard anything.
'There is a five dollar account fee each month which will be deducted automatically from your balance' she said while staring at her computer screen.
I couldn't believe this, you actually get *charged* for having a bank account. I thought the whole idea of a bank account was to keep your money safe and *earn* a little bit through interest. It made me question why anyone in Australia actually *has* an account. Surely it would be much more economical just to keep your money in a pot under the bed? I also got told that I would be charged each time I used my debit card; either to withdraw money or buy goods in a shop. So, let me just clarify - here was a bank which not only charged you a monthly fee for *having* an account with them, they also charged you if you ever wanted to *use* it. This was pure daylight robbery and if I hadn't been in a rush I would have made a complaint.

Jogging through the hoards of city workers, I eventually caught up with the others at the *'Medicard Centre'*. It had been explained to us during the previous day's talk that a *Medicard* was essential and could potentially save us thousands of dollars in medical bills. Flashing it at a doctor or nurse would provide the owner with instant immunity from any sort of payment and, since it was free, this seemed like a much better investment than a bank account. The queue was extremely long and the staff obviously frustrated, but after half an hour or so of waiting we were protected against any possible medical emergency.

With all our administrative worries now over, we decided to take a trip to one of the suburbs guarding the northern entrance of the harbour, called Manly. There was the option of a bus, but by far the quickest and most scenic route was the ferry crossing.

Catching our boat at the Circular Quay port, it set across the harbour at a leisurely pace, giving us another splendid view of The Opera House as the sun reflected against its sparkling cream roof. Everyone on board ran to get a photo just as they had in the Skytower. However, aware that the photo would look relatively naff with another twenty people in the background, I declined the invitation and instead tried to instigate some conversations.

The girl next to me was an ex-challenger named Dawn. A few years older than me, she had just completed her camp placement and, although she still spoke with a strong Manchester accent, her voice was seething in admiration for her now adopted home.
'It's so pretty and beautiful - I often walk there in the evening to relax. It's such a peaceful place and it's impossible to believe you're in the middle of such a fabulous city' she said fondly, pointing towards the Royal Botanical Gardens.

As I listened to her words, my eyes followed the shoreline as we sailed on, studying the number of luxurious houses and apartment blocks that lined it. Soon we were out into open blue water, hundreds of metres from land. I kept my eyes peeled, looking down into the deep blue below, searching for my first shark. I wasn't exactly fearful, just intrigued and hopeful that I could catch a glimpse of one gliding along by the boat. I wasn't sure how I would react to such an image, but I prayed I wouldn't be shocked enough to fall overboard.

With its famous neighbour Bondi on the southern side, Manly rarely gets the media attention it deserves. This is perhaps a good thing as it remains a high class establishment, free from the commercial dirt that accompanies those high profile spots. This was far from tacky – quite the opposite in fact. For those of you old enough to remember, it provided the setting for parts of the 1983 cult film *BMX Bandits* and that was enough to get me excited.

As you exit the ferry port you are confronted by a number of exquisitely paved walkways and fountains, surrounded by some perfectly kept trees. To say that it is satisfying to the eye is an understatement, in the same way that describing the ceiling of the Sistene Chapel to be painted to an 'acceptable standard' would be. It was far nicer than that and I could tell immediately that I was going to like Manly, even though the name left a lot to be desired.

Once again we had decided to tour as a group and so waited for a few of the others to catch up before considering the afternoon's plans. Little to my knowledge, the girls had already made plans of their own. Apparently their shopping needs hadn't been entirely satisfied the day before, so as they rectified this problem, Grant and I grabbed ourselves a little bit of food and then headed straight in the direction of the beach. We sat on some concrete steps talking about our lives pre-Australia, whilst being attacked by a couple of determined seagulls. This was one of the first times we had really discussed home and it worked well in settling some slight homesickness we were feeling. Eventually this conversation diverged into something more fitting of two young men in Australia as we came to the unanimous decision that Australia had a much higher proportion of 'hotties' than England and for this reason, our choice to come here was almost certainly the right one.

Grant left at this point as he had a reunion with an old friend in the city and the rest of us decided to go for a swim. Now, to say that I required a bit of encouragement is an understatement. I wasn't just worried about the man-eating creatures in the water, there were also a number of strong 'rips' or currents to deal with as well. I had been informed to swim between the flags and that way a lifeguard would be watching in case of any problems. Apparently there were shark nets, but with little evidence of these I was slightly apprehensive to say the least. To be honest, I couldn't imagine the lifeguard wrestling a great white to the death after it had got hold of my arm.

Surprisingly though, the girls twisted my leg and I eventually decided to venture into the water. Immediately, I was pleased with the decision as the ocean was so luxuriously warm I felt strangely relaxed and the waves were the perfect size to excite but not cause any discomfort or drowning sensations. It was a great relief as well, providing a slight reprieve from the baking sun and with hundreds of people in the water, I considered my chances of survival to be rather high.

Having had a few unsuccessful games at *Frisbee*, we left the sea and dried almost instantly. I lay on my towel for the rest of the day and looked around, people- watching as I gazed. Many adults glided along the esplanade either rollerblading or jogging under the shadow of the tropical palm trees. Others watched from their deluxe apartments, enjoying the scene of the perfect golden beach below that seemed to stretch endlessly in either direction. School finished and the children made their way down to the beach to play a couple of games of cricket – quite in contrast to the children of England who appear to get their thrills from smoking on street corners. The word 'perfection' now had new meaning - this was the lifestyle for my family and me. I only wished they were here to experience it.

Again I found myself walking along Goulburn Street and back to *Scruffy Murphy's* for the second night in a row. It was a strange feeling for this would be the last time I would see many of the people from our *World Challenge* group. It was such a strange mixture of emotions. A few days ago I hadn't known these people at all, but the pressure had been there to become pals. Now, just as we were beginning to get used to each other, we were being separated.

As I met the others, I soon realised that there was more to *Scruffy's* than I had seen the previous evening. Now above the bar, I was standing in a huge restaurant area serving traditional 'pub grub' and took my seat near Grant and opposite a couple of the girls as my steak and chips was served. I thought it best to go for a traditional Aussie dish, even though I was in an 'Irish' pub.

I had had enough of beer the previous day and so a few of us invested in a number of bottles of tasty chardonnay and duly drank freely without a care in the world. It was such a nice feeling to be able to let yourself go, to not have to worry about driving home or going to work the following day. So I drank a little more. The evening soon flew by and as nostalgia began to set in, we exchanged contact details, be it not very accurately in my case. To be honest, the wine had got to me so much, I could've been writing down any old number and it would've seemed correct.

We soon got motioned out of the restaurant and down to the bar, which was just beginning to fill up. Sian, Grant and I, along with a lovely pleasant girl named Emma, made our way to the flashing jukebox in the corner and searched through a number of classic favourites before selecting a few that caught our fancy. The one that sticks out in memory is *'Summer of '69'* by *Bryan Adams* whose cheesy appeal convinced me that playing a very dramatic air guitar in the middle of the dance-floor would be an incredible idea. Needless to say, it is a memory I do not wish to recall.

An hour or so passed before it was time to say my drunken goodbyes. Having done so, I then stumbled over to the door. A few of my friends joined to help escort me home. At the hostel I made it to my room (I think), lay on my bed and closed my eyes.

CHAPTER 6

The train shuddered again, sending vomit-inducing vibrations straight through my body. I could smell the stale beer plastered across my clothes. As I was now appreciating, the previous night's shenanigans had not been ideal preparation for the eleven hour train journey to Melbourne. If I hadn't been busy avoiding the sunlight, I might have been shocked by that statistic – eleven hours! And yet, consulting a map we were only covering a tiny fraction of this great, expansive land. You could watch over seven football matches in that time.

In total, six of us (including me) were heading south-west for Melbourne on this fateful morning. Of course, Grant was there sitting next to me and chatting away about all the cars he would love to own and seemed completely oblivious to my delicate condition. Immediately in front of us were Sian and Emma, who seemed determined to sleep and achieved this in some of the most awkward positions imaginable. I would later realise that Emma was quite a perfectionist in the art of travel sleeping - indeed it seemed to come naturally to her. Through my reasonably rough and uncalculated calculations, I think she must have slept for about ninety percent of that journey using a technique that was so abrupt it could even be seen as offensive. Nor did there seem any feasible and humane way of waking her. We sang, we shouted and we even flicked her ear, but it soon became apparent that Emma would only wake up when she was ready to wake up. Further towards the front of the carriage were Harry and Rich who were on their way to The Grampians, northwest of Melbourne. Harry soon followed Emma's example and discovered that the window was not as uncomfortable as he had first suspected. Unfortunately, I had no such luck and so stretched my long legs out in the ample room provided, pretended to listen to Grant's endless chatter and settled for a bit of kangaroo spotting. From the talk Thea had given us, I was under the impression that the country was ridden with the things swarming the rural areas in an act of savage brutality. It didn't take long to realise that I was badly mistaken.

The drought that had gripped the country for years had taken an obvious toll as fields of brown grass repeated themselves endlessly in front of my eyes. Then suddenly, just like a mirage shining in the distance, Melbourne emerged on the horizon. Dry sparse fields soon became suburbs full of nice, pleasant gardens and streets lined with green, watered grass and large exotic plants. To my surprise, most of the houses were bungalows and all were covered in the same maroon tinted tiles. We were creeping closer to the city centre as the magnificent skyscrapers came into view, but still I peered out and saw families relaxing in their tranquil city gardens, enjoying barbeques and drinking beer without a care in the world. From my experience, suburbs in England can never quite achieve this state of total relaxation as the residents struggle to escape the curse of the city and the subsequent stress on their lives. They are stuck in the middle, not knowing where to belong. But this was not the case now, on my first visit to Melbourne. A tranquil and trouble free life was booming from the faces of the people I could see, even with the shadow of the big city looming only metres away. This was the life for me.

The train circled round the city and then with a sharp turn, made a mad dash for the centre. The sun was now behind us and I couldn't make out the city at all. Instead, all I could see was a great shining light against a mass of blue sky. If I was a religious man, I may have taken it as some kind of Divine welcoming sign. The Telstra Dome stadium then passed by as the station readily approached. It was truly a magnificent sight, a great piece of architecture and it seemed very surreal to be sitting just metres away from a spot I had seen on television so many times in the past.

Slowly rolling into Spencer Street station, the train gave a relieved breath before coming to a halt. It was then that we realised we had not been given any instructions from Thea on what to do upon arrival. So there we stood; six tired British travellers, in an unfamiliar country with no idea where to go. To try and lighten the mood, I suggested that it was quite an exciting situation, however the others' look of disapproval suggested they disagreed.

Deciding to make our way into the brave outdoors, we stepped out of the station and were immediately approached by a lady. With shoulder length blonde hair and a slim figure, she was a lovely looking person and probably a lot older than her appearance would have you believe.
'Um excuse me, are you guys from Gap Challenge England?' she said confidently.
'Yes, yes we are' we all replied in unison with a great sense of relief.
As we introduced ourselves and explained how tiring and kangaroo-free our journey had been, we were joined by a man.
'Hi I'm Greg, the manager from Lady Northcote Camp. I'm here for Sian, Emma, John and Grant (the Australians seemed to like exaggerating the 'a' sound in his name, much to Grant's displeasure quite understandably)' he said in a very kind voice.
He was of average height, average build and spoke with hardly any accent at all. Your 'average Joe' I suppose you could say. A man whom you could pass by on the street and then forget his face almost instantaneously. However I was slightly confused
'Grant and I are supposed to be going to Licola Camp, how come we are going with you?' I enquired.
'Well, Licola is *very* far away even in Australian terms' he explained calmly 'basically they haven't been able to make it down to the city to get you guys, don't worry though I'm sure they will in the next couple of days or so'.
It was the 'or so' part of the sentence that worried me. Grant and I had been so thrilled to finally be arriving at camp after such a long wait and here we were being told we must delay our arrival by a further few days 'or so'. But there was nothing we could do about it, and besides, it would give us a bit of time to explore the sights of Melbourne and get to know the girls a little better. Having thought about it for a few minutes, it appeared to be a blessing in disguise.

As we chatted and got to know Greg, Harry and Rich did the same with the lady who had first introduced herself to us. It turned out that she was their manager and host for the next twelve weeks and, like Greg, appeared to be a very pleasant character. She was anxious to get away as it was already approaching 7pm and the journey back to The Grampians was extremely long. We wished each other good luck and went our separate ways.

It was dark by the time we arrived at the Lady Northcote camp a few miles west of Bacchus Marsh, which in turn was west of Melbourne. Greg had got us lost a few times on the way here, but at least the diversion had provided us with a little tour of the Melbourne Docklands. The journey had taken just over an hour, although it didn't feel like we had travelled far at all compared to the mammoth distances we had covered in the past week.

Even though Greg had seemed remarkably interested in our stories, the conversation in the car had been quite polite and somewhat limited due to our tired state. Like almost all Australians, he was positively brimming with patriotism and recommended hundreds of places we should visit during our trip.

With no sign of civilization in the surrounding countryside, the camp felt rather lonely in the dead of night, with the only light coming from the thousands of stars matted across the sky above. Effectively it wasn't really a camp at all but more of a cute township or shire providing everything it needed to survive with all the resources necessary to be almost entirely self-sufficient. There was only one thing missing – residents. Apart from Greg and his family, we were the sole inhabitants of the camp that evening and would be for the remainder of the weekend. As we drove through the camp grounds I wound down the window and was confronted by an orchestra of tropical and unfamiliar noises coming from the native gum trees.

'There's the lake, girls' Greg said pointing towards a large manmade waterhole about fifty metres in diameter 'you'll be spending a lot of time pulling children out of there' I saw the girls give each other an intrigued, if not slightly worried look.

The car took a sharp left turn along a dusty road, gradually coming to a halt outside a wooden camp lodge shaped like an 'L'. I tentatively stepped from the car onto the ground - there was no grass beneath my feet, only dust. Marching towards the front door I glanced up at the porch light to see hundreds of moths colliding with the beautiful lamp above. They wouldn't survive long, especially if the huge huntsman spider creeping towards them had anything to do with it. Even I was apprehensive about walking beneath it, suspecting it had enough body strength to grab me and indeed, take me against my will. Therefore, it came as a relief and, may I say, a happy surprise when I made it to the front door with all limbs still attached. The doorway itself was made up of two panels – one was just a normal household door, although a lot thinner than those in Northamptonshire, and the other was an outer door made from netting, designed (I hoped) to deny bugs and creatures any sort of access to the building. I was very thankful.

As my eyes adjusted to the light, it became clear that we were standing in the kitchen. It was very basic but Greg had stocked it full of rations suitable for breakfast, with a wide selection of bread, jam and juice. The main living room was big - so big that swinging a cat around would prove to be a completely untroubled event. This therefore appealed as an appropriate place to finally unpack my incredibly unorganised backpack. The others followed in suit and quite soon we gave the house a real student feel with piles of clothes and dirty washing scattered randomly across the carpet.

Coming from the living room were two long corridors stretching at right angles to one another. On either side of these dark corridors were a number of symmetrically placed rooms, all of which appeared lifeless and empty too. The house was designed to accommodate nearly fifty people, but with only four in our group, there was a mysterious and eerie sense in the air. In effect, walking to the bathroom alone soon proved to be quite an ordeal. But we soon realised the great benefits we had in front of us as well. During each night, every one of us could have slept in two different rooms and not even bumped into one another. Not that this would have been the most logical thing in the world, but it was possible nonetheless.

However, our young and corrupt minds soon took control over our more rational senses as images of horror movies and ghostly stories began to manifest within our imagination. As a result, we concluded that sleeping in the same room would prove the better and consequently safer option. Grant and I were disturbed a few times during the night as, according to the girls the water boiler sounded just like someone sneaking in the front door, however apart from that, I slept like a baby (this saying has always confused me as, according to numerous stories from tired looking parents, babies seem to spend the whole night crying uncontrollably).

The following day was Saturday and although I had been in Australia for five days now, this was the first time I felt like I was seeing the true side of it. Having examined the poor quality of Australian Saturday morning television for thirty seconds, I had decided that checking my e-mails was a much higher priority.

Although there was a large area of watered grass, most of the camp was dry and desolate, especially in comparison with England. I looked towards the clouds and into the covering trees in the hope of spying my first koala. I was unsuccessful on this particular occasion and instead spotted a few tropical and florescent parrots, which, I decided, were an adequate enough substitute.

Greg informed us of an engagement that he and his family were attending during the remainder of the day. Surprisingly, he left us with his master set of keys which gave us free rein of the entire camp. It was very trustworthy of him, as he had only known us for the best part of eighteen hours. I have barely enough confidence to leave my friends in charge of my house and I have known them for eighteen *years*. There were bikes, canoes, bows, arrows, basketballs and table tennis facilities all at our disposal, not to mention a kitchen stocked with enough food to feed five thousand (and I'm not talking about five loaves and two fishes). However, the result of this newfound freedom and responsibility was not exactly met with the immediate relish one would expect. Instead, overwhelmed by the huge choice and unsure which to try first, we subsequently found ourselves still in the office come lunchtime. Then there was a knock at the door
'Excuse me mate, who the bloody hell is Lady Northcote?' a large bearded man asked politely walking into the office.
Well you can imagine our surprise. We didn't know who this man was, what he was doing here or who 'the bloody hell' Lady Northcote was. I glanced at Grant hoping he would answer and in turn he stared at Sian.
'Oh sorry, we're doing sort of a treasure hunt and one of the tasks is to find out who Lady Northcote is' he said in a chuckling voice, having seen the blank looks on our faces 'there's quite a few car loads on their way'

'Sorry, we only arrived today' I finally said, as the uneasy silence reached its peak 'we haven't got a clue who Lady Northcote is, but take a brochure and hopefully you'll find what you need.'

This was not ideal, but he smiled and seemed pleased enough. After his departure we decided that we should try and readily equip ourselves for the hoards of determined treasure hunters closing in upon us and find out once and for all who Lady Northcote was. Failing that, we simply decided to leave reception and relieve ourselves from this harsh burden of responsibility.

The exploration of the camp continued to fascinate the four of us, along with throwing up one or two unwelcome surprises. As we cycled past a small waterhole Grant reflected 'that's a nice little pond, I wonder if there are any fish in it', to which I replied 'it's a sewage lake'. He hadn't noticed the signs (or the smell come to think about it). I did consider the possibility of not letting him in on my little secret and maybe encouraging him to go for a swim, however having taken into account the torture my nostrils would go through, I decided against it.

As evening drew in, we decided to go and explore the culinary delights on offer. The dinner hall was deserted and as I walked across the polished floor, my footsteps echoed against the wall. We had every variety of food at our disposal; it therefore came as a bit of a surprise that I found myself carrying a bowl of tuna and sweet corn pasta with onions and peppers added for a bit of extra tinge. From all the food that was possible and all the potential presented to us, this choice was far from the top ten. As I looked down at my plate there was one thing that came to mind – human vomit.

Still, I tucked in and it didn't taste quite so bad, besides I concluded it was good practice for student life. The kitchen that was positively dancing in the euphoria of cleanliness only moments before was now a shadow of its former self. The work surface resembled some sort of modern art with a series of random ice cream, milk and mayonnaise (experimental idea, not recommended) blobs covering its face. Deciding I needed a bit of air, I made my way to the door of the kitchen, but as I pushed through it quickly, I came to an abrupt halt. Looking straight forward, about two inches away from my face was the hairiest and biggest spider I have ever had the misfortune to nearly collide with. I do not say this lightly, for I have been to museums and numerous Zoos, but this was like a mammoth in size. It stared back at me with numerous yellow eyes piercing my gazing stare. This was undoubtedly a heavyweight of the spider world. Maybe it had managed to get hold of some spider steroids, I wasn't sure of that but I was certain I didn't want to take it on in a fight.

As I backed down, I subtly tried to slide round the side of the web but soon realised it was watching and anticipating my every move. In the two hours we had spent creating a tuna mess, this crafty beast had managed to construct a web across the entire width of the doorway, which although worrying was also rather impressive. However, if I was in any doubt that all the creatures in Australia were after my blood, I wasn't anymore. Backing away slowly into the kitchen, I was reluctant to take my eyes from the fiend.

Safely in the comfort of the kitchen, I assessed my dire situation. The other door appeared to be a much safer option so I made a sprint for it, taking far more care than I had before. The coast was clear so I made a dash for freedom through the darkness. Bang! 'What the hell??!'. Opening my eyes, I saw the stars through a gap in the trees. I was lying on the floor. What had happened? Had something tripped me? I peered around and found myself slumped half across a hole about half a metre deep and a metre wide. The darkness had camouflaged this dangerous trap and I had evidently slipped along the sharp edge. But how did it get there? In my mind there were two possibilities; either the spider, as part of its cunning plan, had dug it, or alternatively it had fallen from a bush and created this crater with its sheer weight. The animals were out to get me, of this, there was now no doubt.

Bacchus Marsh was silent and lifeless as it had been the last time we were there two days ago. It was now 8am on Sunday morning and as I peered down at the immaculately kept main street, there didn't appear to be any signs of life. The train station was a good size and as a result seemed to be out of proportion with the rest of the town.

During these first few days on Australian soil, I had not needed a diary, a watch or a telephone. Sian was there instead. She had the dates of every single event of interest chiselled in her brain (by this I mean that she had remembered them, not that she had performed some sort of painful and weird chiselling act to her head – that would be hideous). It was therefore her careful planning that led us to acquire four ground passes for the final of the Australian Open tennis championships.

The train arrived on time, much to my pleasant surprise and I duly took a seat opposite Grant and slept. I awoke to the sound of screeching brakes as the train slowed approaching Spencer Street station. During my sleep, our carriage seemed to have packed itself full of passengers, all of whom wanted to alight at Spencer Street. The four of us got broken up for a while, but Grant was easy enough to follow and definitely stood out in his glowing white and red England jersey.

As the crowd soon dispersed, Sian led us through the underground station towards daylight and the street above. There was a lot more life here than at Bacchus Marsh as trams and cars sped between the various sets of traffic lights. We passed a large group of ravers doing the 'walk of shame', still wearing their luminous clothing and sucking their stereotypical ultra violet dummies.

Looking for a way into the city, we stood at a tram stop which was inconveniently placed in the middle of the road and watched as a series of trams passed. Many seemed to be fairly new, however every so often an antique wooden one would glide by, looking as if they had been stolen from eastern Europe.

On the plus side, our journey was complimentary as our tram soon arrived and sped off towards the arena allowing us to sample the multitude of culture throughout the city of Melbourne. This was my first real taste of the city and at this initial stage of evaluation, I wasn't really sure what to make of it. On the one hand, with ancient wooden trams gliding along past my sleepy eyes, it felt like I was in Prague. However, the skyscrapers soaring into the clouds above were telling a much different story.

The tram jerked around a corner at a considerably complicated junction and ploughed on towards Federation Square, flinging us forward every twenty seconds or so as it stopped at yet another set of traffic lights (whoever designed these Australian cities was certainly suffering from some kind of traffic light fetish). Sian was acting as our personal tour guide for the day and she soon pointed out Federation Square approaching at a stuttered pace on our right. From my first glance, I concluded that this was Melbourne's answer to Circular Quay - an arty, cosmopolitan and lively place packed full of restaurants and fancy cáfes selling hundreds of varieties of coffee. It certainly wasn't as large or as alive as its Sydney equivalent (for starters, I didn't see one clown or street performer within the vicinity) but it certainly matched it for cultural fulfilment. The whole area was skilfully designed with a number of calming fountains, modern sculptures and ergonomically pleasing benches. The buildings were highly abstract, with a large proportion constructed entirely out of glass. There was nothing uniform about their shape, on the contrary it was difficult to deduce whether this was an intentional art ploy, or whether the foundations were merely sinking. The courtyard area created was as peculiar in shape as the structures that surrounded it. This immediately begged the question 'why Federation *Square*?' and the only feasible answer I received from my fellow travellers was that 'Federation Almost Hexagon But Not Quite' does not exactly have the same appeal. It seemed very lively though, and as I pushed my face against the glass, a sense of adventure had been created within my psyche which made me eager to explore its offerings. Although I wasn't aware of it at the time, this was my first taste of the pleasurable and enriching feeling of excitement that this highly fashionable city can induce.

The excitement in our voices was brewing as the tram continued to strive on towards the arena and we contemplated various excuses we could use in order to get into the dressing room and possibly meet the players. This is turn prompted Grant to explain (once again) that, not only had he met Jonny Wilkinson, he had also gone to the same school as he.

Along the left hand side I now noticed a number of parallel streets, running perpendicular to the tram, that were home to a number of pubs and bars. It was rather confusing as, far from being unique, each appeared to be a clone of its neighbour. I soon realised that I was peering into the famous grid system of Melbourne's CBD - an area divided into blocks, divided by many long straight roads which should be incredibly easy to follow. In actual fact, the opposite is true. With so many roads travelling in the same direction and sharing so many resembling features, a maze of confusion is created which is guaranteed to render even the most experienced boy-scout disorientated.

Thankfully however, our tram continued to bypass this pool of puzzlement and instead travelled along the riverbank south of the city centre. A banner advertised that there was an art exhibition taking place in a building on our right hand side and Grant was fascinated to see that the artist shared the same name as his history teacher. I suggested that he was perhaps following Grant in order to claim back an overdue book, but this was not met with a smile. After careful consideration, I decided to end the conversation assuming that either Grant had a history of not returning library books, or alternatively that my joke was not funny. To be honest, I think I know which one is more likely. Worrying that I was losing the audience, I quickly instigated some topical tennis conversation again, as the tall buildings began to disperse and a weather front that was worthy of an English winter was revealed. Could it be that the sun does not *always* shine in Australia? Far more confusing than these unexpected clouds however, was the bizarrely impractical road system the city seemed to have inherited. From what I could see, it appeared that any car wanting to turn right at a junction was required to get in the *left-hand* lane before performing (with the help of a minor miracle or two) an elaborate manoeuvre across the lanes of traffic. To say it was impractical, treacherous and bloody scary is an understatement of dramatic proportions.

Gleaming modestly in the shadow of the magnificent Melbourne Cricket Ground (MCG), we caught our first glimpse of the Rod Laver arena. Having had the pleasure of visiting Wimbledon, I noticed that the Australian Open was situated in the same way. Both are so perfectly tranquil, they are worthy of a stately home and reminiscent of the countryside. For this reason, they are welcomed in the city but somehow seem oddly out of place.

Outside, there was a young man selling over-priced programmes, but this didn't bother us because it was the occasion of a lifetime (well I say that now, but I didn't actually buy one in the end – they were *far* too expensive.). Piled on his head was a mass of uncombed ginger hair, which contrasted greatly with his bright, immaculately kept uniform. However, there was something strange and pleasantly different about his attitude that definitely set me back and surprised me. As Sian raided her bag in search of the correct change, the boy did not demonstrate a lack of patience or annoyance, but instead began chatting to us as if we had been friends for years.

'I recognise your accent' he said turning to Sian 'you're from Wales, aren't you? Me and a few of the guys went on a rugby tour there last year, what part are you from? We went to the north near Prestatyn'.

'Yeah it's gorgeous up there' Sian replied, obviously pleasantly surprised by his talkative nature.

'And how about the rest of you guys, are you from Wales too?' he said looking round at the rest of us.

'No!' Emma immediately protested 'we're English - I live near London'.

'Ah Pommies, I should have known. You didn't *seriously* think Henman was going to make it *this* far did you?!' he replied with a huge, smug smile on his face.

'Do you want me to remind you of Leyton Hewitt's performance?' I said in an equally mocking way. On this note, he wished us a good day and we continued towards the gate. I found it fascinating, and to some extent warming, that such friendly banter could occur with someone I had known for only twenty seconds. And I owe it all to Tim Henman's incredibly poor tennis ability and lack of testicular fortitude.

I remember as a young lad (back in the day!) setting my alarm for 3am -much to annoyance of my parents – and watching the likes of Boris Becker and Pete Sampras in the Australian Open final. It seemed a world away then - possibly even a different world - but here I now stood, in the very arena where those famous events had occurred. Unfortunately I didn't have a ticket for the court, but using my incredible powers of persuasion along with my boyish good looks, I had managed to convince a steward to let me in for a photo. As always is the case, the arena seemed so much smaller than the television portrays, but the camera definitely hadn't exaggerated the dazzling qualities of the green seats. Grant, Sian and Emma stood on the outskirts of the stadium and waited for me to return from the photo shoot.

We walked around beneath the grey painted sky, overwhelmed by the carnival atmosphere that was gradually increasing in front of our eyes. Sian and Grant soon discovered the merchandise stalls and found it necessary to blow their money on a couple of 'essential', brightly coloured t-shirts. I'm not particularly a tacky t-shirt fan, but I definitely thought that a memento of some kind was important. This is how I came to own an Australian Open tennis shaped yo-yo - an item which (so far in my life) has proved to be about as useful as a *'one-legged man in an arse-kicking competition'*. This has yet again confirmed my suspicion that all merchandise is designed effectively without any kind of practical use. In other words, all merchandise is intended to be useless.

As Grant was trying to find himself a hat, Emma and I took a seat in one of the beautifully designed gardens and people-watched for a while. It was a fascinating activity especially with so many different nationalities within one area. We saw a number of Swiss fans in confident mood, holding giant flags and convinced that Federer's brilliant dominance would prevail. The Russians were very few in numbers and those that were present kept a relatively low profile compared to the Swiss. Obviously they didn't really fancy Safin's chances.

There were of course, a high-number of Japanese and Asian tourists, each one being strangled by the thousands of pounds worth of video and camera equipment strapped round their necks. Emma and I were laughing about the tacky hat Grant was contemplating buying, when just at that moment, a tiny Chinese lady caught our eye. It appeared as if she had purchased every single item of merchandise that was available. From head to foot, she was covered in the Australian Open logo without any exception at all. We stared in disbelief as, in her Australian Open hat, t-shirt and trousers she attempted to carry ten or twenty other bags full of items around with her. I was convinced that all her purchases must have exceeded her body weight about ten times. It was as if the Australian Open was her sponsor. This made us laugh heavily and bought Grant's purchases right back into perspective. Having thought about it for a while, I suggested to Emma that maybe the lady had taken the saying 'shop till you drop' a little too literally.

As the final commenced, we took our seats and watched the match on a giant screen situated thirty metres in front of us. There was a large grass area where all the Swiss fans had congregated, creating a huge mass of red and white flags, which fluttered and shook every time Roger Federer won a point. The final itself was no contest at all. This wasn't because of Safin's inability to play well, it was purely down to the unstoppable play demonstrated by the Swiss champion much to the delight of his hoards of supporters. Although the final had been quick, this had been an incredibly memorable and enjoyable occasion and one which I never thought I would experience. The only sour note of the day occurred when we returned to the train station. Sian looked me up and down with a very sympathetic look
'Oh dear, that's going to be painful' she said in a concerned voice.
When I checked my face in the mirror, it quite closely resembled a fried tomato wearing sunglasses. Although this sounds selfish, I was thankful that

Emma's skin had taken a similar battering and I wasn't going to be the sole focus of all the jokes. Even through the clouds, the powerful Australian sun had successfully disembowelled my fragile white skin leaving me looking like a typical English tourist. The one piece of advice I had been given before my departure was 'do not under estimate the ferocity of the sun Down Under'. I guess some people just have to learn the hard way.

CHAPTER 7

It had been over an hour since we left Traralgon, but eventually our Toyota Hilux arrived in Heyfield. My immediate impression was that this mountainous town was incredibly cute. In every direction there were immaculately kept lawns and impossibly straight flowerbeds. It seemed like quite an old-fashioned and close community which kept trend with the other Victorian towns we had passed through by housing a long, wide main street lined with local convenience shops. There was a hardware shop, a butchers, a bakers and of course a very busy pub.

Our host Simon had arrived on Monday evening looking tired and exhausted. The five-hour drive did not seem appealing that night and so we decided to catch forty winks and then jump on the road first thing in the morning. Leaving Emma and Sian was upsetting and I couldn't help feel this emotion was somewhat dominating my gap year. It seemed that, no sooner had I settled into a group than I was being torn away from them and forced to make alliances with others. This was somewhat frustrating and made the thought of bonding with anyone seem rather pointless. But as I quickly learned, this is how things are for the long distance traveller and although you are constantly in contact with people, the loneliness you feel inside can be great. Some people cope by shutting others out completely for fear of losing yet another friend. I was determined to avoid this technique as its risks were plentiful and could easily result in pit of self-destruction. However, like any skill you learn to perfect the art of saying goodbye and I eventually did this by perceiving it not for its negative qualities, but as the beginning of yet another adventure. I suppose deep down I was just missing home.

We were now four hours into our journey and looking forward to stretching our legs. Two more minutes disappeared (along with my mobile phone signal) and already we had reached the other side of Heyfield. Simon turned to us both, laughed to himself and then said in a sympathetic tone
'I hope you don't get car sick, this is where the journey really begins'.

    Gum trees flashed past the window in their thousands, springing out of the dusty ground as we weaved around them along the coiled mountain road. If there was one thing I was sure of, it was that Romans definitely hadn't built it. But that didn't bother Simon in the slightest and he definitely wasn't slowing for any corner. The road itself wasn't in the greatest condition and the edge of the mountain was always close - a little too close you could say. On more than one occasion, I did peer down out of the window only to be faced by a sheer one hundred million foot drop. Although exaggerations can be expected from my account, I can assure you it was high. There was nothing between the fall and me apart from a pane of glass and I couldn't even see the road beneath us because we were so close to the edge, or more to the point, hanging over it. Then my stomach began to turn.

Wilderness passed the car window like a repeating piece of scenery from a 1950s movie as we got higher into the mountains and civilisation soon faded into oblivion. The brown thirsty fields appeared again in the valley below. Then, after an hour or so of mountain driving, we rounded our final corner and a sea of green, lush grass hit our eyes. We had finally arrived at Licola.

CHAPTER 8

Originally built as a logging town, Licola was once a thriving place, reaping the rewards produced by a rapidly expanding economy. Most of the original buildings still stand today, however the once energetic settlement has been reduced to a permanent population of just six. This gave the place an extreme sense of isolation which was somewhat intimidating especially on that first afternoon. As we drove past the wooden 'Licola' sign hanging from a nearby tree, I couldn't help but feel I was in the middle of a Clint Eastwood film. I knew Heyfield was nearly sixty kilometres away, but learning that only six people could cope with the conditions enough to actually *live* in Licola, sparked up nightmarish images of a town where the locals willingly encourage their disabled but freakishly strong son to play with his chainsaw dangerously close to your genitals.

As if to support my nasty suspicions, I recall the first visit I made to the village shop. It was owned by an elderly couple whom we seldom saw and apparently sold everything from fishing equipment to cuddly, novelty teddy bears. Well, what else could you need, isolated in the mountains? Anyway, I tentatively made my way across the road, careful to avoid the one car that normally passed daily, and made my way into the shop. The bell

rang as the door closed behind me but nobody else seemed to be there. It was actually quite pleasant and sold a variety of confectionary delights (all extremely overpriced of course) as well as a good selection of beer. As I poked my way around the items for sale, I suddenly heard a voice behind me 'Yees?' Can I help you?" it said in a croaky voice that sounded like it hadn't spoken for years.
'Oh, hello' I said looking at the lady in front of me. I suspected she was a lot younger than she looked 'My name's John, I've just moved into the camp across the street. Nice to meet you' I said holding out a hand which she shook suspiciously. As she looked me up and down, I couldn't help feel I'd fallen into a scene from *'The League of Gentleman'*.
'I seeee. What do you want?'.
'Ummm' I said rather taken back by her directness. Could she really be that busy that she didn't have time for a quick chat? 'I'm just after some stamps' I finally mustered up.
'Some, whaat?' she said, obviously confused by my request.
'Stamps. I want to send a letter back to England'.
'What is it that you want?'.
'STAMPS!' I shouted back in frustration 'I want some stamps – you know, a square piece of paper, normally sticky on one side which you lick and place in the top right hand corner of an envelope in order to cover postage costs'.
'Oh you mean staaamps' she said back in a particularly weary tone.
'I'm pretty sure that's exactly what I just said, just not in such a dreary way'.
'Well I haven't got any stamps, have I?'.
'Umm...what?' I replied in astonishment 'what do you mean? This is the shop isn't it?'.
'We don't just have stamps lying around. I'll have to order some in. Should be here next week when the next delivery arrives'.
And with that, I left. She was one of only six permanent residents of the town, but I never spoke to her again. To be honest, that shop scared me a little so I avoided it like the plague from that point forward. It was the first afternoon. Recalling the story to Simon some minutes later, he found it hysterical and called his fiancée Kate who laughed along too. As joint managers of the camp, Kate and Simon were not what I was expecting at all. Both in their early thirties, their love for nature and desire for a different way of life had led them from Melbourne to Licola, where they had transformed

the camp into a highly successful activity centre for children over the past two years. I asked Kate if the isolation was a problem
'Yeah it can be sometimes, but then you just go for a walk and look around at your surroundings and you realise you're living in one of the most beautiful spots on Earth'.
Their friendliness, passion and love of Licola gave me great hope for the next few months. Suddenly life appeared to be a lot more optimistic. It was a strange sensation as I had only been there for about an hour, but was already suffering from such a huge array of emotions. Then Simon said
'Don't worry if you're feeling a little unsure about this place now. Everyone feels that way when they arrive because it's such a huge change of lifestyle. But believe me, the spirit of this place is like magic and it will definitely grab you'.
I think it already had.

Later that afternoon, another team member arrived, named Cherry. She was your typical Australian girl with bright blonde hair, tanned skin and an incredibly vivacious personality. Pulling up in her battered white van, she beeped the horn, jumped out and gave us all a hug. I had never seen someone inspire so much confidence in the company of new people before and that was slightly disconcerting to begin with. However, after thirty minutes in her company it soon became apparent that this was down to Cherry's incredibly energetic outlook on life. We had known each other for less than hour, but already she was doing impressions of our accents
'Don't worry guys, if I take the piss out of ya, it means I like ya' she said with a thick Australian twang.

Kate decided to take all three of us for a tour of the camp so we could begin to appreciate its unique characteristics.
'Right on the footsteps of the Alpine National Park, Licola provides the gateway into the extreme Australian bush' she said as we followed, listening intently 'Licola was built as a logging town and this is what forms the basis for our camp today. The track we are standing on used to be the old main road and these' she said pointing towards sixteen pristine wooden houses, all lined up along the road 'were the worker's family homes. This is now our guest accommodation'.

It was a truly amazing experience to think these were once the houses used by the loggers themselves. It was like living in a piece of history, but then, I suppose that is what we are doing every day. Surrounded by mountains on three sides and the beautiful Macallister River on the other, Kate was opening my eyes to what an incredibly special place this was. Guiding us through a line of trees she then led us to a wooden chapel which I was somewhat surprised about. Apparently it had been created by the workers as a place to worship, but had unfortunately fallen into disrepair. Thankfully though, recent work had restored it well, although I was assured it was rarely in use. Part of the original saw mill tower was still standing and Kate showed us that before leading us towards the generators.

'What are the generators actually used for?' I enquired.

'Everything. There isn't any mains electricity. We generate our own power, pump our own water and treat our waste'.

I knew we were out of touch with civilisation, but no mains electricity? God, what else was in store?

The new camp facilities were located right at the centre of the oval shaped grounds. These included pretty much everything we needed in order to survive in this extreme environment such as kitchens, toilets and even a little hospital. Of course, there were other amenities needed for running a school camp such as a large sports hall, a reception area and a huge dining hall with a balcony overlooking the acres of green playing fields. Grant and I were given our own self contained flat which was conveniently attached to the hospital. It had its own kitchen, bathroom, washing machine and veranda. Pushing Grant and Simon out of the way and running to the door like an obese child chasing a doughnut, I managed to get in first and pick the room of my choice. Grant laughed at the time, but the smile was soon wiped from his face as I reclined on my luxury king-size bed whilst he peered angrily at his inadequate single. I was quite generous though and offered him a small section of my walk-in wardrobe to store some of his clothes. What a lovely fellow I am.

It was then that I noticed a television in the corner. Reaching for the plug, I felt like I was grabbing out to gain one last link with real civilization. But every channel was the same - static. Although impressed that I was listening to the remnants of a Big Bang some 13.7 billion years ago, I was ultimately disappointed that *'Neighbours'* would be absent from my life.

'Sorry mate, we can't get any television signal up here. Or radio for that matter. We've got loads of video tapes though, so you can enjoy them' Simon said, sensing my frustration.

With such large grounds and the added advantage of a natural river, Licola incorporated a whole range of recreational activities. Across the wide open oval there was archery, high ropes and a rock-climbing wall. I hadn't really been sure what high ropes were before, but the clue was in the name. Quite simply, it was a series of cables arranged into a mini assault course twelve metres above the ground and supported by a number of large telegraph poles. Obviously there were a few more technicalities, but that's the general gist. In addition to this, there were canoeing facilities on the river (i.e. canoes) and a swimming pool although Kate informed me that it was never really used as they encouraged the children to embrace nature and use the river instead. Recalling the story concerning the young quad biker made me a little apprehensive about this, however I was assured that there wasn't a crocodile for a few thousand kilometres. There had, however, been a number of duckbilled platypus sightings so I looked forward to that with inquisitive anticipation.

The remainder of the evening was spent meeting the rest of the staff which was somewhat daunting. As well as Kate and Simon, there was another camp co-ordinator named Barry who was in charge of organising the sponsored camp for disadvantaged children. Taking care of all the food needs was Mick the chef, who was a lovely guy but a typical 'Pommie Basher' especially when it came to discussing sport.
'Ah, a Pom! You wouldn't have won the world cup without Jonny Wilkinson you know?' he said upon meeting me.
'Yeah, but we did have him!' I replied, going along with the banter.
'What about the Rugby League though mate? We destroyed you in that!'.
'Unfortunately for you, nobody cares about Rugby league' I said, to which he had no response.
I felt victorious, but this was not to be the last sporting discussion Mick and I would have over the forthcoming months. The other permanent program staff were three girls named Tessa, Lisa-Jane (or LJ) and Jayne. Along with Grant, Cherry and myself, we made up a six-man team destined to change the lives of kids forever. Okay, perhaps that was slightly dramatic - we were

in charge of running all the activities for the school children when they arrived. Tessa had her bottom lip pierced which made me slightly weary of her at first, but soon I realised that, like Cherry, she was a lovely, fun-loving girl. If I had seen Lisa-Jane walking down the street, I would immediately have suspected she was an English literature teacher with her thick-rimmed glasses and intellectual mannerisms. Jayne on the other hand was quite simply terrifying - in a nice way. Is that possible? I'm not sure. She had the best volume to height ratio of anyone I had ever met. But when I say volume, I'm talking about her voice. She could shout and complain about anything in the world and make it seem hilarious. Australian's are famed for their bluntness and Jayne was at the extreme end of the scale. I mean, don't get me wrong, we all loved her immediately, but when she spoke you never knew what sort of insults were going to come out. It was all in good spirit though and a nice welcome to the world of Aussie culture.

Having settled in and conducted a few polite conversations with each other, Kate and Simon arranged a meal for us all. Mick cooked up a traditional Australian dish of frozen pie served with ketchup, whilst we all sat out on the balcony bonding. The first children would be arriving the very next day - how was I expected to teach them when I was in such unfamiliar territory? Thankfully, Cherry assured me she'd get us through and even volunteered to start teaching us a couple of essential knots. Having decided I wasn't too keen on killing a child on my first day of work, I duly accepted her invitation.

As we feasted on disgusting camp food (I would soon get used to it), we all told our own individual stories of how we had ended up in Licola. I looked around at the mountains as the sun began to set behind them. It was a simply incredible view. We carried on drinking and chatting into the night as the pale blue sky transformed itself into a deep black, illuminated by a sea of stars.
'The night sky is amazing up here - there's no artificial lighting for over sixty kilometres' Simon said pointing out The Southern Cross constellation.
'I'm going to study astronomy at University' I said 'but I've never seen a night this clear before. Shame about that cloud' I said indicating a long thin cloud that had just appeared, splitting the sky in two. 'Wait a minute....it's not…is it?' I said. Simon waited for the penny to drop.
'It is. That my friend is not a cloud, it's The Milky Way'

For all my years of astronomy, I had never seen The Milky Way in England. But here I was in a place so isolated, so clean, and so un-touched that I could see something over thirty thousand light years away and deep in our galactic centre. Licola had gifted me a unique window through which the past was truly accessible. Never before had the distant light from these heavenly objects pierced my eyes quite so dominantly. This defined prominence in the sky reiterated just how insignificant our planet was in relation to the great universal pond. All of a sudden, our isolation seemed somewhat trivial in comparison as Licola provided me with a strange warmth that finally felt like home.

I'm not sure if the loggers had heard of bricks or whether they were merely trying to use the resources they had available, but their wooden houses certainly were cold. With its position in between three mountains, the sun didn't rise in Licola until late morning giving it a really chilly environment anyway, so the fact that we only had paper for walls didn't exactly help matters. Having been fooled by every Australian television program, I had assumed prior to departure that the country's temperature rarely fell below 20 degrees Celsius and had subsequently packed the thinnest sleeping bag in a somewhat foolish attempt to save luggage space. As I'm sure you can imagine, the effect of combining all these factors was somewhat undesirable and resulted in a very cold night sleep. This on its own may not have been quite so bad, but when the sun did eventually pop up from behind the mountains, it did so with vicious vengeance. Obviously frustrated by not being able to cook us from the early hours, it was as if it had stored up all that excess energy and released it at the first given opportunity. As a result, the temperature and humidity would soar up before I'd even had a chance to remove my jumper and drain my energy until simple movements felt utterly impossible.

  On the very first morning, I had been assigned breakfast duty which I hadn't been particularly happy about it, but due to the arctic conditions found myself wide awake at 6.30am anyway. Having only just finished school myself, it was bizarre to now be considered as an authoritative figure. I immediately had sympathy for my old teachers. Wearing approximately fifteen layers, I ventured out towards the dining hall and improvised a pathetic plan to organise a hoard of rioting twelve year olds into an orderly fashion. Having just about got them settled, the kitchen then served pancakes with gallons of Maple Syrup which only succeeded in pushing their energy levels right back up. Luckily though, the ultimate responsibility for their discipline lay with the teachers, so I sneaked out the side door and let them handle it - after all, they'd be receiving a wage packet at the end of the month and all I would get was a pat on the back.

The camp programs we ran usually lasted 3-5days and were designed to encourage team building as well as personal development. As a consequence, they were incredibly popular with schools looking to provide a great bonding experience for their younger students. As an added bonus, it gave the predominantly city based children a great opportunity to let off steam and experience 'the great outdoors'. The teachers would therefore deal with the children and provide their entertainment in the evenings, leaving us free to do whatever we liked.

However, days were still hard and often lasted from 7am until perhaps 9pm, if you were on dinner duty. Even if you hadn't been put on for breakfast co-ordination, you were expected to set up various activities and perform safety checks an hour before the students were due to arrive. Of course this wouldn't have been too bad, but the fact that the work was voluntary made it all the more difficult. I knew this is what I'd volunteered to do and was happy to offer my time, safe in the knowledge that my generous contribution was helping to make a difference to these kids' lives. Yeah right! Cherry, LJ, Tess and Jayne were making the same contribution and getting a damn fine wage for their troubles! The long hours, combined with the draining heat made the job even more difficult. I don't know how to explain the weather in Licola for the heat was like nothing I had experienced before. During that first week, temperatures at midday were constantly reaching the high-thirties, but it was the way it suffocated you and extracted every morsel of energy that was the problem. When you are on holiday with a lovely sea-breeze, this type of temperature is seen as a blessing, but in such a dry climate with no protection, it was simply unbearable.

Groups of 12-15 students would arrive on hourly rotations at your specific activity, during which time you would have to give a safety brief, and then, standing in the blistering heat, belay each one through. In addition, as an instructor I was kitted to the teeth in safety equipment, and although this made me feel incredibly important, it was nevertheless rather sweaty to

the point that my helmet could have quite easily been used as a swimming pool by lunch.
'Do you know Harry Potter?' I would be asked without fail by each group.
'Yep, he's my next door neighbour' would be my response.
'How about the Queen?'.
'Yeah , I used to go out with old Lizzie. All three of us have dinner together on Wednesdays actually - the conversation is thrilling. We all have so much in common'.
This is an example of a typical conversation I would have at least thirty-six times each day. With the teachers there as a disciplinary figure, we could afford to relax slightly. As a result, (most) of the children responded far more positively to tasks than I had anticipated and treated us program staff like the 'cool older sibling'. Okay, maybe I added in the word 'cool', but definitely older sibling. From my point of view, this was something I had not anticipated but made the experience all the more enjoyable. I found I wanted to be there despite the early mornings, plague of flies and extreme heat.

Sometimes we would conduct night hikes through the bush and to the top of one of the large hills. Once there, we would get the children to conduct a moment silence. Being from the city, they had very rarely been in such a peaceful environment and highlighting just how isolated we were seemed to make a great impression on them. It was a simple exercise but one that made you realise the great impact you were having on their lives, if only for a short while. But the impact wasn't just on the children, it was on me too as I found myself interacting in a real Australian community. No longer did I feel like a simple traveller passing through - I was living, working and building relationships with the natives and this gave me a marvellous feeling of acceptance.

For the next few weeks this is really how camp continued. I developed my training skills quite substantially and was soon running high ropes, canoeing and rock-climbing under supervision. In addition to this, I created some games for the low ropes and archery, which allowed me to run them on my own. I'm not sure if I was covered by insurance, but this was Australia! Who gives a damn? If a child had fallen off and broken an arm, it would've been their own damn fault!

Of course, there were a few subtle social differences that took a bit of getting used to. For example, telling a student to 'shut up' was considered incredibly offensive, whereas calling them a 'little bastard' was considered endearing. I also learned that when an Australian says 'thongs' he is not talking about incredibly small underpants, but is instead referring to flip-flops. I wasn't aware of this on my first day and was subsequently rather shocked when Kate asked me to make sure the children weren't wearing thongs. Thankfully, noticing my severe discomfort she explained the cultural differences between the words, otherwise I would probably be writing this book from a cell deep inside Melbourne prison.

CHAPTER 9

As they were school camps, weekends were usually left completely free. However, due to the marathon drive to get just about anywhere, we mostly spent them in Licola. Of course, here and there the odd person would head back home, but Grant and I spent three of the first four weekends in the mountains. Upon arrival, this had not seemed like a good option at all – in fact Grant and I had run to Melbourne on that very first weekend to escape the severe confinement of Licola – however after a while we had developed such a great community, it seemed like a waste to leave. After all, with the crystal clear waters of the Macallister river to swim in, huge green fields to play football and some of the greatest hiking terrain on the planet right on our doorstep, why would we want to watch dire television?

That being the case, we actually started to discover that instead of waiting for us to come back, the city folk would instead come to us. On just the second weekend, Cherry's boyfriend and mother drove up along the winding road with their car jammed to the limit with booze and steaks. Tess' friend also made the pilgrimage and with Mick hanging around too, we had ourselves a little party weekend.

'John Boy!' Cherry shouted to me in her best *'Little House on the Prairie'* accent, before changing to an incredibly posh Englishman 'do come and help will you – there's an awful lot of alcohol here'.

'I would do, but I love seeing you struggle' I said, watching her attempt to drag a crate of *Victoria Bitter* 'I knew you Aussies couldn't handle your alcohol'.

'We'll see who can handle their alcohol' said Jamie, Cherry's boyfriend, before throwing a bottle of *VB* in my direction. These were the first words he had ever said to me and I immediately knew I was going to like him. Unbelievably, it was ice cold.

'How is this beer so cold, you've only been here thirty seconds?' I enquired.

'I've got an Eskie cool-box packed full of ice – you've got to be prepared for these situations'. Indeed you do but I was still incredibly impressed by his approach to alcoholic beverages 'so, are you boys into football – like real football?' he enquired.

'Aussie Rules?' I asked.

'No real football, as in The English Premiership. I'm a Coventry City fan – follow them like mad. I even got the 1987 FA Cup final imported on DVD. No, I hate all this Aussie Rules - give me *real* football any day'.

From that moment forward, I could tell this was going to be a good weekend.

We drank all day, played football and then made our way to the river for a pre-barbeque swim. The others went ahead, whilst Grant and I made our way across to the shop to purchase some more alcohol. However, remembering the infamous stamp incident, I decided to keep my distance. Without too much incident, Grant emerged from the shop with three bags full of cider and looked rather happy with himself. We were both topless due to the immense heat and I couldn't help think that we had succeeded in bringing a nice English Friday night to the Australian bush!

However, our pride was soon dented upon reaching the river when our freakishly white 'Pommie skin' was mocked by the enviously brown Australians. Not letting it get us down though, we ran and dived off the platform into the beautiful pristine waters of the mountain spring. Hearing the commotion, Daryn the caretaker (who could have easily played the part of Pluto in a Popeye film) came across to investigate. Informing us that he had just purchased a dart board, we were all invited round for a tournament later that evening. I suspected that if we continued to drink as we had so far, Daryn would soon regret that decision.

With the barbeque positioned right by the river bank, it was set up for the perfect evening. Mick rustled up some of the largest steaks I have ever seen, along with an impressive array of sausages, burgers and a range of salads (which were left relatively untouched). So, beer in hand and steak on plate, I sat and enjoyed my first true 'barbie' experience. I must say it was brilliant and actually rather cultural, if not slightly overfilling. Having been comprehensively beaten at darts, Grant and I hung our heads in shame with the only consolation being that we had made a number of small holes in a gloating Australian sportsman's wall.

But it was all in the spirit of the community we had managed to create in this tiny cove on planet Earth. I felt like I had gone back in time – to the time your grandparents always talk about – the time before television. I had always considered this to be somewhat of a myth, but here in Licola I was experiencing the effects of living in a world not dominated by such a convenient form of entertainment. As a result, we had been put in the somewhat daunting position of having to use our creativity to produce games for our own amusement. We could not hide behind the spirit crushing television anymore. And as I sat around the fire with all these new people, my life felt positively enriched because of it.

The next morning I went through to Grant's room and he was asleep, still fully clothed and lying in a very awkward looking position. It looked like the Australian spirit had got too much for a few people. With such a long drive ahead of them, the others left early nursing a number of hazy hangovers. I wasn't sure how the whirlwind, mountainous drive was going to affect them, but suspected the outcome would be slightly negative. I had been sensible however, and following an early morning swim in the river, felt very upbeat. With the help of the others, we decided to consult the paper in order to find out if any momentous events were happening in our area. It turned out that there was nothing of the sort and the best thing we could find was 'The Paynesville Jazz Festival'.

'I don't really see myself as a Jazz person' I said 'but I'm up for checking it out'.

'Yeah, I reckon you're right' said Tess 'we might as well go and check it out - it's not too far away, so if it's shit we can just come back anyway'.

'Okay cool. How far is it by the way?'.

'I don't know - a hundred and fifty k's I guess'.
'And that's a short drive to you?'.
'When you live in this country, anything under two-hundred k's is considered quite close'.
So, on the spur of the moment and with none of us being that enthused by the prospect of a Jazz Festival, we piled into Tess' 1974 Gemini and set off on the mammoth journey. It was further away than London is from Peterborough, but was still one of the closest places to us. The roads were far more treacherous as well, but it was nice to have an outing now and again.

Using Tess' tape player, we listened to a little Jazz on the way in an attempt to capture the essence of the trip. After two and a half hours though, I was just about sick of it. We had arrived in Bairnsdale - the first settlement we had come across of any significance and only a few miles from Paynesville. Since it was pretty much in the middle of nowhere, I was convinced it would be brimming with characteristics worthy of a town otherwise forgotten by modern society. I'm not sure if I was imagining a world where people still wore top-hats and loveable shoe-shine boys roamed the streets, but I was ultimately disappointed. Not that it wasn't pleasant, you understand - it was simply dull. The grass was green, the sky was blue and the streets were clean, but it ultimately lacked any kind of individuality. Just like Traralgon, it was divided into a segmented grid with the same old shops lining the streets. In fact, I suspect if I hadn't been concentrating on navigating so hard in order to escape the sound of the jazz flute, I could easily have thought we were 120kms west *in* Traralgon.

That said, I was extremely hungry and my spirits were lifted slightly when the local café supplied each of us with a delightful English muffin. With life seeming slightly more positive, we squeezed ourselves (literally) back into Tess' rust-mobile and travelled the remaining distance south towards Paynesville.
'Looks like it knows we're coming' I turned and said to Grant.
'Why's that?' he asked.
'Look' I replied pointing towards a point in the sky just above our car where the black clouds were gathering 'the weather's trying to make us feel at home'.

That, combined with the overwhelming smell of fish and chips made Paynesville just like any other traditional English sea-side resort. Looking around, it appeared there must have been more chippies in this town than sheep in New Zealand. Unlike most sea-side resorts however, it had one fundamental flaw – it wasn't on the sea. Well not directly anyway. There was of course lots of water and a little beach which would have fooled all but the canniest of men, but being a shrewd sort of chap, I decided to investigate. Consulting the map that had provided me with so much comfort throughout the journey, I noticed that the beach was actually approximately 5km out from the town, running parallel to the shoreline. The huge volume of water we were observing was actually just a trapped lake, unable to re-join the sea because of the sand barrier blocking its path. Apart from the fact that it was unnaturally calm though, you couldn't really notice any difference.

Gathering our thoughts and excited at having finally arrived (which had seemed unlikely due to the condition of the car) we followed the one miniature sign pointing towards the jazz festival.

'The sign says it's down this way Johnny' Cherry shouted in her strong Australian twang as I started walking the wrong way.

'What sign?' I shouted back.

'That one' she replied pointing to a tiny piece of A5 paper strapped to the bottom of a lamp post.

'Oh. That's not a great omen is it?'.

We were expecting big stages, massive stars, flashing lights, huge bouncers who could crush your head if you dared queue inappropriately. But all we got were two old men in a pub. That was it – the entire festival was two old men - one on the trumpet and another with a saxophone. Granted, they were rather good for the half a song we heard, but then they packed up and left – the end of the Paynesville Jazz festival. That's right, we drove for 150kms to listen to a style of music I detest, performed by two men who were blatantly cheating death, for thirty seconds. And what's more, the pub charged us two dollars each for the privilege! Cherry had just been to the bar when they were finishing up and was unaware of the sudden change of events

'That was a real good tune actually' she said passing me over a bottle *VB* 'I think we're in for a good afternoon'.

'Think again' Grant said.

'What?' Cherry replied slightly confused.
Then the two jazz stars got up to the microphone,
'Uh-hmm. Thank you very much Paynesville' they shouted into the microphone from the corner of the bar 'see you again next year'.
Well, Cherry's face was red with rage as she, quite rightly, marched straight back to the bar and demanded her two dollars back. I was too embarrassed for the sake of a loaf of bread but admired her confident nature as she strolled back. Thankfully for all our sakes, the bar staff had made a compromise and offered her a half-refund which she duly accepted.

The bar emptied quickly after the festivities had finished and Paynesville was transformed into somewhat of a ghost town. I looked over at the seafront and noticed a company running boat trips to the other side of the lake – the problem was that their jetty was so long, people could almost jump to the island. However, it is things like this that give a town certain quirky characteristics that make it stand out from the likes of Bairnsdale. Granted, the stagnant salt water may have made it smell pretty bad, but it was these ridiculous eccentricities that made it seem like a far more entertaining place. It then started raining. Little did I know this would be the last precipitation I would see for the next ten weeks.

CHAPTER 10

The next week our work load had increased substantially with the number of camps literally doubling. Consequently, we only had an hour turn around between sending a bunch of kids packing before another load arrived. It was a bit like *'Challenge Anika'*, only without the cool blue buggy. To cope with this demand, Kate and Simon had employed a number of extra staff members to help through the long days. This would change on a weekly basis, but there were four who stayed for the next month called Skipper, Bomber, Kate and Mel.

Bomber was a little older than the rest of us, but was still one of the funniest guys I'd ever met. Like Cherry, he had an enthusiastic love of life. Within a few minutes he had already invited Grant and me on a camping trip 'Have you boys been to Wilsons Prom yet?'.
'Wilson's what?'.
'Wilsons Prom – it's a national park and the most southernly tip of mainland Australia. I'm going camping there in a few weeks and it's a must see so I'm taking you boys with me'.
So that was that, we had a camping trip booked with Bomber.

Everyone seemed to have something wacky about them and Kate was no different – pulling up to camp in her turquoise van with 'The

Sandman' written across the side, I knew immediately she would be a fun character. Like Tess, Mel gave off a strong hippy vibe with long dreadlocks all the way down her back. She was a native of New Zealand, travelling alone and working her way from place to place. As quite a tall character, her presence was quite dominating at first, but then I soon realized that she was probably the gentlest person on Earth. Very friendly and brilliant with advice, I developed a rather close relationship with her as she was so easy to confide in. I also enjoyed mocking her New Zealand accent and was pleased the attention was finally being diverted from Grant and me.

And then there was Skipper from Melbourne. Having trained at college with LJ, he was only a few months older than we Poms. Although he portrayed lots of confidence, I soon learned that he was a deeply modest and humble character. As a result, Grant and I immediately formed a very strong friendship with 'Skip' - enjoying stupid pranks, listening to the same music and generally enjoying the great atmosphere Licola was offering. I suppose we were just grateful to have someone else of a similar age and with the same interests. It amazed me that I could have so much in common with a person who had been moulded by such a distinct upbringing on the other side of the world. He had grown up in a completely different society, playing different sports and learning different subjects. Yet, there we were, enjoying the same type of humour and discussing our incredibly similar relationship issues. It was strangely comforting to know that, although we may have been raised in a different environment, the same emotions range across all humanity.

With more qualified staff on site, we were able to put a number of new activities into operation. One that particularly interested me was called 'The Leap of Faith'. The name was slightly disconcerting as it suggested Divine intervention would be required in order to survive. Imagine my concern then when, in front of an entire class of students, Skipper proclaimed

'Don't worry guys; it's easy if you believe in yourselves. And in order to prove it, Johnny the Pommie here is going to go first and demonstrate it to you'.

I gave him a look that said 'you bastard!' and he just laughed back before throwing me a harness. I wasn't scared. Of course I wasn't - just a little apprehensive. It would have been nice to have had a little warning - but here

I was on stage having never practiced my lines to the play. I knew the genre though - it was going to be a tragedy no matter what I did.

Going over to the pole, I began my ascent quickly trying to seem as confident as possible to the many glaring eyes beneath. After seven or eight metres, the pole began to wobble. Having not done it before, I wasn't sure if this was normal or whether the supreme weight I had gained through camp food was taking its toll. But I had to keep going.

After twelve metres I reached the top and looked around at the tiny faces staring up at me from below. It hadn't seemed this high from the ground. Now for the hard bit - getting onto the platform. Well, I say platform but it was really just a wooden box, forty centimetres square and perched on top of the pole. Under normal circumstance this would be no problem, but being twelve metres from the ground with nothing to hold onto made the situation slightly more challenging.

Not sure how to tackle the problem, I heaved my left knee up so it was on the box. Unfortunately, this put me in an incredibly unstable position and as the wind swirled at such high altitude, I felt myself falling backwards. The crowd below all let out a sudden gasp in unison. Grabbing out frantically, I luckily got hold of the box with my right hand before clawing with my finger nails and somehow managing to pull myself back and hug the pole like a koala. Steady(ish) once again, I pulled back up on the box - first one knee, then the other - before pushing down and standing up straight on the tiny platform.

With my height added, I was seeing things from almost fourteen metres above the ground which was simply terrifying. To make matters worse however, the pole beneath my feet was so insecure, it shook with every movement I made. This in turn made me get more nervous, which of course made the pole vibrate with an even greater amplitude. I believe this is perhaps the most terrifying example of a vicious circle. I looked out straight ahead at the trapeze. It was a four metre jump away which seemed an impossible distance under such circumstances.

'Okay John, just bend your legs, jump and grab the trapeze. You show these guys how easy it is when you believe in yourself' Skip shouted.

I didn't reply as I was too busy being petrified. Steadying myself, I bent my legs before having one last glance at the audience below. Skip had been belaying me all the way up, but he now had three children pulling back on his harness to keep him grounded if I missed. In my head, I had images of me falling to the ground whilst Skip was flung into the air with three twelve year olds clinging to his belt. The embarrassment would have been more overwhelming than the immense pain. But I had come this far and couldn't stop now.

'Right guys, let's count him down before take-off' Skip shouted 'Three..Two..' as all the voices below joined in. '..One…jump!'.

My legs wouldn't move. I hadn't jumped and was still standing completely still on the platform. I wanted to jump, I truly did, but my body wouldn't let me. You see, to leap to our death goes against every natural instinct we have. My brain had assessed the situation and decided 'no no, this isn't right at all. I think I might die here, therefore I'm not going to jump. In fact, why did I even consider it in the first place? It's ridiculous'.

So I was stranded at the top of the pole with the children below staring up with an increased sense of fear. I couldn't let them down though and if I didn't do it, none of them would even try. So, focusing on the trapeze and trusting in Skip, I bent my legs and leapt. I don't know how I finally managed to convince my legs to move, but they certainly did me proud. Swinging in mid-air, I was suddenly hit by the sound of a rapturous applause and cheering. I had made the leap of faith and kept my reputation intact. It was a good day, but one I was not keen to repeat.

Most of the children had the faith to jump, but very few made it to the trapeze. Still, I was impressed (and rather jealous) by their lack of fear. Their minds seemed to be free from conscious thoughts as they put their complete trust in Skip, me and the equipment. It was quite pleasant to come across a group of people who simply trusted, did not take time to consider the potential hazards and just enjoyed themselves. In adulthood that trust seems to fade as many take on a more pessimistic view of life. But perhaps that is just what experience does to you.

The school left later that afternoon. Yet again we were made to feel like film stars as the children lined up to have their photos taken, then cried as the bus pulled away. But for us, work was only just beginning. The next morning we had a group of university students from the USA arriving. They were all over on an exchange with Melbourne University and this was an opportunity for them to bond and explore the real Australian Bush. Before that though, it was our duty to clean the camp in anticipation of their arrival. Working around the clock we mopped, vacuumed and polished, before collapsing on the sofa at around 9pm.

'Right you lazy bastards, time for some staff training now we've got a minute spare' Simon and Kate said walking into the staff house.

'Are you joking? We're absolutely knackered' Grant and I said in disbelief.

'You've worked really hard today guys, but we need to show you some important stuff to do with the water tanks'.

'But they're right up on the hill!'.

'It's okay - we're all going on the mountain bikes so it shouldn't take too long'

Full of resentment, we all got up off the sofa and jumped on the mountain bikes stored outside. It was a beautiful evening with The Milky Way splitting the night sky above, but with no visible moon it was completely pitch black, making the bike ride slightly edgy. Tentatively, we all made our way up the steep mountain track in convoy before getting to the water tanks which were situated on a little clearing looking out across camp. Down below we could see the little lamps from our house glimmering against the dark background. Apart from that though, there were no other lights, no signs of life and no sound whatsoever - just silence and the natural beauty of the surrounding countryside. Unfortunately, the ride had been hard, so I was too exhausted to really appreciate the view. I could sense the frustration in all our voices as we dreamed of being back in our house, relaxing on the sofa.

'John, can you come and give me a hand over here' Simon said, pulling back some tarpaulin from around the side of the water tanks.

'Okay' I said in a weary voice, taking one corner and pulling.

I suddenly felt rejuvenated, for underneath this boring tarp lay some far more exciting objects.

'This is just a little thank you to all you guys for working so hard this week' Kate said, grabbing a bottle of *VB* from the cool box and throwing one to me.

'And this is so you can enjoy yourself!' Simon added holding up two bottles of tequila!.

The staff training had been an elaborate hoax so they could get us to their party venue. They had even sneaked one of the vans up so we could have a CD player and a little music. We sat, we sang, we danced. A few moments before, I had been so stressed by the work, but now I knew what Simon had meant on that very first day as I looked around at the beautiful surroundings and thanked my lucky stars I had been given this fantastic opportunity. Suddenly the magic of this place and its peaceful qualities had completely relaxed me.

Too soon though (as is always the case), time faded away and the party had come to an end. Our spirits lifted, Skip, Grant and I hugged Kate and Simon before jumping on our bikes for the journey back down to camp. The track was incredibly steep, so much so that I had needed to push my bike up most of the way. Strewn with rocks and combined with the sheer darkness of the night, this should have provided quite a challenge, but with youthful exuberance on our side, anything and everything seemed possible. Peddling to increase our acceleration, we literally flew down the hill. The pitch-black of the night made it impossible to see more than two metres ahead and there were a number of close moments as I almost clipped Skip's tyres in front.

Making a sharp right turn at the bottom of the hill, we joined the road and used our momentum on the smooth tarmac surface to maintain the high speed. Another sharp turn and we were into the camp gates, far exceeding the twenty miles an hour speed limit. The darkness now was unbelievable as I followed Grant's white t-shirt across into the driveway and towards the oval.

It was then that I heard the smash. It was the sound of metal crushing after a collision with something far more solid. Almost instantly, I heard Grant's screams as he simply disappeared from my view. 'AAAHHHH SHIIIITTTT'. Braking hard, my bike went into a massive skid as I struggled to avoid whatever it was that Grant had hit. Falling to the floor I scraped my knee along the track, but other than that I felt okay. Running over to the crash site, I found Skip laughing his head off whilst trying to pull Grant from under the wreckage of his once glamorous mountain bike. About a metre away was the offending object – a mammoth-sized boulder about 50cm in height, positioned for decorative purposes between two trees. We had seen it every time we had come into camp, but I guess in the excitement we had just forgotten it was there.

'Are you okay mate?' I said in fits of laughter 'good job you went first hey?!'

'Glad I could help you out mate' Grant replied sarcastically, dusting himself down 'I didn't even see the rock! Even when I hit it, I still couldn't see it because it's so dark. We must've been going at about thirty miles an hour?'.

'Yeah I agree, don't think you'll be riding this bike again though!' Skip chipped in enthusiastically as he examined the wreckage 'you've smashed it right up'.

He wasn't wrong. The front wheel had completely crumpled into a mesh of spokes whilst the forks had completely snapped. That's how fast he was going.

'To make things worse, I went flying over the handle bars unaware of what was going on and then the bloody bike followed and landed right on top of me. Talk about bad luck'.

We all looked down at the bike and then Grant started laughing. Skip and I soon followed before falling on the floor in hysterics. What a crash! However, I did feel sorry for him as, although he'd survived the crash, he now had to try and fix his wreck of a bike before the Americans arrived.

The next morning I got up as normal and began setting up the activities. It was an extremely hot day and the flies were as persistent as ever. I was setting up the rock-climbing with Tess and at one point I couldn't see her legs because they were completely covered in flies. I tried flailing an arm at them, kicking them and chasing them with a stick but nothing seemed to deter their advances towards my nostrils and ears. I now understood why Australians always wear hats with corks dangling from the rim and thought I might invest in one whilst in Melbourne. The cockatoos were showing off as normal in the early morning sun by hanging upside down on the wires of the high ropes. It still amazed me that I was seeing hundreds of these wonderful birds in their natural habitat.

The American students arrived slightly late as many of them still had hangovers from the previous evening's antics. By the looks of things, the winding mountain road hadn't helped their stomachs settle. They were all about twenty years old and obviously excited to be in Australia, which they demonstrated in their unique, confident style.

Having run a number of slightly patronising problem solving tasks, we embarked on the real program for the weekend. With Grant still suffering psychological scars from the night before, I volunteered to run the mountain biking course. This would be a decision I soon regretted. As we set off in the blistering heat, we followed the standard route shown on the ordnance survey map. Depressingly, I hadn't taken into account the steep incline we would have to climb. The terrain along the mountain side was wonderful though and as we followed the track, the gum trees provided us with some limited protection from the sun's blistering heat. I was thankful of this as the sun's energy was draining enough without the added problem of having to create enough peddle power to propel ones-self 9kms up a mountain. Having to adapt to such an extreme environment (and still suffering from some severe hangovers) many of the students found the going too tough and turned back. Most stayed though, as we encouraged each other at every break and pushed our bodies to their physical limits. The stifling helmets made us even hotter, but with a steep and potentially fatal drop on one side of the track, no one wanted to take them off.

Our casual afternoon bike ride had turned into an incredible piece of endurance training, as well as numbing my arse to the extreme. But the feeling of elation at reaching the top was almost as fantastic as the magnificent views across The Alpine National Park. It had been 9kms of intense riding but it was definitely worth it. As the group instructor, I felt like a pioneer leading my explorers to a new, unseen land. As I peered towards the horizon, the luscious green mountains seemed to stretch forever into the distance like waves of sand dunes in the desert. The only negative point really was the smell. I thought it might be coming from me, but looking down to my left, I saw the culprit was a decomposing wombat carcass. In this incredible heat, it absolutely stank and meant the number of flies surrounding us increased dramatically - a measure I had previously considered to be absolutely impossible.

'God, look at that view - it's awesome! Do you come up here every day?' one of the guys asked me.

'No not everyday - that climb's enough to kill me. The Earth seems to make you work hard for views like this, I suppose it makes the experience even more rewarding' I replied but was quickly interrupted by one of the girls screaming.

'Oh my god, I think I'm going to die if these flies don't LEAVE ME ALONE' she shouted before going crazy and kicking wildly at nothing really in particular 'can't the government do something about them? Like, just spray insect repellent all across the country?!' she said once she'd calm down a little. I laughed at her.

'They were sending me crazy this morning as well - but it's all part of being in this wonderful countryside. You'll get used to it I'm sure'.

She looked doubtful 'I don't *want* to get used to it. It's disgusting. I'm going back' and with that, she jumped back on her bike and began the decent back to camp.

Having just about recovered, we all followed quickly; eager to let gravity do its job and take us back to camp with minimal effort and maximum speed. We had been stopping every five hundred metres or so on the way up, but since we were travelling so quickly I told the group we only needed to stop once at the small stream about 4kms down the track. Having explained where some good off-road parts were, we all set off at an incredibly high-speed with me controlling things at the back of the pack to make sure we didn't lose anyone. With only a couple of cars using the route each week, everyone was able to really enjoy themselves by racing on the bendy track and tackling some challenging woodland terrain during particular off-road sections.

Surprisingly unaffected by Grant's crash the night before, I took on some tough off-road terrain, jumping a number of large boulders with quite a bit of confidence. Then, all of a sudden, disaster struck as my front tyre exploded. We were only a few hundred metres into the descent and I was therefore over three and a half kilometres away from the checkpoint. In an attempt to lighten my load, I had given the puncture-repair kit to a guy riding just in front of me. Assuming that it would be someone else who would get into trouble, I had put myself at the back of the group and as a result, was totally stranded. No bike, no water and no pride. Having tirelessly peddled away up this slope, I had envisaged my joy on the ride down as I sailed along pleasantly, with a huge grin across my childlike face. Now, I found myself marching back, expelling even more energy pushing my bike. I just hoped that the others would remember to wait for me at the checkpoint.

Forty-five exhausting minutes later, I rounded my last corner to be welcomed by a sarcastic cheer.

'Jeez man, we were beginning to think we'd lost you' one of them shouted. 'What did you do to your bike dude?'.

'I just had a minor mishap on one of my landings, no biggy' I replied trying to play it cool.
'We thought you might have fallen off the cliff or something'.
'Oh right, well cheers for coming to help me then!'.
'Ah well man, you look like you can handle yourself. Shame you can't handle your bike though'.
'Shut it you cheeky swine! And hand me the repair kit'.
'Here you go man, we're gonna shoot ahead and try out some more jumps!'.
'Okay, be careful - you don't want to end up with a puncture. See you back at camp'.
When I arrived back, all the others had heard my embarrassing story of woe and were sympathetic in their own Australian way. This basically entailed me retelling the story of my hike much to the amusement of my co-workers. I was assured it was all in the spirit of good fun though. In general, this was the whole ethos of this particular camp, with much less emphasis on 'setting a good example' and more on allowing the students to have a good time.

      For this reason, we didn't stop them that evening as they ventured across to the shop and purchased all the alcohol they had available - literally. Being under-age to drink in their homeland, they were certainly seizing this incredible opportunity to drink themselves into a coma uncontested. Would I wake to find toilet roll covering my house? Or maybe a student passed out, naked and upside down in the tree outside my window? Upon arriving in Licola, I never imagined such a place would play host to such a large student gathering – but one was shaping up quite nicely indeed.

'Wake up! John Boy, get the hell out of bed!'.
Grant was knocking on my door, although it took me a few moments to realise this. Yet again I had that familiar dry taste in my mouth as I pulled myself up off my bedroom floor.
'Okay mate, I'm coming' I said reaching for the door handle and pulling it open with difficulty 'what the hell happened last night?'.
'Ha-ha, I don't know about you buddy – you look well rough, but Skip and I ran the camp fire – only about twenty students came but we had a great laugh. They taught us all about 'S'mores''.
'Sam whats?'.

'S'mores – it's where you get two crackers and put chocolate and marshmallow in the middle. Then you melt it on the campfire and stuff your greedy pie-hole'.
Stumbling towards the kitchen I grabbed myself a glass of water and leaned against the side for support 'Okay, that goes a long way to explaining the obesity rate in America. But why the hell have they got such a stupid name?'
'Because apparently once you've had one, you always want S'more!'.

Waking myself up from the daze I was in, I made my way outside with Grant towards the main staff house. All the others were suffering too. I asked Cherry what the hell had happened.
'Ah I'm not sure, I remember Tess, you and me walking up to the houses to make sure they weren't partying too hard, but then everything goes a little blurry. Tessa Babes, you got any ideas?'.
'Ah yeah' she said 'there was a huge party just getting started in one of the houses. I think there must've been about sixty of them there. They invited us in for a quick drink and we ended up playing drinking games until about 3am'.
'Really? Oh god, I think I do remember. Didn't you start doing some of your flame twirling?' I asked having suddenly remembered Tessa on the oval showing off her skills. I had never seen her use her fire spinning equipment before, so I was impressed she had managed it safely in such an intoxicated state.
'Yeah, I tend to do that when I'm drunk. It's perfectly safe though, I swear'.
'How the hell do you learn how to do something like that? It must be quite painful if you get it wrong?'.
'I just practiced with the equipment when it was unlit. Still, it's quite scary the first time you do it with real flames. Getting drunk gives you the confidence you need I suppose!'.

We all ventured out onto the main bit of camp. Even though we had had such a rough night, we still had a full day of rotations to run, although it didn't look like many students would be turning up. Venturing down the main street, I could see beer bottles all over the floor and a couple of disorientated Americans wandering back to try and locate their beds.

Cherry and I were in charge of the high ropes and by lunchtime our student count was at a stunning four. Oh, how I longed to be back in bed like everyone else! It was a shame really that the last day would be forgotten by most, as it was truly beautiful, even by Licola's standards. However, I was relieved I didn't have much work to do. By 2pm we decided to call it a day and proceeded to walk down the main street, striking a frying pan to wake everyone up. After all, we didn't want them missing their bus.

Rising slowly like zombies, they eventually packed up and having exchanged numbers with Grant and me, jumped on the bus for the journey back to Melbourne. I suspected (for the second time in two days) their hangovers were not going to be helped by the considerably bumpy, mountain terrain. I was definitely disappointed to see them leave as they had turned Licola into a lively, pulsating place once again. Now, with them all gone it seemed incredibly lonely and the isolation began to affect me once more. However, Grant and I didn't have time to dwell on such feelings as we had a Grand Prix to go to - next stop, St Kilda!

CHAPTER 11

We were nearly 2kms away but I felt like I was playing chicken in the middle of the track. It was a bit annoying to be honest, as I was looking forward to my first lie in for weeks, but in truth the nails they had used instead of feathers in my pillow had woken me up long before. It was Saturday morning and I was lying in a twin room in *The Coffee Palace* hostel, St Kilda. We'd paid well over the odds for our room, but looking out at the crowded streets below, I realised what a prime position we had acquired. The cars had obviously begun their practice laps as the powerful purr of their jet engines dominated the surrounding air. This only made to heighten the excitement of the fans in the street who were wildly anticipating the start of another Formula 1 season. It was only 10am and they were already out in their masses, waving flags and letting off fog horns right next to my ear. Unfortunately though, we had only purchased tickets for the actual race itself so found ourselves with a free day.

Keen to explore the cosmopolitan metropolis of central Melbourne, we grabbed a bus into the city. This was a decision I regretted almost instantly for the bus was packed with Formula 1 fans. Furthermore, each and every one of them on this particular bus appeared to be obese, sweaty and topless. Believe me, unavoidably rubbing up against four of them whilst

locked in a moving tin can, is probably the most unpleasant experience imaginable. Twenty minutes of torture later, we arrived in central Melbourne and stood admiring Federation Square before venturing under-ground to the tourist information centre. What exactly did this sophisticated city have to offer? Before my question was answered however, my phone began ringing:
'Hello?'.
'Johnny! How's it going?'.
'Ummm..yeah it's going quite good. Who is this?!'.
'It's Emma. God, it's only been a few weeks and you've forgotten me already!'.
'Emma! Sorry, I haven't got your number in my phone. We haven't had any e-mails from you guys so we assumed you weren't coming'.
'Sorry about that, our internet access has been pretty limited. Anyway, are you here in the city? We're here for the Grand Prix – have you managed to get tickets?'.
'Yep we've got tickets for tomorrow and we're in the city right now, where are you?'.
'Brilliant! We're at the Queen Victoria Market. Come meet us'.

The Melbourne residents I had spoken to had all displayed a great sense of enthusiasm whilst discussing The Queen Victoria Market, so I was rather surprised to discover there wasn't one signpost for it. Having departed the tram in what we believed to be the correct area, Grant and I began scanning the streets for any clues we could find. Even more bizarrely, when we stopped members of the public to ask for directions they would talk passionately about the great vibe surrounding the place, but when asked to clarify *where* it was they would simply wave their arm in a hazardous and ultimately confusing circle, before moving on rather quickly. It was as if it had been created within the imaginations of the locals, built on top of a ludicrous legend, much like the foundations of the Mormon church.

    We didn't exactly stumble through the back of a wardrobe, but with a bit of luck we eventually found our destination. I would tell you where it is but I am sworn to secrecy. However, I will tell you about it. Located under a large roofed area, it had the look and feel of a rather traditional market such as Covent Garden in London. Unfortunately, that is where the similarities end. For although there were a few stalls selling relatively stylish merchandise, they were sadly out-numbered by people trying to flog appalling, fake BMW jackets, English football shirts and Gucci sunglasses. The problem was that every single stall (and there were *a lot* of them) was trying to get rid of exactly the same rubbish for exactly the same price. Now, I'm no consumer expert but I'm pretty sure that one of the essentials in business success is to locate a 'gap in the market' and exploit it. They had certainly filled a gap in the market, but only in the literal sense. So if you're searching for consumer diversity, it probably isn't the place for you. If on the other hand you're on the look-out for a counterfeit *Rolex* watch then I would highly recommend the place.

It was a shame really as intertwined throughout these rip-off stalls were a number of incredibly talented and modest artists. Their work was superb with some great watercolour landscapes really capturing the cultural essence of the city, though I couldn't help feel they were having their reputation damaged by the people surrounding them. Grant and I stood and admired their work for quite a while until the air of tackiness was too overwhelming and we left with nothing. If they had been located at a slightly more up-market crafts fair, I'm sure their talent would have been given the credibility it quite obviously deserved.

Having taken so long to actually find the market, Sian and Emma had moved back into the city for a spot of lunch. Keen to catch up with them and partake in some clothes shopping that was a little more classy (after all, who wants to buy clothes they could easily make themselves with an old curtain, some scissors and a roll of double-sided sticky tape?) we jumped back on the tram towards the city centre. I found it strange that there were never any inspectors on the tram - were the city council merely hoping that everyone was honest enough to buy a ticket? If so, then they were very much mistaken as I had never seen it happen and, in an attempt to fit into the culture, I decided to follow the example set by the locals.

Arriving in the centre, we browsed a number of the shops selling traditional Australian clothing (long flowery shorts) before diverting down a side street to a café. There, we met with Sian, Emma, Rich and Harry for a spot of lunch and a catch up. At first the conversation was nervously polite as we exchanged mild stories from the past few weeks, but as we eased into each other's company the atmosphere became much more relaxed.

A few hours later and we were still chatting as the day began to draw to a close. It was then that Emma suggested we make our way to Melbourne museum to see one of the old *'Neighbours'* sets which was being preserved there. For those of you who aren't familiar with the soap opera Neighbours, be thankful for that fact. Beginning in 1985, the programme is set in the fictional Melbourne suburb of Erinsborough and has given acting debuts to many idolized pop stars - the most famous of who is Kylie Minogue. With the sun always shining, the people always brown and everyone enjoying life, it is an incredibly popular show on UK television primarily because it provides the viewers with a short break from the torrid onslaught of rain. So, although I wasn't proud of the fact that I was a viewer, I was nonetheless rather excited by the prospect of visiting the old set. I think the others felt the same way and although we all tried damn hard to hide our enthusiasm, it was obviously a difficult task.

The museum itself was a fantastic building, constructed with some very initiative ideas and adventurous architecture. But, I couldn't help feel it was overshadowed slightly by the pristine gardens surrounding the vicinity. Open spaces beautifully landscaped, they provided a wonderful escape from the bustling city, which seemed to simply evaporate into thin air as soon as you stepped through the gates. The noise of traffic disappeared and the spectacular concrete walkways vanished as their dominance was replaced by an air of tranquillity.

'Quite a setting' for such a spectacular piece of soap opera history I mused. The museum probably had some far more historically significant finds displayed in it, but we all made our way straight for the prime relic. Instead of representing how badly educational priorities have diminished in modern society as many people would argue, I think this behaviour just indicates what sad prats Grant and I really are. Besides, this was part of my childhood. With a devastating fire destroying a lot of the original set, this integral piece had been saved by the rescue services. Subsequently, the production company had commissioned a brand new set to be built and so this piece had become surplus to requirements. It was Jim Robinson's kitchen! I was standing in Jim Robinson's kitchen! What a wonderfully surreal moment it was. Having taken some funny photos in various comedy poses, I looked around the back of wooden frame and noticed that a number of the famous crew members from the glory years had signed their names, creating a remarkable piece of television memorabilia. Walking towards the exit, I didn't bother looking at any other displays as I knew none of them would live up to the adrenalin rush I had just been given. Judge me if you will, for I am a satisfied man!

That evening St Kilda was transformed into a town in celebration. Where the main road once ran, hundreds of fans now stood flying flags and blowing horns with great anticipation for the race ahead. As some exuberant Italians ran over and hugged me for no apparent reason, I felt like I had fallen into Rio de Janeiro during carnival season. I had expected a lot of support, but this was ridiculous. I for one can understand the passion that is felt for ones team on such a large occasion – but showing so much dedication to a car manufacturer that you are willing to follow them around the world just seems a little too extreme. They are not a person you can watch perform, respect and aspire to be. Neither are they a team of individuals who come together to form an identifiable, strong unit. They are simply a manufacture's brand name just like *McVities* biscuits or *Charmin Ultra* toilet paper. Do *they* get such fanatical support? Do people spend their lives following around 'Team Charmin', supporting them through their long running battle against *Andrex* in the 'softest toilet tissue' world championships? I think not. So why do people do it with Formula 1 cars? Why do people feel so much devotion and sense of familiarity with a particular model of automobile? I don't have the answer, but what I do know is that, as a result, we found it very difficult to get a seat in any restaurant. In most of the places we tried, simply finding a place to stand proved very challenging. With so many people around, it was perhaps a bad sign when we found a place that was relatively quiet, but we were so relieved and hungry that even the bucket of grease that constitutes a *KFC* meal would have seemed appealing.

    It was an Italian restaurant, situated along the main strip of bars and cafés which seemed to cook and present their food in a rather authentic way. The waitress positioned us on a nice round table towards the back of the restaurant before running back with a couple of menus and a carafe of wine. I immediately loved the place - we had only just taken our coats off, and they were already throwing free alcohol at us. Lots more wine and a splendid risotto later, Rich and I got back to playing some of the incredibly immature but forever humorous comparison games we had enjoyed on the train. It was great to see the guys again - we hadn't heard from Harry or Rich since that first day in Melbourne due to their limited internet access. I think they felt rather frustrated and stranded by this lack of communication and were subsequently enjoying interacting with a few familiar faces. Hearing their stories of woe, Grant and I were again grateful that we had been placed in a community that had provided so much warmth.

    I had been considering my independent travel after camp for some time and now seemed quite a good opportunity to raise some enquiries with the others. Due to some interview Grant had to attend back in the UK, it had become apparent that our post-camp plans would not coincide. Although this was slightly disappointing, having lived with him for three months I thought I would probably be looking for a change anyway. Sian would have been a great travel partner, but having already completed her round-the world tour prior to camp, she had booked a flight home a few days after the end of term. Harry was in a similar situation and Rich already had plans with some old school acquaintances. Luckily however, it seemed Emma and I had similar time scales, budgets and goals. Since we got on really well and shared the same unique, although horribly embarrassing sense of humour, it made perfect sense that we went together. Plucking up the courage, I turned to her to give my proposal

'Emmmma, I've got a proposal for you. Not that I want to marry you, no offence' I slurred.

'Okay, you haven't started this remarkably well John' she replied, laughing.

'I was just wondering what your plans for after camp are and whether you want to be my travel buddy?'.

'Ha-ha, of course, I'd love to. My plan was to stay in Melbourne for a few days before heading back to Sydney. I'm not sure from then, but I definitely want to experience the whole east coast'.

'Emma, that is music to my ears as it's exactly what I had planned too. So, shall we make it official?'.

'Lets'.

'EVERYONE' I said tapping my glass with my knife and standing up 'Emma and I have an announcement to make' everyone was looking at me with eager faces 'we are now official travelling buddies. Isn't that great news?' I never got an answer as they had all lost interest and returned to their individual conversations, but I was certainly a very happy man.

With such a great carnival atmosphere in the air, our evening continued long into the night. I don't remember too much from it to be honest, only the great sense of surrealism that surrounded the whole situation. I had never been a huge Grand Prix fan, but as a child I had always risen early to watch the first race of the season in Australia. Like the Tennis, it seemed like a completely different world and one I certainly never believed I'd get to experience. I knew loads of my friends would be tuning in early on Sunday morning to watch the spectacle unfold - unbelievably, I would *be there*, just metres away from the action, close enough to get a headache from the fumes and have my eardrums destroyed by the roar of the engines. Why though? My home in England is a measly one hour drive from Silverstone and the thought of paying it a visit had never crossed my mind. It was because I realised this may be my only opportunity. In essence, it is this belief alone which provides the essential foundations needed to create a memorable gap year. If you can convince yourself that the chances in front of you today will simply fade into oblivion tomorrow, then your whole trip will be encapsulated with a sense of *carpe diem* - seize the day for it may be your last. This is exactly what I was attempting to do and, although financial considerations needed to be addressed, I was determined to turn all my opportunities into memorable realities. By becoming part of the crowd at this Grand Prix, I can forever say 'I was there'.

Time slipped into insignificance during our night out in St Kilda and as a result we didn't stumble back to bed until the early hours of Sunday morning. This would have been fine had Grant not insisted on shaking me violently at 6.30am shouting 'come on, let's get down there now so we can get a good seat'. Doing exactly as any normal person would, I ignored him and went back to sleep. Shaking me again, I could detect an extreme sense of frustration in his voice as he shouted at me to get up again.
'We're going to be late!' he said 'come on!'.
'It's…' I replied trying to find my watch '6.45am you arse. The race doesn't start until two. That gives us…lots more hours sleep'.
'We need to beat the rush and get a good seat, get up!'.
'I'll beat your face in if you don't shut up and let me go back to sleep'.

But he was persistent enough and I eventually found myself again standing in the middle of a vibrant St Kilda, waiting for a bus and nursing a killer hangover. Grant and I weren't really speaking at this point since he had shouted at me angrily for stopping to style my hair. To be honest though, the silence was blissful and allowed me to rest my eyes peacefully for the duration of the journey. Since part of the main road was being used as the race track, it was subsequently (and thankfully) closed, meaning the bus ride to Albert Park entrance took far longer than normal. Even still, upon arrival I consulted my watch and was severely depressed by the thought of being up this early on a Sunday - the day of rest apparently.

Calling Harry and Rich, it appeared that they had been sensible and were still in bed asleep. Like us however, Sian and Emma were full of life and already in the grounds, so we eagerly made our way across the park to find them. Prior to 1996 Albert Park was, well, simply a park. Covering over 550 acres of land, the rural haven incorporates a huge lake, numerous grass playing fields and even a golf course. When this was announced as the new site for the Australian grand prix (it was previously held through the streets of Adelaide), the locals understandably panicked at the thought of their park being transformed into petrol heaven for a few days every year. Far from that however, it appears that the revenue generated from the event has been pumped back into its conservation. There was certainly no sign of dilapidation on this chilly autumn morning, as we hiked around the lake looking for a good place to set up camp for the day. As we picked a spot on a hill just past the second corner, I sat and looked back across the water. For some reason, there was a very distinctive air of natural calm surrounding the place with many birds singing and ducks swimming in their normal sedate lifestyle. I couldn't help feel sorry for them, sitting their completely oblivious to the dramatic changes that were about to be made to their relaxed, untainted environment.

There were hundreds of stalls throughout the park selling incredibly overpriced merchandise. Of course, Grant was there in an instant. Fondling his way through horrible t-shirts, hats and beer holders, Emma and I sat back to see what monstrosities he would find to waste his money on. Surprisingly (and much to our disappointment), he managed to limit those retail impulses and only ended up purchasing a t-shirt and matching baseball cap. It goes without saying that he put them both on straight away, and although it made him look like a little boy on an outing from a home, I'm sure he was a lot warmer than me. With the weather we had experienced recently, the locals were taking the spell of cloud cover as a blessing and a welcome break from the torrid onslaught of heat.

We continued to follow Grant as he made his way through acres of clothing stalls, food outlets and advertising stands, taking an interest in it all. Then I saw a shop selling earplugs. Confused as to how anyone could make a business selling tiny pieces of sponge, I made my way across.

'Hello there. Cold day isn't it? So, what are you selling?' I enquired.
'Earplugs mate, two dollars a pack' the fat man behind the stand replied.
'I'm sorry, for a minute then I thought you said you wanted two dollars. Obviously I must've misheard you – I mean, one dollar for a tiny piece of sponge would represent the biggest rip-off since they started selling popcorn' I said, genuinely confused.
'Nah mate, it's two dollars for a pack. If you don't buy some you'll regret it once the race starts'.
'I very much doubt that my friend and even if I do, I'll just look down at the two dollars in my hand and smile'.
With that, I turned my back and began to walk away from the stand expecting the others to follow me to the moral high ground. Richard did, but to my astonishment the others didn't. They did exactly the opposite in fact and *willingly* handed over their money.
'Boys, you really should get some of these - it's going to be really loud when the race starts' Sian said.
'That may be so Sian, but I am willing to accept my fate if it means I don't give into these thieves who make a living by bumping up the price of essential items when they realise people have no other option. It's like creating a cure for cancer, but then charging people millions of pounds because you know they'll have to pay it in order to stay alive. I won't do it'.

Rant over, we returned to our space on the grass eagerly anticipating the start. With the pre-race entertainment coming to an abrupt halt, the glistening cars made their way onto the track. I hadn't expected to feel much emotion upon seeing them, but then I realised that right in front of my eyes was something representing the very peak of human engineering capabilities. I thought about the years of testing, designing and heartbreak that had gone into producing these near perfect cars and couldn't help but admire the finished product with the utmost respect. The speed of them was immense as they stormed along, gripping the tarmac track with impossible accuracy that seemed to defy the laws of physics. My eyes strained to keep up and all I saw was a sudden blaze of colour as they raced past us, blurring my vision. Even the pure roar produced by their powerful engines seemed to struggle to keep up, echoing behind the car and causing the ground beneath my feet to vibrate majestically.

The practice lap was over and my head was pounding. Turning to Rich, I could see he was thinking the same thing. I tried to shout to him, but no words could be heard over the sound of the cars. He understood though. Sneaking off so nobody else had the opportunity to say 'I told you so' we ran over to the ear plug man and (with a great sense of relief) swallowed our pride. Racing back to our position, the cars were just taking their positions on the grid and there was a tremendous sense of excitement filling the crowd. All the start lights went on and engines fired to full power. Then just like that, they were extinguished and these fantastic machines were released from their cage like an over enthusiastic greyhound, finally escaping its restrictive chain.

Usually, with so many cars converging on such a small first corner there is a lot of drama in Australia (hence our choice of position – everyone loves a big crash, don't they?), but on this occasion they all passed through problem free with the two Ferraris leading, much to the pleasure of the thirty Italians standing in front of us. I don't really have much more to report, on the contrary, I have nothing more to report as this is how it stayed for the entire race - a Ferrari one-two finish. Not that we could tell, as without a big screen to see, it was difficult to make out which car was winning. Every so often, there would be a flash of colour scream past us followed by the roar of a jumbo jet engine and a loud cheer. The problem was, we couldn't tell whether that person was winning the race or coming last. After sixty or so laps, it's quite difficult to keep track of how many times each competitor has passed you, especially when you can't really see them properly. So I gave up trying to work it out and instead concentrated on reading the facial expressions of the Ferrari enthusiasts who were listening to pocket radios. After a couple of hours, they all leapt into the air and began hugging each other, so I assumed the race had ended.

After the cars had completed their laps of honour, all the fans began climbing the huge metal fences. Men, women and children clawed their way up and over in order to get onto the track in an incredibly dangerous and potentially fatal manoeuvre. I took the opportunity to have a sit down and take in the wonderful, joyous atmosphere. I had thoroughly enjoyed this day out. Would I do it again? Probably not. Don't get me wrong, I can see the appeal of a fast car race, but I wouldn't want to go to one every other week. I'm sure many people will disagree with me, but let's face the facts - can a sporting event really be that great if you don't have anyone to support, nobody really knows who is winning and you have to wear two pieces of overpriced foam in your ears just to prevent a brain haemorrhage? Still, at least I can say 'I was there'.

CHAPTER 12

Half way along the road between Licola and Heyfield, we had heard about a retreat camp known as 'Wollangarra'. This is where Grant and I found ourselves heading now. We had been working hard for the two weeks since the Grand Prix, so it was nice to finally have some more time off. Having promised to take us camping, Bomber was now living up to his word as he prepared our equipment back at camp for the trip to Wilsons Prom. However, we still had time to kill, so Cherry and her family had included us in their afternoon of exploration.

Like Licola, Wollangarra is an outdoor education centre following the philosophy of 'growth through challenge' with a particular emphasis on rustic living. However, it achieves this on a far more drastic level. Built by students, it is located in a snug valley, separated from the real world by a river (and a long walk). In order to stress the importance of the surrounding natural environment, Wollangarra is an entirely self-sufficient community, and this is why I was so eager to experience it. There was a cable crossing the river, attached to the rocks on our side and a tree on the other. Sliding along it was a two- person, very rickety looking, wooden seat which Grant and I jumped on. Pulling ourselves along the cable some ten metres above the ground, we arrived at the other side and sent the pre-historic cable-car back for the others. This was the only way to access the camp. Jumping from the tree, I landed softly on some lovely, fresh grass. Although this may seem relatively normal, due to the drought I had not seen green grass (apart from Licola) for months as all the surrounding land was brown and barren. Emerging from the trees, I was then hit by a sea of colour. Like an oasis in the desert, the luscious bright grass surrounding the camp encompassed hundreds of varieties of exotic flowers which hit my eyes with such shock that I almost fell backwards into the flowing river. With such dull, sterile land smothering the hills around us, the fruitful world in front of me created quite a defining contrast.

With the others just about to cross the river (we nearly lost Cherry's mother at one point) we made our way into the heart of the camp. None of the instructors seemed to be there, though we were sure they wouldn't mind us taking a look around. All the buildings were constructed entirely out of recycled materials, the main one being built with a nice big central courtyard. Growing along the overhang of the roof were grapevines, with huge bunches of ripe fruit just hanging off them. Chickens and rabbits ran all around us, obviously taking advantage of the fertile land the students had created. As I experienced this unfamiliar atmosphere, I couldn't help but feel so happy to have found this unique place where humans and nature were working so closely and successfully.

Keeping with this philosophy, there was no electricity or gas in the retreat as the occupants coped with candles and fires. Walking into the main room, the smell reminded me of an old Victorian house I had visited as a child. Lining all the chairs were thick rugs to keep the locals warm in winter and jars of pickles and jams to feed their hunger. Far from being in the warm Australian mountains, I felt like I had stumbled into a nineteenth century Alpine ski lodge. As soon as I walked outside however, I was reminded of the ferocious heat of the Australian sun. Even by normal standards, this was a startling hot day, easily in the 40s and I could feel my energy being drained.

Setting up a picnic, we ate lunch on a veranda attached to the separate barbeque building that was across the main lawn. Intrigued as to how the inhabitants grew their own food, Grant, Cherry's uncle and I made our way down to the organic vegetable garden by the river. It was relatively modest in size, but as I wandered round I couldn't help be impressed by the diversity of vegetables they were growing. Looking to investigate further I walked deeper into some longer vegetation and it was then that I heard a frantic rustling up ahead. Stopping dead in my tracks, the grass in front started shaking violently and moving straight in my direction – it was just like a velociraptor attack in *'Jurassic Park'*. Thinking back to my initial training and attempting to remain calm, I stood as still as I possibly could. It is a strange sensation as it goes against every natural instinct you possess. My mind was willing my body to run and escape the danger as quickly as possible, but I knew that move could be fatal. Remaining still, the bushes continued to rustle as the noise got louder converging on my feet. Three metres. Two metres. One metre…I dared myself to look down at the ground and as I did, I saw it. Its black body shot out from the grass, followed by its long tail as the rat sprinted across my feet, not paying any attention to my presence. I sighed with relief as my heart kicked in and started beating again.

But then a shuddering thought crossed my mind – what was it running from? From where the rat had just emerged, I noticed the grass move again. This time though, the movements were not of an animal frantically panicking – they were subtle, calculated and produced with purpose. Right then I knew exactly what was coming. Holding my breath, I remained as still as possible and waited for my fate to reveal itself. The nearest hospital was a river crossing, two kilometre walk and eighty minute drive away, so any sort of attack would pretty much mean certain death. It was exactly that thought that was passing through my head when I felt it touch my leg. Before I looked down, I knew exactly what I was about to witness. It was a brown snake – generally considered to be the second deadliest in the whole world. With its tongue periodically flicking to taste the surrounding air, it had slithered in between my feet with its dark maroon body following. It moved with the focus of a predator – a predator out to kill. Two metres of its body passed between my feet before it was finally gone. Fearing to move, I remained perfectly still for a few more moments before I heard a shout to the left. With such drama unfolding I had forgotten that Grant and Cherry's uncle were here.

'Look here guys – it's a bloody brown snake!' shouted Cherry's uncle with incredible enthusiasm 'lets catch the bastard!'.

With those words, he ran through the undergrowth chasing it in a style Steve Irwin would've been proud of. For so many obvious reasons, this seemed like the most stupid thing to do. Stupid in the same way as playing around with the wires of an armed nuclear bomb 'just for a laugh' would be. It is simply madness. Thankfully though, the snake evaded his lunges and we were able to return home venom free.

Five hours later and our Subaru car was finally pulling into Tidal River some 230kms away. Bomber was an experienced camper and seasoned traveller, so his claim that Wilsons Prom was 'the must see place in Victoria' made this trip rather exciting. Having once described Southend-on-sea as 'a place that rivals Auschwitz as the most depressing on Earth', I knew his astute travel analysis was fairly accurate. In his mid-thirties, Bomber (his real name was Anthony, but nobody used it) was a bachelor, freelancing in outdoor education at schools and camps. One of the main reasons he was so good at it was because it was his passion. It is a rare thing to be able to combine a hobby with a job, but Bomber had achieved this feat and appeared very happy as a result. Throughout our entire journey, he had entertained us through singing songs, telling comedy stories and playing a huge game of 'Horse'. This involved spotting horses in the fields, pointing at them and shouting 'horse' as loud as you possibly could. The first person to do this would receive ten points. Of course, other animals were included along the way, such as a tortoise which Bomber spotted and subsequently landed himself fifty points – that lucky guy. To be honest, it did seem a little like he was making up the rules as we went along, although he assured us that it was purely experience that had seen him romp through to a two hundred and fifty point victory.

    By the time we arrived, the site was bathed in darkness, so we set up camp quickly on the sandy floor and cracked open our beers. Earlier in the night Bomber had introduced us to a truly fantastic Australian invention – the drive-through off-licence. We drove in, ordered our beer and ice and then simply waited as it was carried to our car. Then we drove off, stocked full of alcohol and having wasted no additional calories in the process. Why had no one in England thought of this before? It is quite simply a genius idea – now, we no longer have to put any effort into getting booze, we can simply roll from the sofa into the car, have someone else load the alcohol at the shop, before driving home and calling our wives to move it into the fridge. Marvellous stuff.

Getting the gas-stove burning quickly we settled down for a bit of food after our long journey. Whilst chopping some peppers, I noticed Bomber examining something on his arm

'What's up mate, you look concerned' I enquired.

'Nothing mate, just checking out this mole on my skin – if it goes black it's a sign of skin cancer'. He must've seen my concerned look 'don't worry though John boy, it's just one of the hazards of living in this beautiful place. Believe me, there's a flip-side to most things and this is one of Australia's'.

'Yeah and the fact that every animal is trying its hardest to kill you' I added, trying to lighten the mood.

Bomber wasn't depressed though, as it was something he and most Australians had come to live with. They simply saw it as an inevitable consequence of their life, but not a life-threatening one if precautions were taken to catch it early. I found it difficult to contemplate living in the knowledge that you had a 33% chance of developing skin cancer. It was surprising with how well they were coping with it – their behaviour was admirable.

Following a good, fulfilling meal, we were all feeling rather lethargic so I suggested a stroll down to the beach to finish off the beers. It was 11pm so the walk wasn't exactly straight forward, but as we emerged onto Norman Bay, I immediately knew it was worth it. We couldn't see the ocean, only hear the roar of the waves and feel the earth trembling as they crashed onto the sand. Taking refuge in a small gap in the sand dunes, we took out a beer each and just sat. The lighthouse flashed intermittently in the distance as a cruise ship sailed across our view. Above us, another incredible canvas of stars again revealed themselves to provide a perfect backdrop. It was nights like this I had dreamed about when planning my gap year. Now I was here and the reality was even better.

'Quite a night hey Bomber? So, why do you love it here so much?' I asked.

'It's difficult to describe really, hopefully you'll understand by the end of the trip. I suppose it's just such a unique place. You get that a lot with this country – just when you think you've seen it all, something else of interest emerges. You'll see tomorrow'.

And with that, Bomber quite spontaneously (as he was inclined to do) burst into a rousing rendition of a Collingwood football song.

Wilsons Promontory is a national park situated at the most southerly tip of mainland Australia. With an abundance of diverse wildlife it stretches over 90 square kilometres incorporating wild bush land, mountainous walks and some glorious beaches. As with many national parks in the country, there is a strong Aboriginal spiritual connection with some archaeological records suggesting it was occupied up to 6500 years ago and was possibly used as part of a walkway to Tasmania during the ice ages. Having read this information in a local brochure, I could immediately see why Bomber spoke so highly of it. I had already experienced the 'diverse' wildlife having had two particularly aggressive possums fight outside my tent for what seemed like the entire evening. Still, it was nice to be up early to witness the sunrise before toasting some hot-cross buns on the fire for breakfast. I had been in Australia for two months now, but it was still hard to believe all the things I had achieved in that time. There were more experiences to be had though.

Eager to get my own back on Grant from his early morning wake-up call during the Grand Prix, I grabbed a frying pan and wooden spoon. Attempting to keep in my childish laughter, I sneaked into his tent, positioned it by his ear and banged as loudly as I possibly could.
'WAKE UP GRANT! TIME TO GO WALKING!'.
'You're....an.......absolute......bastard' is all he could muster in response.
Happy that I had finally returned this most annoying favour, I walked across to the modern shower block for a wash. However, having spotted about twenty leeches climbing up the wall of my cubicle, I quickly left. Determined not to have my blood extracted, I decided the sea would provide a much better alternative for a wash. It was then that I remembered that the waters were shark infested – so it was a toss-up – leeches or sharks? For some bizarre reason that still remains a mystery to this day, I chose to take my chances with the great whites.

The beach we had been on the previous evening was Norman Bay, so we decided to hike north and visit the much-talked-about 'Squeaky Beach'. Thinking there may be some kind of exciting fable behind such an unusual name, I asked Bomber about the origins.
'So where does the name come from – is it some kind of Aboriginal legend?' I asked.

'Ha-ha, no mate, it's because when you walk on the sand it makes a high-pitch noise. It's a little bit like a squeak actually'.

I was quickly learning not to read too much into place names in Australia as they're usually fairly straight forward. Take '90-mile beach' for example – it's a beach that stretches for 90 miles. Simple.

So with our rations packed and map in hand, we began our 1.5km hike along the headland. The first half provided us with some spectacular views across Norman Bay, which was nice since we had enjoyed it thoroughly but not actually *seen* it. High above the sea, we had stumbled across a couple of fantastic look-out-points and took the opportunity to have some photos taken. The dense green vegetation along the two headlands provided a perfect frame for the contrasting blue sea and crystal white beach. Across the bay, I could see the ocean vary in colour like the surface of a marble, before becoming clear as the waves broke and blended into the sandy beach below. It was such a wonderful view but what made it even more spectacular was its relatively modest nature. For although this was such a beautiful spot, there were only ten people walking across the 1km beach which gave us an exclusive sense of remoteness. With our hiking gear on, it almost felt like we were explorers who had just discovered this new, natural and unspoiled land. And it was this that made Wilsons Prom special. I was finally realising why Bomber had talked it up so much. Yes it was a great place for hiking and seeing some lovely beaches, but there was more to it than that – it was a *real* place not dominated by tourism and contempt to be accepted for what it was. The tourist board had not constructed huge billboards saying 'Hey come to Wilsons Prom – it's swell!', they were happy to let the fine, natural beauty of the spot speak for itself. Thankfully, they had identified the pure essence of the place and realised that by increasing visitor numbers, this would be completely destroyed. So on that note, I issue you this warning – do not visit Wilsons Prom, for your presence will ruin the experience for everyone else. Thank you.

Continuing up to the top of the headland, we took a rest on a strange rock formation. As I looked behind me to the left, I could see Norman Bay with Squeaky Beach on our right. It was a strange sensation to be standing right out in the middle of the sea, trying to imagine a time when this was one solid stone face. Through years of erosion, the two huge bays had been produced giving testament to the sheer power possessed by the ocean below.

'Bomber, why is the sand so squeaky on that beach?' I said pointing towards Squeaky beach 'and not on Norman Bay? It just seems strange when they're both so close together'.
'I've heard it's something to do with the quartz content in the sand. But I can't be sure mate'.
'Just how squeaky is it?' Grant asked.
'Honestly? You probably won't notice it' Bomber said with a smile.

Much to our disappointment, he was right. Climbing down from the rocks, I must admit I was quite excited and imagining some sort of orchestral noise occurring when my foot made contact with the quartz sand below. Sadly, I was let down. There was no squeak. There was no noise at all really. I was ultimately a very frustrated victim of false advertising. Not to worry though, for it was a splendid beach and I only had to share it with five others. There was a man walking his dog, a couple walking hand-in-hand, Bomber and Grant. Just like earlier, I truly appreciated the remoteness but couldn't believe such a beautiful spot had remained this untouched.
'Come on Granty boy, let's go for a swim' I said dumping my stuff on the beach.
'Watch out lads cos there's some strong rips around here. You don't want to end up like poor old Harold Holt' Bomber said as we ran off down the beach.
'Harold who?' I enquired, stopping suddenly in my tracks.
'Harold Holt – he was Prime Minister of Australia back in the 1960s. One day however, he decided to go for a quick dip in the sea near Portsea and was never seen again'.
'He just disappeared?' Grant asked 'was it a shark attack?'.
'Nobody knows – he simply vanished. Experts in the area think the most likely scenario was a drowning as there were some really strong rips around'.
'What exactly are rips? Grant asked again.
'They're strong and unpredictable currents which can easily deceive and drown the most experienced swimmer. So you guys watch yourselves'.
'But how the hell are we going to see them? How can we watch out?' I demanded.

'Hmmm, good point. Well, if you feel yourself going under just make loads of noise and pray someone comes to help you. Sure as hell won't be me though, I'm going for quick nap'.

With Bomber's words still ringing, and the unfortunate death of Harold Holt in my mind, I only ventured a few metres into the water. Of course, this decision was made a lot easier for me by the freezing temperature. Even so, the strength of the currents around the beach was very apparent, almost knocking me off my feet on numerous occasions. Determined not to meet such an unfortunate end, I made my way back to camp and threw my wet towel on Bomber's smiling, sleeping face. Grant too had been a little put off by the story of woe, so we decided to stay on land for the remainder of the trip.

With that in mind, we got the map out and planned the afternoon's activities. Having run over a couple of ideas, Bomber made a suggestion:
'Well guys, we've got very limited time here so you're not going to be able to see much. I think we should do what we can to try and take in as much as possible. And where can you do that? Up there' he said, pointing behind us towards the top of Mount Bishop 'from up there, you can see The Prom at its very best'.
'Okay Bomber, it's just the name that puts me off – Mount Bishop. You see, it has the word 'mount' in it which suggests a lot of effort will be required to reach the summit' I said in response.
'Don't worry, it's not too bad a climb and we don't need to go all the way to the top – I know a great look-out point. Trust me, this will be the best way to see this place'.

We began the hike by crossing the inlet at tidal river. Apparently (as the name would suggest) it varies in depth quite dramatically during different tides and has been known to flood sporadically. Thankfully for the young toddler paddling along the shoreline, it was rather shallow on this occasion. Reaching the base of the mount, I peered skywards towards the rocky peak, contemplating the task in front of us. For the past two months I had been encouraging children to challenge themselves and now I found myself in a similar situation. Focusing on the glory that would greet us at the top, we set off at a quick pace entering some typical Australian bush land. The climb wasn't too steep during these initial stages which allowed us to enjoy the wonderful wildlife in the surrounding environment. Our first sighting (and my first in Australia) was a Kookaburra sitting nonchalantly in a nearby gum tree, making a noise that sounded distinctly like an overweight man laughing. After a quick photograph session and a few cricket bat jokes, we soon continued on our way, progressing deeper into a forest that looked distinctly like the Amazon rainforest. It seemed that even in this short 3km walk, the diversity of the Australian countryside could be seen in all its glory. From the open, light and relatively dry Kookaburra filled land, we now found ourselves deep under a thick canopy, navigating around ferns larger than John Prescott's lunch box.

     Stopping for a sandwich, we sat down and ate at 'The Quaint Place' which had a lovely view dedicated to the lives of those rangers who had served The Prom throughout many years. We sat in silence and simply admired the setting in front of our eyes. Then, just as I was tucking into a piece of cheese, I saw something from the corner of my eye. A flash of crimson I thought, but when I turned there was nothing to be seen. Going back to my lunch, I tried to ignore it, thinking it must simply be a trick of the light. But then it happened again - this time though the colour was a deep purple. I tried to ignore it again, but in an instant I was surrounded by four of the most colourful birds I had ever seen.

'What are they?' I asked Bomber as they all began to converge on my sandwich.

'Rosella parrots' Bomber shouted back 'they're native to Australia'.

I had never heard of them, but here in front of me, scavenging at my feet like city pigeons, were four of the most flamboyant birds I had ever seen. Even the rainbow itself could not produce such rich and elegant colours. They were the sort of magical creature a child would produced in his colouring-in book and you would simply reject it as being a part of their overactive imagination. Incredibly, they were real and trying to steal my lunch. I felt bad for kicking (be it rather gently) something that displayed such impressive flair, however, nobody takes my food without a fight.

     Passing back from The Amazon, we resumed our climb towards the summit and hit a landscape that looked somewhat like The Rocky Mountains of Colorado. This truly had been a remarkable journey so far and I couldn't believe the best was yet to come. Finally, we had reached the peak. Well, it wasn't really a peak – more a gathering of rocks that formed an impressive overhang facing west. With Mount Bishop producing such an air of permanence and stability, these rocks appeared awfully vulnerable, but Bomber assured us that we had to venture out if the view was to be appreciated. To me, that sounded like the exact speech a serial killer would give, just prior to pushing his unsuspecting victims off a cliff. Still, 'the view will probably be worth it' I thought and duly began climbing up the sides of the huge boulders with Grant. There were no safety railings or nets - it was simply us and nature. Pulling myself up, I resisted the temptation to glimpse a peek and instead gave Grant a hand up onto his feet. When we eventually turned however, the view was quite simply breathtaking. In fact, it was more than breathtaking – it was awe inspiring. Looking across the sea front, we could see the beaches we had so happily walked along earlier that day and could just about make out others enjoying them now. Tracing a line with our hands, we mapped out the route we had taken along our hike from Squeaky Beach. I was impressed with our achievement as this wonderful secret garden soared to an even higher level in my estimation. Along the way, all its enchanting qualities had revealed themselves to us, but now we stood and tried to take them all in at once. The result was overwhelming and indescribable. I actually considered not writing about it at all, as there are simply no words that could possibly do it justice.

We each sat on our own rock and looked out towards the sea. Being so far out from Mount Bishop itself, I felt like I was simply floating gently through the air.

'Do you ever get bored of this place?' I asked Bomber.

'Mate, I'll tell you now that this is one of those places nobody could ever possibly get bored of. Not because there's so much to do, or so much entertainment going on, but because every time you come back it fills you with such an overwhelming feeling. I'm not even sure what the feeling is – you can't describe it to anyone, but everyone feels it. You know what I mean? It's an incredible feeling and one I only really experience here. That makes it worth coming back for and so I could never get bored. It is one of those truly special regions on this Earth and should be treasured – not just by Victorians, but by everyone'.

And with that, two Wedge-Tailed Eagles flew out from the cliffs and circled high above our heads.

We left early the next morning just as the sun was rising on the horizon. Luckily, there was still time to complete our Australian wildlife tour in style as six kangaroos and two emus crossed the road in front of our car. As I watched these defining national symbols silhouette themselves against the tender red sunlight, I thought about Bomber's words and felt a real sense of satisfaction - for in this small corner of the country, I had experienced the real Australia. This was not a place you read about in tourism brochures or saw on postcards. Nor was it a marketing trap set up for commercial gain. It was genuine Australia, finally revealing itself to the world in one small, enchanting flash. I felt lucky to have captured it.

CHAPTER 13

When a train conductor describes somewhere as 'rather close', you would be forgiven for thinking it was within walking distance. Nevertheless, you wouldn't necessarily expect to be travelling for more than say, ten minutes. Pulling into Bendigo station two hours and over 150kms later though, I was reminded once again of the vast scale the Australian people work on. Believing I would be alighting relatively quickly, I hadn't actually taken a seat at the Spencer Street station in Melbourne, but instead stood by the door with keen anticipation.

Having returned from Wilsons Prom, we had endured two weeks of solid work with a school for disabled children before conducting a sponsored camp for those who come from financially strained backgrounds. Both were incredibly rewarding experiences, but ultimately very exhausting. It was quite a relief to be offered a week holiday, so we all accepted with relieved enthusiasm.

Fancying a change of scenery and taking advantage of some distant relatives' hospitality, Grant had flown to Hobart for a week of relaxation in Tasmania. Although I was happy he was going to spend Easter in a lovely furnished family home with a comfy bed and a never-ending supply of food, this did nonetheless leave me in a little bit of a pickle. Depressed and facing the prospect of Easter alone in a hostel room that had the uncanny knack of making a prison cell seem luxurious, Skip, Tess and LJ had mercifully come in for the rescue. Like a child burdening his divorced parents, I hassled them for attention, forcing them to take on the responsibility of entertaining me over the next week. Skip had volunteered himself for the first leg and very kindly invited me along on a camping trip to Bendigo, where we could light big fires whilst drinking copious amounts of alcohol, relatively consequence free and without caution.

It was early evening when the train eventually pulled into the station and the town was alive with that strange bubbly energy that seems to accompany funfairs on their travels. Discussing our plans for the evening, we decided to take a walk around the rides - not so much to have a go on 'The Big Wheel' but more to soak up the enjoyable festivities. Perhaps it was the dazzling lights and vivacious atmosphere, but I certainly warmed to Bendigo much more than expected.

Like other settlements in the area, its origins dated back to the great gold rush in the late 1850s. In contrast to its brothers though, it had a deep sense of character that was still evolving. Far from mundane, the buildings lining the street actually displayed a large variety in their architecture, making me feel like I had finally arrived in a real town. Yes, the large boulevards still existed, but they were surrounded by huge Victorian stone buildings, decorated with beautiful carvings worthy of an avenue in Paris. The proud cathedral was not made out of wood, nor was it painted in any obscene colours – it was made with thick stone in a traditional gothic design.

I loved Bendigo, for this was not the result of a scribbling in a mathematician's notepad during coffee break - it was an ever-changing example of artistic flamboyance. Okay, maybe I am exaggerating ever so slightly, but I was just so happy to find a town whose design wasn't inspired by a depressingly logical mind. The fact that the high street wasn't merely a never-ending, perfectly straight stretch of repetitive tarmac, periodically intercepted at right-angles by hundreds of cloned roads and littered by a few thousand pedestrian crossings, was just wonderful. A typical English town (with the exception of Milton Keynes) proudly exhibits pieces of inspiration from many different people, ranging over hundreds of years and incorporating a great diversity in style. Many would say that the result is simply an untidy mess where the confusing streets and alleyways will take you in every direction except the one in which you wish to travel. But, I say to you my friends, you have failed to realise that it is this fantastic characteristic that creates the brilliant sense of adventure and unpredictability for which our towns are famed - for even the simplest stroll has the potential to turn into a three day expedition through the unknown. In contrast, Victorian settlements are somewhat smothered with an aura of inevitable certainty. Of course, there were still areas of Bendigo that were dominated by this terrible grid formation, but certain parts around the CBD had escaped unharmed, and these were the parts I cherished with joyful enthusiasm.

Skip had loads of female friends, so he had invited two along for a little variation in conversation. It surprised me that Kylie and Jess (being typical city girls) were willing to come camping in the middle of nowhere. To be honest, I don't know many women who would eagerly sign up for a night in the wilderness in England, but add to the mix redback spiders and you've got yourself a scenario about as appealing as a honeymoon in Baghdad. I was keen to get their take on things so fired a few questions at them as we enjoyed a schooner in one of the bars:
'Does the fact that every animal in this country is out to kill you not play on your mind slightly?' I asked.
'Well, how long have you been here?' Kylie asked.
'About three months now'.
'And during all that time you've been working in the bush. So how many animals have attacked you?'.
'Ah, I see where you're going with this, but even if a serial killer hadn't attacked me yet I still wouldn't want to sit next to him on a bus'.
'Okay fine, but how many spiders or snakes have you seen?'.
'Well a brown snake groped my foot the other day, but I haven't seen any spiders. Well, actually we had loads of massive spiders in our flat in Licola but Skip said they were just huntsman and not to worry'.
'Umm' Skip said suddenly joining in our conversation 'about that – I wasn't actually sure if they were huntsman or not, I just didn't want you to panic'

'Right' I said in disbelief 'so in order to stop me panicking, you sent me to bed with a huge, potentially fatal spider. Good thinking – I mean, how can I panic when I'm dead?'.
'Sorry dude, you're fine though so I wouldn't worry about it – nobody in Australia really thinks about it'.
'It's true' Kylie said 'we've been brought up around all this wildlife and you generally just forget about it. It's best not to let yourself worry. I haven't seen a snake in years'.

I couldn't help think that this comment may have been tempting fate. Fortunately, this proved not to be the case as our first evening passed completely snake and spider free. Still, if someone had said something like that to me before this trip had begun, I would've said 'yeah right – forget about the deadly assassins all around me?! No chance!' It was true though – the thought about snakes and spiders had generally slipped to the back of my mind, so much so that I never even checked my boxer shorts when putting them on in the mornings. To be honest, I wasn't sure if that was a good thing or bad thing.

Our camp site was located in a small area of bush next to a river. In order to get there, we turned off the road into a field, crossed that for about half a mile, before meandering our way through some trees. Basically, it wasn't what you would call an 'official' camping spot.
'Are we allowed to camp here?' I asked Skip 'I mean - will anyone mind?'.
'This is OZ mate, nobody minds where you camp as long as you clean up after yourself and don't start a bush fire' he said while ferreting around in the back of his car for something.
'What if we *do* start a bush fire?'.
'Hmmm, I don't know really. I suppose we'd just have to drive and get away from here as quickly as possible. The public don't take kindly to that sort of thing so it'd probably be best to distance ourselves from it. Don't worry though, my car's fast so we'd have no problems'.
On saying these words, he finally emerged from the car with his find - a giant chainsaw. Grabbing the pull cord, he fired it up with a huge grin and announced that he was off to find some fire wood.

Why is it that we men get so excited by the prospect of burning things? There must be something in testosterone that turns us all into raging pyromaniacs. Talk to men about football and some will show an interest - talk to men about breasts and many will show an interest. But talk to men about fires and I guarantee they will shake uncontrollably with intense excitement and anticipation. Sweat will drip down their forehead as you report the height of the flames and how the crackles from within were produced with deafening volume. Maybe it is that caveman instinct attempting to free itself from the chains of oppression in which modern society holds it. For some reason, the people who govern our land have seen fit to outlaw random acts of destructive satisfaction, causing those natural urges to remain suppressed beneath our peaceful demeanour. It is my theory that fire provides a unique opportunity to release these feelings and allow them to blossom once again. Am I trying to rationalise the irrational? Perhaps it is just an unexplainable truth, but a truth nonetheless and one I was very aware of when I saw Skip return with a mountain of wood. This was going to be a big fire.

  Unwilling to settle for just big however, we set off into the wilderness with one goal in mind - make the *biggest* fire imaginable. The girls were oblivious to our efforts and remained seated by the radio as we gathered fuel for the furnace. They wouldn't understand anyway. We trekked across bush land looking for that ultimate trophy, until finally, we found it. Rounding a corner, we found a felled, dry tree trunk lying in the long grass. I wasn't sure what type of tree it had been, but it certainly wasn't a conventional one with many irregular branches and knobbly shapes coming from the body. I was however perfectly aware of its potential. About a metre in diameter and two long, it possessed the capability to make all our dreams come true. Attempting to lift it, we soon realised that help would be required. Unwilling to cut it open with the fear of disturbing a deadly spider's home, we instead used the brute force of the car to drag it into position. The girls were shocked by the sheer size and even more shocked by the effort we had put in just for a log. But this wasn't any log - it burned all through the day and long into the night with heat so intense we had to sit ten metres from its mesmerising flicker. Taking advantage of the huge energy it radiated, we cooked three meals (including Easter lunch) before huddling around and exchanging ghost stories long into the night.

  Then, in the middle of one of skip's more elaborate stories, I suddenly caught of glimpse of headlights through a gap in the trees. They were moving erratically as if the car were travelling across uneven ground. What's more, they were coming towards us. Looking at our watches, we saw it was nearly midnight.

'Who the hell could this be? Shit, they're coming straight for us' said Jess obviously quite scared.

'Get a couple of knives, it could be a mental case' chipped in Kylie. I tried to calm the mood.

'I tell you what guys - look at us - four youths having a fun day camping in the middle of nowhere and then we completely vanish. This is just like the start of horror movie'.

'Ah shit mate, shut up' Skip shouted as he reached around for a weapon. All he could muster was a spatchelor though as the lights continued to home in on us and we could hear the high revs of the engine. Standing in a line, each gripping a different kitchen utensil for protection, we waited for the inevitable. I had never really considered how I would react in such a situation. Thinking back now, I am surprised I didn't run away as my mind was telling me to do.

The lights got so bright I could see the whites of Skip's eyes as they illuminated his face.

'Guys this is really scary, I think we need to do a runner' Kylie said slowly in a terrified voice.

'And leave all this stuff here? I'm not leaving my car here for them to smash to pieces. Whatever it is, I'm sure we'll be able to sort it out' Skip replied with an authoritative whisper.

The car was much closer now – less than twenty metres as it made its way through the bushes just as Skip's car had earlier that day. It couldn't be a coincidence, they were coming straight for our location. Ten metres now and we could see the white body of the 4x4. Then it stopped ten metres away from us with the headlights right in our face to blind our vision. The door opened and a voice spoke

'What the hell is going on here?!' it said. We looked at each other looking for something to say.

'What? Who the hell are you?' Skip shouted back 'we're just camping'.

'Ah bloody hell' replied the voice as the driver killed the lights and started walking towards us 'I'm the ranger from around here – some drivers reported a fire in the woods so I came to check it out. Bloody hell, that's *one hell* of a fire!'

'Jesus mate, you scared the hell out of us' I said with a sudden sigh of relief. The girls were now laughing at how scared they had been just moments before.

'Sorry guys, I just wanted to check out what was going on. You scared me too to be honest'. Turning, he examined our camp 'that fire's bloody impressive, how'd you move that tree trunk?!' he said, obviously impressed.

'We towed it with the car' Skip said 'do you want a beer mate?'.

'Now you're talking my language'.

We had a few drinks as he told us some of the funny things he had caught campers doing throughout the past few weeks. He stayed for an hour or so before declaring 'I probably should get back to the wife'. It was certainly a marvellous experience and one that made me admire this country even more. I couldn't imagine a warden (or whatever he was) being so laid-back at home. Usually, people abuse authority, but like most Australians he had shown an element of common sense along with the great ability to have a laugh.

Then, without warning, the heavens opened and it started to pour. This was the first rain I had seen in months and I could feel the countryside dancing for joy as it fell. I went back to my tent for some cover, laughing at Skip who was sleeping in just a 'swag' – a full body sleeping bag incorporating a small mattress. These are incredibly popular with campers, especially on tours of Uluru as they keep you 'in touch with nature'. As the water drained through the feeble face netting, Skip confirmed this claim to be true. A better friend would've invited him into the tent, but I was laughing way too much to think about such trivial things.

CHAPTER 14

The Great Ocean Road - is it a great road along an average ocean or a great ocean next to an average road? It was a topic of discussion and one we debated heavily as our car travelled south-west out of the city towards Torquay. This was the second instalment of my Easter week adventure and I was thoroughly looking forward to it.

Having arrived back from Bendigo, Skip had fed me and then shipped me off to LJ's as he had some interviews to attend. It is difficult as a traveller, as you do not wish to burden people with your presence, but then any opportunity to spend a night in a bed not infested with cockroaches must be ceased upon. Mel and I hadn't exactly asked Lisa-Jane for her hospitality, instead we had merely subtly implied that it would be a large help to us and our diminishing funds. The fact that she had a lovely suburban home with a swimming pool may have swayed our decision ever so slightly too. Anyway, we spent an enjoyable couple of days visiting good shopping spots around Melbourne as well as seeing the gaol where Ned Kelly was hanged, before Mel flew to Cairns to continue her travels around Australia. I was sad to see her leave as her energetic and optimistic outlook had never failed to cheer me up. But more than that, I envied her incredible lifestyle.

'Where are you going to stay when you get to Cairns' I had asked her.

'Lisa's got some grandparents up there and she's arranged for me to have a bed at their place while I get settled down. But after that - who knows? I'll go wherever the wind takes me'.

Many people may view this as a rather wasteful lifestyle adopted by those unsure of their role in life. But I saw it as an incredibly brave adventure conducted by someone unwilling to waste her life in an office. She travelled from place to place until she got bored, and then simply moved on - what could be more rewarding than that? Drifters like Mel should not be looked down upon and pitied by society, but instead admired - for they are the only people daring enough to live life to the full. Everyone dreams of a lifestyle encapsulated by *carpe diem*, but little do they realise that it's only people like Mel who can truly achieve it. I hoped I would see her again on my travels. Now though, I had my own mini-adventure to conduct.

Being locals to the area, LJ and Tess had travelled along The Great Ocean road many times as children, but had since become oblivious to its charm. It's understandable really as most people never really appreciate the something that's on their doorstep – for example, here I was touring Australia and I hadn't ever been to Scotland. With my tourist-like enthusiasm acting as a catalyst, both seemed to have had their wilted spirit restored as we embarked on the trip with a great sense of anticipation.

Stretching for over 300kms, the road provides debatably the most spectacular coastline scenery in the world, through an area incorporating world-famous surf beaches, The Otways Rainforest and (le pièce de résistance) the lighthouse from *'Round the Twist'*. With the surfboards loaded on LJ's roof-rack, we arrived at the road's gateway in Torquay. Taking advantage of its status as a famous surfing town, the streets were dominated by commercial billboards advertising expensive beach merchandise none of us could afford. Each of the famous brands had its own huge, extravagantly built department store which we looked around with interest. Deciding that food for the next two months was a far greater priority, I resisted the temptation to purchase a pair of overpriced boardshorts even though the devilishly attractive assistant insisted I should. Apparently they would've made me look like 'a spunk' on the beach, but I don't think she'd noticed my freakishly white skin. Escaping the prowl of these dangerously irresistible sales women, we jumped back in the car quickly and sped off along The Surfcoast Highway.

This particular section of The Great Ocean Road takes you on a 45km tour of some of greatest beaches on the planet, before terminating in the next settlement of any note, Lorne. As a surfing novice, I was keen to experience the thrill of riding the waves. Having watched the film *'Point Break'* continuously up in Licola, I couldn't really imagine a better place to have my first lesson than the legendary Bells Beach. So, 2kms into our tour and we were already turning off The Great Ocean Road to partake in a little recreation. Unfortunately though, all we got was a feeling of utter disappointment. Don't get me wrong - the beach itself was beautifully set in a little cove and surrounded with some splendid natural fauna, but this beautiful setting was not the one I remembered from all my hours of *'Point Break'* viewing.

'Sorry LJ, I think we've taken a wrong turn somewhere – this isn't Bells Beach' I said as we parked the car.

'It is mate - what are you talking about?'.

'No it's not. I've seen Point Break – where the hell are the steep, pine cliffs?'.

'That wasn't actually filmed here you idiot! I don't even think they filmed it in Australia'.

Yet again Hollywood had lied to me. Determined not to let it ruin my day however, I got out of the car to look at the waves I was about to thrust myself into. With this, Bells Beach dished out yet another disappointment, for it was more crowded than the pitch during a game of Aussie Rules. The waves did indeed seem spectacularly huge (probably too much for my sake) but each was being ridden by about twenty individual surf enthusiasts. This was the first time since Manly I had seen a beach in Australia quite so busy, which surprised me considering the sheer number of them along this coastline. Nevertheless, knowing I would have absolutely no control of my board and worried it might result in me killing someone in such a crowded environment, we made the decision to continue on our journey towards Lorne and find a more secluded spot.

This first section of The Surfcoast Highway was inland by about 1km and so provided quite an anti-climax for the start of The Great Ocean Road, despite providing some charming countryside views. It was just the lack of ocean that worried us slightly, however this all changed upon arrival at Anglesea. Hoping to take part in some water sports, we soon found ourselves a quiet little beach just west of the town. Having unloaded the boards, we were just preparing for my first lesson when the sun suddenly disappeared and the heavens opened from above. Having not seen much rain for months, Victoria was certainly trying to make up for it now. Running back to the car, Tessa shouted back at me.

'Where the hell are you going?'.

'Into the car – it's raining!' I shouted back, surprised at her question.

'Don't be such a Pommie wimp! Come on, the rain won't hurt you'.

'It's bloody freezing! You're okay, you've got a wet suit on – I've just got my feeble English skin'.

'Come on, surfing in the rain is way more fun anyway. You're going to get wet in the water so what's the problem? Plus, sharks never attack people when it's raining so you'll be fine'.

She had a good point – not about the sharks (this was blatantly a damn right lie), but about the whole 'getting wet' scenario, plus I admired her perseverance so decided to give the surfing a shot. Luckily, one of her friends had joined us and she just happened to be a qualified instructor which was rather convenient. Lying on a surfboard drawn in the wet sand, I acted out her instructions on how to 'catch a wave' and the technique for standing up. I wasn't sure why I was learning how to stand up, as I was convinced that such a complex skill would be beyond me. Quite naively though, I thought it all seemed rather simple. A little too simple perhaps, but I was still full of optimism as I ran towards the rough looking sea. Then I remembered the sharks and stopped in my tracks.

'Tess?'.

'Yes'.

'Are there any sharks around? It seems a little stupid to use a beach without a shark net'.

'You've got nothing to worry about – just put the thought of sharks out of your mind. They don't even like the taste of humans anyway and usually only eat an arm'.

'That's really put my mind at rest – thank you. But seriously, have there been many attacks around here?'.

'None for years that I've heard of'.

'Right, there are two things in that reply that worry me. For starts you said 'not for years' which suggests there have been some before, which in turn suggests that sharks like it around here. The other thing you said is 'that I've heard of' which, since you don't read the newspapers, makes your statement irrelevant'.

'Just get on your board and shut up'.

She was right of course – I mean, why worry about going into water infested with something generally considered to be the greatest hunter on the planet. Some people may even refer to it as 'the perfect killing machine'. With ten other surfers in the sea however, I calculated that my chances of being taken were only 10% even if a shark did attack and so began paddling out towards the breaking waves.

This in itself may seem like a relatively straight forward exercise, especially when watching the professionals from the beach, nevertheless I soon discovered that it was deceivingly difficult. Having been embarrassingly flipped over a couple of times by breaking waves it became apparent that your timing was imperative. Unfortunately, it appeared that mine wasn't. Every time I thought it was a good opportunity to paddle out, another wave would pick me up and ceremoniously dump me upside down into the water below. Imagine (if you will) going to play basketball and then realising in front of loads of onlookers that you can't even catch a ball and you can start to gauge the sort of humiliation I was feeling.

Like a mother helping her dribbling child, Tessa thankfully came to the rescue and helped me control the board past the breaking waves so I could finally excel. Obviously I didn't, but I was a lot better than my efforts to paddle out would suggest. The highlight came towards the end when, after a number of failed attempts, I almost stood up. Looking out to sea, I had seen one particularly large wave approaching and prepared myself for it carefully. Spinning my board around quickly and paddling as fast as my arms could manage, I was picked up by its incredible power. With a sudden burst of energy, I was flying along at what felt like a hundred miles an hour. Grabbing the sides of the board, I pulled myself up and was just about to let out a triumphant cheer when my foot slipped, I fell backwards the board shot out from underneath me. Emerging from the freezing sea and coughing up pints of salt water, I attempted to get my bearings but before I could, another gigantic wave took out its fury on my head. This pattern of events inevitably continued until I was eventually beached on the sandy shoreline like a piece of discarded driftwood. And that, I'm afraid to say, is as good as it got.

It was great fun though and I was slightly disappointed when the experience was cut short due to a large rash developing on my chest caused by the abrasion of the board. Thinking about it, I had probably been tempting fate earlier in the day by saying that rash vests were for wimps. I'll know never to make that mistake again.

After having some food in a café made entirely out of corrugated iron, we continued on our trip from Anglesea towards Lorne. Immediately, all the doubts I had concerning the greatness of this road were forgotten as we embarked on some of the finest scenery I have ever seen. Hugging the ocean for the entire span, the road meandered around the steep cliffs. As dusk approached, the subtle light accentuated the definition between the contrasting green cliffs and powerful grey sea creating an incredible backdrop. The road was so close to the sea at points that, as I peered out of the car window, it almost felt like we were driving through the raging waves.

Rounding a headland, the sun began to set and the clouded skies were illuminated, creating an inspiring red and purple canvas above our heads. Asking LJ to pull over, I jumped out and captured the image before it vanished for all of eternity. Taking a moment to gather my thoughts, I looked out across the swirling ocean which seemed to have calmed since earlier. Instead of waves crashing into the cliff below, the whole sea seemed to be rocking periodically in elegant unison. As the light dissolved, the intricate details of the massive cliffs became clear as they provided a perfect framework for this overpowering picture.

Unfortunately, night fall was approaching and LJ was keen to get on. We continued past The Split Point lighthouse where *'Round the Twist'* was filmed and onto Lorne – described as the Surfers Paradise of The Great Ocean Road. I could see why people would say that, although the overall feel was ever so slightly more tasteful. Desperate to get to a camping site before nightfall though, we drove through relatively quickly and didn't get a chance to experience it enough to pass any significant judgement. Continuing along this glorious costal road, we eventually arrived at a small settlement called Wye River where we set up camp near the beach and squeezed into a tiny two man tent for some well deserved rest.

The problem with tents is that although they form a visual barrier, they don't stop sound by any reasonable degree. As a result, it is quite difficult to sleep when the couple in the tent next to you start having a huge domestic. Well, it was for me anyway but LJ and Tess seemed to be immune to the torrid abuse they were firing at each another.

It was 6am and I was now wide awake so decided to go for a morning walk along the beach. It was completely deserted apart from one solitary surfer riding the waves quite far out from the shoreline. Frustratingly, he made it seem so easy and didn't get dump-tackled once.

Wye River was a beautiful little spot surrounded by lush green hills with many small houses desperately clinging to their steep sides. With the mesmerising sea moving gently in front of me, I was taken back to my childhood as the scene reminded me of the setting for *'The Goonies'*. All that was needed now was for a pirate ship to float by and a strange monster wearing a superman top to shout *'hey you guys!'*. Suspecting that it was most unlikely, I returned to the tent to wake up the girls. An hour later we were on the road again and moving quickly towards The Otway Rainforest.

Continuing along the coastline until Apollo Bay, the road then veered right inland towards this splendid national park. Before we knew it, we were surrounded on all sides by dense, green, tropical vegetation. Of course I was expecting this, but the transition from rugged coastline to compact forest was relatively sudden in its nature. I felt confused - as if my brain couldn't adapt to this extreme change in such a short space of time – one moment we were driving along by the cold ocean and the next we had somehow ended up in the rainforest. Usually there is some kind of gentle acclimatisation, but here we were being spoiled by one spectacle after another. As if encouraging you to saver the intense beauty of your surroundings, The Great Ocean Road thoughtfully meanders the long way through The Otways National Park. Naturally, if you were in a rush to get somewhere this would probably be the most frustrating design ever conceived, but we enjoyed the prolonged period of time it provided us in amongst the giant ferns. Looking around hoping to spot some unusual wildlife, it was hard to believe I was in the same country as the sparse barren hills surrounding Licola.

We then faced a dilemma – turn left and travel directly south to the Cape Otway Lighthouse, or continue on our path towards The Twelve Apostles? I had read quite a bit of literature concerning the lighthouse which was the longest running on mainland Australia until it was decommissioned in 1994. Constructed in 1846, it was seen as an essential piece of engineering to help ships on their difficult and dangerous journey through the windswept western gateway of the Bass Straight known as 'The Eye of the Needle'. However, since the next region of shoreline was known as 'The Shipwreck Coast' it appears all their efforts may well have been in vain. Still, it was a nice symbol and represented an important piece of Australian maritime heritage so I was quite keen to see it. Unfortunately the others were not and I was subsequently outvoted. Still, it gave us time to enjoy a relaxing lunch in a delightful little bakery in Johanna before setting off for the real tourist attractions.

The power of marketing is a wonder to behold. Nobody thinks they are taken in by it, yet we all are. Here we were making a 200km pilgrimage so we could have our photos taken in front of some limestone stacks. When you think about it that way, it seems like pure and utter madness. I'm sure we all loved studying the processes of erosion in geography class, but making such efforts just to witness its effects seems a little extreme.

Prior to the 1950s when the world wasn't dominated by such media propaganda, these stone stacks, standing 20-30 metres from the shoreline, were simply known as 'The Sow and Piglets'. However, looking for a more appealing name in order to boost tourism in the area, this was soon changed to 'The Twelve Apostles' despite the fact that there were only nine of them. But my God did it work. I was expecting a small lay-by, perhaps with a roadside hot-dog van and a tiny platform on which to take photos. Instead, there was a huge car park in the shadow of the ultra-modern visitor centre and hundreds of metres of intricate walkways linking many look-out-points. No wonder everybody I had met seemed to have an incredible photo of The Twelve Apostles – I just thought they had been adventurous enough to climb out onto the delicate cliffs, but it seems they had put in far less effort.

On closer inspection though, I was pleasantly surprised to see that these amendments had been implemented with a large amount of dignity. Thankfully, the visitor centre was not a hoard of cheap, tacky t-shirts featuring the statement 'I love Victoria!' but instead presented a number of elegant poems written about this astonishing coastline.

As we crossed the road, I suddenly began to get quite excited by the prospect just in front of me and realised just how strong the effects of their powerful advertising had been. Having seen so many photos, I suppose I had developed a strange sense of familiarity with the scene, even though I had never visited it before.

There they were in front of me – The Twelve Apostles standing proud and solid amidst the crashing waves on the inaccessible and untouched beach below. The wind was so strong that we all had to hold onto the railings to stop ourselves being knocked over, which gave testament to the extreme conditions this stretch of coast dishes out for those hoping to sail it. I wouldn't describe the sight as Divine like many people, but thinking about what these stone stacks had achieved was certainly inspiring. Unlike the rest of the cliffs around them, these small pillars of strength had not fallen into the sea beneath. Under continuous, immense pressure they had been tough and defiant in the face of adversity. For me, they were not a mythical symbol of religious descent, more importantly, they were a defining example of resilience, courage and spirit. As if to reiterate my point, I recently read that one of the largest ones has fallen down. It seems strange to name something that is slowly eroding away after such important religious icons, although thinking about, it probably provides a good representation of how our modern society is changing.

In 1878, the Loch Ard ship set sail from England on its way to Melbourne. It took about three months before the passengers on board saw the great land of Australia from deck. Relief short lived, imagine their dismay when, just a few miles from entering the Bass Strait, they hit a patch of dense fog. I think you know that luck is not on your side if, having just entered an area of ocean known as 'Shipwreck Coast' you have your visibility cut to just a few metres. It would be like wandering into a bear trap testing field blindfolded, which I think you'll agree is a situation nobody wants to find themselves in. So, it is no surprise (although I'm sure it was to the passengers) to hear that the ship never made it to Melbourne and instead crashed into a reef just off Mutton Bird Island. With a strong, swirling ocean pounding the hull, the ship sank within fifteen minutes, preventing any life boats being launched effectively. Shockingly, only two of the fifty-four on board survived. One was an apprentice named Tom Pearce who, having found himself washed ashore in a small cove, swam back out to sea in order to save a screaming woman named Eva Carmichael. Alive but deserted and cold, the two found themselves on a small beach just ten minutes west of The Twelve Apostles, and this is where we found ourselves now. When we got out of the car and walked across the headland, there was an eerie silence in the air. Now named after the wreck, Loch Ard Gorge is a fabulous place to view the extremities of coastal erosion. High above the devastating ocean below, we had a fabulous view of the caves, arches and stacks being carefully carved by the relentless sea. Seeing the extent of this damage only made the survivors' story seem even more miraculous.

 The beach itself was a tiny circular cove, surrounded almost entirely by steep cliffs with only a small gap for the sea to approach. Modern steps have been built down to the beach, however these obviously wouldn't have been present when Eva and Tom were washed ashore. I tried to imagine what it must've been like for them and how, in a cruel twist of fate, their spirits would have been crushed having discovered that they had been washed into an impenetrable cove. As far as I could see, the only feasible escape route would've been back the way they had entered. To this day, I still do not know how they escaped but it is an interesting problem to try and contemplate.

 Still, although I had read the story and was standing in its menacing setting, the reality of it had not registered with me entirely. I suppose I treated it as some kind of mythical story. Then, we came across the graves of four of the unfortunate and the reality of it became hauntingly apparent. The mood was suddenly very sombre. In a somewhat ironic act of nature, the sun then appeared, brightly illuminating the golden sand and transforming the sea into a warm bath of turquoise. It was hard to believe what sinister acts it was capable of.

With time running out we made one final stop just down the coast at 'The London Arch'. As the name suggests, it is a huge limestone arch located in the middle of the ocean. I had never seen waves this big in my life, and although we were fifty or sixty metres above the beach, the destructive force of the waves could be felt as their crushing vibrations transferred up through the cliffs and into my feet. The power they portrayed was simply devastating.

'Those waves are so powerful' I mused with LJ.

'Yeah, you can see how strong they are just there' pointing at the arch 'it used to be called 'London Bridge', but the bridge collapsed back in 1990 and trapped some tourists!'.

'Really? Was anyone killed?'.

'No, thankfully nobody was walking across the bridge when it collapsed, but the tourists needed to get rescued by helicopter. It just goes to show how much force those waves possess'.

With that, we jumped back in the car and started back for Melbourne. It had been a wonderful few days allowing me to experience majestic scenery, exciting legends and the thrill of (almost) riding the waves. The answer to my very first question was now blatantly apparent - this was a great road next to a great ocean.

The next week we were back in Licola for the last few days of the season. Our last camp was cancelled, so we spent our week reflecting on the past few months. Ending the placement in style, Kate and Simon purchased all the alcohol the shop could provide and we all danced the night away! With no neighbours around, we could simply make as much noise as was humanly possible, which was all the encouragement I needed to get on the karaoke machine. Nevertheless, I was ultimately very sad to leave. This incredible little town in the mountains had provided me with the comfort and stability I associated with home. The people too had made Grant and me welcome, incorporating us in their very special Australian society. I appreciated everything they had all done for me and would miss them deeply, but it was time to take this country by storm and unlock some more of its secrets.

PART 3

CHAPTER 15

As I woke and opened my eyes, reality soon hit me and I realised that for the first time I truly was homeless. The safety and reliability supplied by camp had disintegrated away leaving me as an independent, excited traveller. I was at Skip's house as he had kindly offered to take Grant and me in for a few days before my departure to Sydney. The thought of having to leave my friends again was getting me down, but I supposed it was all in the spirit of the adventure I was pursuing. Besides, it provided me with an honourable excuse to spend lots of money, get drunk and have ample amounts of fun during my final few days with my new found mates.

Skipper's Sunday was going to be dominated in typical Aussie fashion with a football match, and since we were honorary Australians, Grant and I thought we should do the same. Of course, we weren't willing to risk our life on the field (the game is simply madness) and didn't want to waste our time watching amateur rubbish, so we bought ourselves 2 tickets for the huge derby match between Essendon and Collingwood, to be played at Melbourne Cricket Ground (MCG). Since Simon was such a huge Essendon fan, he had groomed us into his way of thinking so that is whom our loyalties lay with.

Skip lived in a suburb named Seaford. It was pleasant, but there didn't really seem to be much to it in terms of entertainment. This was fairly typical of the Australian outer-city areas, with a series of confusing, identical streets, lined with pleasant and delicately designed toy bungalows. Without a central point within the town, there was a distinct lack of community and this feeling was repeated by the settlements we passed through on our way to Melbourne on the train.

Like everywhere in the world, there was graffiti covering the fences along the track. This didn't so much surprise me, instead it just sparked intrigue. I mean, what is the universal reason that induces an attraction between graffiti artists and railway lines? In every country in the world I can guarantee there will be at least one piece of artistic drivel lining the fences that parallel the track, but it remains a mystery as to why. With Grant jamming on his air-guitar whilst listening to *Green Day* on his MP3 player, trying to come up with an explanation for this seemed like the best way to use my time. Unfortunately, I never actually came up with a feasible answer.

The MCG is massive. There are no other words that do it justice. This fact was never more apparent than when Grant and I climbed the steps to our seats and watched the pitch slowly fade away into a distant green memory. This was possibly the longest set of stairs known in human history and as sweat started pouring from my brow, I half expected to see a few heart attack victims sprawled out along my path. To my relief, this never occurred, but I feel it is my duty to issue a health warning to all prospective fans travelling to the MCG - train hard before-hand. This is the only sports arena in which the fans must be fitter than the players and where they issue you with a complementary can of antiperspirant at the turnstile. Nevertheless, although we were breathing heavily and were surrounded by the stench of exhaustion, it was well worth it as we took our magnificent birds-eye-view seats.

As the crowd grew, so did the tension and a chorus of nervous applause went up for the war veterans being driven around the pitch on Anzac Day. I thought it rather fitting that the soldiers of the past were paving the way for the soldiers of this modern time. Granted, they were not dressed in immaculate uniforms or carrying rifles - instead they had replaced these with a series of multi-coloured vests and pairs of impossibly small shorts. But make no mistake, this was definitely war.

The game itself is based on a few simple rules which truly invite carnage. Let's start with the first of these rules; 'A player cannot, under any circumstances, be sent off'. Now I'm not an Aussie Rules expert, but this rule might as well be written as 'kill each other in any way possible, we don't care'. The second rule states that 'if you catch the oddly shaped ball and shout 'mark' then no other player can tackle you, except (of course!) if the ball has not been kicked to you originally or has touched the ground in between the original kick and you collecting the ball, in which case all players (from either team), managers, supporters and grannies are invited to pull, punch, shoot or maim in order to get possession'. Following so far? Good. If you do manage to survive the riot, then the only way you can score is to kick the ball between the two huge posts, in which case you gain six points. If however you miss the goal, you still get one point – just for trying. Add to this mixing bowl a couple of hundred water boys dressed in fluorescent pyjamas, three umpires who all look uncannily similar, two dozen physios – all of whom are allowed on the pitch whilst the game is in progress - and (finally) you've got yourself a game of Aussie Rules.

With all this in mind, you would be forgiven for believing I was describing some kind of kamikaze carnival and I suppose it is true that the number of people on the pitch at any given time puts the population of China to shame – but I tell you what, it makes a bloody entertaining game!

Seventeen days later (give or take), we emerged from the stadium apparently victorious. Unsurprisingly, I was actually just very confused. As we began the decent back to sea level, I heard one supporter – an elderly man, with a thick grey beard- talk about how Jimmy Herd had dominated the game and since he was the captain of our team, I took this as a good sign. Grant was his normal upbeat self as he relayed moments from the match to me in his truly unique and enthusiastic style.

'Glad we got one over stupid Collingwood' he said, with a beaming smile and wearing his tight Essendon vest.

'Yeah, I'm well chuffed' I replied, not really understanding how someone could feel so much passion for a game we didn't really understand and which had no real historical significance. Don't get me wrong, I understand the fervour and desire that comes with a derby match – many a time have I sat at White Hart Lane screaming my English hooligan face off at Spurs against Arsenal. However, having only been in the country for a few months, I wasn't really sure where my allegiance fell. Grant did. He was convinced and obsessed – I suppose I respected him for getting so involved, but it would take me a little longer to get so passionate.

That night we enjoyed a lovely meal in a small Italian place named Raginthino's and discussed the game with Skip. After a couple of beers, my passion had certainly increased.

The next day was my last in Melbourne. However, it promised to be one of the most exciting. To be honest, I'm embarrassed to say that it was this prospect that had provided Australia with most of its appeal whilst planning my gap year. We were visiting Ramsay Street – home of the world-famous Australian soap-opera *Neighbours* and I couldn't contain my excitement. I had been dreaming of this for years and now, after such a long wait, it had finally arrived.

Quickly knocking back a couple of aspirin, I ran over to a sleeping Grant and jumped on him chanting 'Neighbours day, Neighbours day...!' The look on his face suggested he wasn't half as chuffed as I thought he might be, but I couldn't contain my excitement. Skipper had declined our invitation to join us on our *Neighbours* extravaganza deciding it was 'a Pom thing' so Grant and I merrily made our way into the city alone.

An hour later we found ourselves standing directly opposite Federation Square facing a true monstrosity – the *Neighbours* tour bus. Talk about a sore thumb sticking out, this was the ultimate of broken limbs. From the front it appeared to be a relatively normal, white coach. However, as it slowly began to turn the corner, its side was revealed in a single moment of unbelievable glory. Painted in huge letters across the side were the words '*Neighbours Official Tour Bus*' along with a couple of cheesy photos. There was no chance of being inconspicuous in this.

With an embarrassed smile, a red face and around twenty other Brits, I climbed up the steps onto the bus of humiliation. Grant said the laughing and pointing from passers-by would subside eventually - he was wrong, it continued all day. I eventually began to embrace it by giving each of our tormentors a big thumbs-up and an energetic grin - not only was I sitting on a huge cheesy bus painted with Alan Fetcher's giant face, but I also appeared to be a mental case.

As we took our seats on the bus, I turned and looked behind me only to be greeted by the beaming smiles of Sian and Emma. It was a pure coincidence but nevertheless, a very nice surprise. Over the past three months we had kept a little contact via e-mail but only seen each other on one occasion at the Grand Prix. There was loads of catching up to be done as we exchanged stories about the adventures of camp and the travels both parties had participated in recently. It turns out the girls had been given some money for their work on camp and had used it to explore the west coast of Australia for a week or two – a trip I was incredibly jealous of. They told us tales about Perth, swimming with whales and explained in detail how Emma suffers from very severe sea-sickness - a fact I would learn first-hand later on.

As with most things associated with *Neighbours,* most of the supporters and enthusiasts are British. In fact, the Australians don't really like it at all. I suppose they experience the environment in everyday life and so the show itself just fades into insignificance. Not for the British though. *Neighbours* has always had a huge following in the UK - granted the acting isn't brilliant and the story lines appear to repeat every few years, but the dream of that perfect lifestyle really seems to capture our imagination. For most people, the normal day consists of boring work, combined with grim skies and rain, so I suppose this seemingly perfect Australian suburban life provides a brief escape from reality. This, I concluded, explained why everyone on the bus was British and equally as excited as myself.

Having completed an hysterical viewing of our 'favourite Neighbours' deaths' on the bus DVD system, we rounded a corner and turned into Pin Oak Court. For most of you, this name has absolutely zero significance. However, this is the *real* name of the cul-de-sac we all know as Ramsay Street. As the afternoon sun beamed down through the trees, the street slowly came into view and my dreams were realised. You see, the street itself is not impressive, it is just like any other normal Australian suburb but the familiarity of it is the confusing thing. Every day since I was ten, I had sat and watched this little corner of the world so it felt remarkably normal, but I had never actually been there.

As we posed for a photo with a mock Ramsay Street sign, the door of one of the houses opened. We all stood in stunned silence, staring intently to see whether Harold Bishop would wander down the steps and onto the street to participate in a little power-walking. To our disappointment, the woman's face was unfamiliar and there was no power-walking to be seen. It was then that our guide explained that the houses were in fact lived in by normal residence and were not owned by the studio. Number 24 Ramsay Street is in fact number 6 Pin Oak Court. However, don't let this dishearten you, it certainly didn't me. Ramsay Street might not truly exist and it is in fact far smaller than it seems on television, but I was standing in a piece of history, and that, my friends, is something to be relished.

As the bus pulled away, we waved goodbye to Pin Oak Court and continued on toward the studio, where we were told we could purchase merchandise

'Can I borrow ten dollars?' Grant asked in a cheerful tone 'I've seen something'.

I reluctantly gave him the money wondering which piece of horrendous merchandise he would return with. Believe me, he didn't disappoint. As he skipped back down the bus, he was already showing off his brand new purchase with a huge grin on his face - the sort of happiness shown by a six year old when he finally gets the toffee apple he's been begging for. I turned to Emma and Sian and we all cracked up in hysterics - it was impossible not to. Grant was wearing a bright blue t-shirt and printed across the front was that famous saying *'Good neighbours become good friends'* followed by a massive hand giving an enthusiastic thumbs-up.

'How much was that?' I asked, unable to hold in my laughter.

'Thirty dollars' Grant replied in the most serious tone I've ever heard.

Well that set us off again - all three of us in absolute stitches until I finally collapsed off my chain onto the bus floor. Grant wasn't really seeing the funny side.

'Thirty dollars!' I finally managed to muster whilst fighting for breath, 'for a t-shirt that's going to get you bullied!'.

'Don't be stupid' Grant said with a slight smile now appearing 'I'm going to wear this on the town tonight!'.

I couldn't breathe from the laughing, but it was well worth it. I couldn't believe he'd wasted thirty dollars on yet *another* item of crappy merchandise

- I think he owned a t-shirt, baseball cap or towel from every event we'd been to over the past three months. One day I asked him 'how are you going to get all this rubbish home?' and his reply was 'don't worry, I bought an Australian Open rucksack, I'll just send it home in that'.

Fast forward four hours and a group of English teenagers slowly converged on St Kilda in a trance of *Neighbours* madness. As Grant and I wandered up the street towards *The Elephant and Wheelbarrow*, we could sense the anticipation amongst the other British travellers surrounding us. Unfortunately, this was short lived as we saw the queue outside the 'traditional English pub'. Thankfully, we had pre-purchased tickets and merely strolled past the line of frustrated fans who were being forced to wait. I felt very smug it must be said.

      Inside the pub, the room was packed and filled with an electric atmosphere. As I waited to be served, I got talking to a number of other travellers who offered advice on where to travel once I got to the east coast. In truth, it wasn't terribly useful as everyone had a completely different place to recommended and issued contradictory warnings on places to avoid. 'You've gotta visit Nimbin mate, you'll have the time of your life' one person would say 'but stay clear of Noosa, it's way too expensive, like going home to London'.

I immediately made a mental note of this, thinking it was definitely going to come in useful. Unfortunately, I had to erase this note two seconds later when a tall drunken guy (everyone at *Neighbours Night* seems to fit this description) who had been listening to our conversation, shouted in the most enthusiastic voice I have ever heard

'Noosa is awweeeesssssoooommmmeeeeee, do NOT listen to this man cos he's pissed off his face. Only go to Nimbin if you're looking to get high my friend. Otherwise, Noosa is the place to be. Oh and Airley Beach is wickeeeed too, but guess what?'.

'I don't think I'm going to guess this am I?' I said in response, wiping a few particles of his lager saliva from my cheek.

'It don't got a beach! You see why it's funny man? Its name's Airley Beach, yet it doesn't have a beach. Only in Australia my friend'.

I thanked them both for their incredibly confusing, drunken, contradictory advice. I think it was at this point I decided to make no formal plans whatsoever.

Making my way over to Grant, I found him sitting at the table we had been allocated. We hadn't been able to get a table with the girls, but he had befriended the people next to us and was already showing off his new t-shirt, explaining to them that 'yes it was genuine *Neighbours* merchandise'. Well you wouldn't want to be wearing a *fake Neighbours* t-shirt now, would you? I quickly joined in the conversation, content to listen to their travel advice but forgetting it almost instantly. The party consisted of three men and one woman in their mid-twenties from the London area. I wish I could recall their names, but unfortunately the night's entertainment began just as they were telling me and I ultimately missed it. Don't get me wrong, they were a very nice group of people, but they just couldn't compete with Ryan Maloney (a.k.a Toadfish Rebecchi) who had just appeared on stage. He was quickly followed by Alan Fletcher and Natalie Bassingthwaighte or Karl Kennedy and Isabelle Hoyland as they are more commonly known.

As they stood in front of a few hundred chanting fans, they sang songs and told jokes – it was probably one of the most surreal moments in my life – especially when Toadfish claimed to Dr Karl that the only reason he was fat was because 'every time he shagged his mum she gave him a cookie'. Believe me, hearing a pillar of modern society and preacher of morals swear was rather shocking to say the least. But with an incredibly fun atmosphere and a genuine sense of enjoyment from both the audience and the stars, I loved it.

Having finished a few sketches, the actors made their way round individually to every table and met every fan in the entire pub. It was incredible dedication and that impressed me even more. I can't exactly remember what I said, but I remember thinking up an incredibly witty comment as Ryan Maloney was approaching our table, only for it to be met by that kind of polite laugh and look which blatantly said 'that's only the 264th time I've heard that joke this evening and if I hear it one more time, I will actually crush your testicles like a bunch of grapes'. Grant shook his head in embarrassment (and it was *he* who was wearing the t-shirt) which kind of condemned me to silence.

Nevertheless, Ryan and Alan were incredibly down to earth, normal guys who shared a drink and a good laugh with us and Natalie Bassingthwaighte was beautiful - even more so than on television. I like to tell everyone that she came back for a second photo with me, but in truthful reflection it was I who was following her, like one of those annoying little dogs you really want to kick just to see how far it will go. Then, as quickly as they had appeared, the stars disappeared and the fans started filing out of the pub. Our *Neighbours* extravaganza was over and now I had another eleven hour train journey to face.

CHAPTER 16

I decided not to say goodbye to Grant and Skip, instead I said 'see you later', for it made the whole experience seem a little more positive. Now I was moving on to the next stage of this incredible adventure. During the few days I had spent in Sydney previously, it had really excited me and I was desperate to get back. Melbourne was a warm and loving city, the sort of place that made me feel at home, but Sydney had Circular Quay, Bondi and a big aquarium – what other reasons did I need to return?

Thankfully, I was not alone. For Emma too had been captured by the pull of Sydney and so we decided to meet up upon arrival and plan our route along the east coast. I liked Emma a lot it has to be said and I was pleased it was she who had decided to accompany me. Although shy at first, we were now quite good friends as her sarcastic comments and dry humour really started to flourish. In that sense, we complemented each other very well and so I saw her as the perfect travel partner. I'm not sure whether she saw me in the same way, or whether it was just lack of choice, but nevertheless here we were. At 8am that morning I boarded the train bound for Sydney, fresh in the knowledge that Emma was still in bed, would rise about two hours later, pack her stuff at a leisurely pace, catch a flight to Sydney, potter around a little in the city and grab some dinner all before my train was anywhere near arriving. Still, you'll have to offer more than an in-flight movie, a meal, luxury reclining seats and a quarter of the travel time to squeeze thirty dollars out of me.

It had been arranged that we would meet with a few of the other gappies who had also finished their placements recently. Our hostel was *'Wanderers on Kent'* in the middle of the city which was rather expensive but very clean, quiet and pleasant – although the key card lock system seemed to try its hardest to break-down every time I used it.

Having settled in to our room, we found ourselves back in *Scruffy Murphy's* almost instantly and my extra thirty dollars soon evaporated into thin air. I don't mind spending my money on beer though, it makes me happy and my mother always says happiness is the most important thing in life. Unfortunately, I didn't feel quite so happy the next morning. Why do all brilliant things have a downside? Alcohol gives you an undesirable urge to hug a toilet, all nice food has more calories in it than the average American, driving your car fast gives you speeding tickets and a hefty fuel bill, diet coke gives you cancer and running around the streets naked will land you a jail sentence in a tiny little cell with a huge, but strangely affectionate man named Winston. It makes no sense. If anyone can find me something pleasurable which has no negative side effect whatsoever, I invite you to write to me.

Anyway, being a nostalgic bunch, we sat back in the same seats we had three months previously and exchanged intriguing stories from the past few months. It seemed like only five minutes since we had left, but so many incredible and potentially life-changing events had occurred in this time. Although we had only really known each other for a few days in early January, we had formed quite a close bond during those first intimidating days and so being in their company was rather pleasant. Thankfully, for everyone's sake, I didn't venture back onto the dance floor on this occasion.

I was very eager to visit Bondi as it is so famous and we had skipped it last time. As the others had already visited the day before our arrival, Emma and I decided to catch the bus out on our own. I can't recall ever seeing it rain on *Home and Away*, but it positively pissed it down on this particular day. Ultimately, this destroyed my spirits and I subsequently wasn't too impressed with it at all. If I were at home, the thought of venturing to the beach on a day like that would seem absurd. However, I was at Bondi and you can't go without sitting on the beach. I must say, it seemed strange sunbathing in the rain, not that this should come as a major surprise. On a positive note, the beach was huge, clean and unsurprisingly deserted – obviously everyone else had far more sense than me. On a hot, summer day I could imagine how great this place would be, but I just didn't feel any magic on this particular occasion. There were tacky gift shops selling postcards and fast food restaurants all along the sea front. For me, it just didn't seem to capture the Australian essence. In comparison to Manly, it was poor and had no chance of stealing my heart. I don't base this assessment all on exterior beauty of course, but I just didn't feel that healthy vibe and love of life I got in Manly. Maybe I'm being too harsh – I suppose I was just annoyed that the English weather had followed me to one of the most famous sunspots in the world.

In order to save a few pennies we decided to move to a cheaper hostel near the station. To save even more money we decided to walk it. Unfortunately for Emma, she has child size legs and compared to my Peter Crouch style anatomy, they just couldn't keep up. This was to become a theme for the trip with my freakishly quick pace leaving Emma behind as she struggled to pull her packed suitcase through the busy streets. She wasn't best pleased to say the least. We eventually arrived, pink faced and happy at our new hostel called *'Footprints'*, fresh to the news that a man had been shot dead right outside our new abode on the previous night. For a moment we began to think that this was not the place for us, but then we noticed they gave away free fruit at reception and our mood soon changed. It was clean enough and the dorm rooms were very spacious – we stayed in the largest which was named 'The Church' because of its stain glass window. Unfortunately it had a large hole in it and I couldn't help wonder whether this had been caused by a gunshot. Realising how cheap the price was though, I decided it would be sensible to put this thought to the back of my mind.

The next few days were spent exploring the sights that Sydney had to offer. I was keen to visit the aquarium again, but it soon became apparent that nothing much had changed, plus The Waratahs were playing and I was desperate to see a genuine brutal Australian rugby game. Tickets were cheap at only ten dollars from a tout outside the stadium who informed us that this was quite a big match. Sitting behind one of the posts, we had a great view and came close to many of The World Cup stars such as Loti Tuqiri. We even saw a huge punch-up as the Highlanders came from behind to beat the home side. So much controversy and excitement and even the sun decided to pop out. I was slightly confused as to why the locals were referring to it as 'footy' – I had become accustomed to this being used as a reference to Aussie Rules, but then who was I to argue? If they wanted to call this game in which you primarily use your hands 'footy', then they were welcome to.

I respected Emma, I really did, but up until this day I had never understood hers, or in fact anyone's, enjoyment of The Ballet. This is why her suggestion that we could go and watch Swan Lake that evening at The Opera House wasn't exactly met with beaming enthusiasm.
'Trust me, you'll enjoy it' she said with a big grin across her face.
'Well, I am a cultured modern man' I replied whilst being dragged down toward Circular Quay.
    It was then that the implications and possibilities of this outing actually revealed themselves to me. You see, I still wasn't that excited about the prospect of the ballet, but instead realised that, if I did go, I would enter a unique and very desirable club. I would be included in a handful of people who can look at one of the billions of photos of Sydney Opera House and say 'I watched the ballet there once, it was delightful!'. Consequently, I soon perked up and with a new injection of energy, strolled down to the harbour.
    We met a number of our other friends in the foyer and approached the ticket office merrily. It was then that we were informed that Swan Lake was sold out, not just for tonight, but completely sold out – every show, every day for the next forty-five years. We were gutted. However, we were then presented with a life-line as the attendant informed us that a number of standing tickets would be available once all the aristocracy had taken their seats. It sounded ominous to me – I think the door staff were just making a sneaky bit of money on the side. But regardless of the arrangement, I was happy. Please don't judge me - yes, I had departed with twenty dollars to see a show I wasn't the least bit interested in, but I was in Sydney Opera House watching Swan Lake – how many of *you* can say that? Seriously, the only

reason I really went was that it provided me with some top quality gloating material.

After three hours of standing, my legs and back ached like mad and to be honest, the last thirty minutes couldn't have gone fast enough. However, I was surprisingly impressed by the show which was performed with admirable perfection. For me though, it was purely the setting that made the evening as good as it was.

The following day Emma decided she would climb The Harbour Bridge, not by herself you understand, but with the assistance of some professionals and some interesting grey tracksuits. They run the bridge climbs every day and it's not until you peer up and see the little ant-like creatures crawling across it, that you get a real perspective of how huge that piece of iron is. I would have loved to have done it myself, but since I didn't have $150 spare and grey really isn't my colour, I decided to take a walk and leave Emma to do all the climbing. Instead, I took a wonderfully relaxing walk through the pristine gardens of Hyde Park and subsequently got lost for a number of hours. It was a beautiful setting though, so I didn't really mind.

Coming face-to-face with yet another huge spider with lethal looking yellow markings, I finally decided that enough was enough and made my way to an information booth for a map. Navigating my way through this tropical oasis, I emerged back onto the busy city streets and walked to The Travellers Contact Point on George Street. Remembering how helpful they had been during my previous time in Sydney, I consulted some of the staff who offered me an incredible deal which involved a flight to Cairns and a *Greyhound* bus pass all the way down the coast. It sounded like an incredible journey and at only $450 it seemed like a bargain - besides I fancied a bit of sun. So I booked Emma and myself on a flight the very next day and cheerfully made my way back to the hostel.

Now the next part of my story was one that surprised me, but I'm not really sure why. You see, when I was about fifteen I remember my sister and her boyfriend wanting to get away from England and have a bit of a holiday. They decided upon Kenya – a beautiful country, far from England and certainly out of the thoughts of most people in our little corner of Northamptonshire. Upon arrival, they walked through the doors of their hotel and guess whom they saw? That's right - our next door neighbours. Now, I don't know about you, but I hear stories like this *all* the time and for some reason I am still shocked and normally say 'Gosh! It's a small world isn't it?'. We hear so many of these stories, so why are we still surprised when we are told them? The surprise should be when someone comes back from holiday and *doesn't* tell you a story such as this. For that reason, I wasn't going to include this little tale, but since everyone else seems be telling them, I thought I might as well have a little go.

Anyway, to the story - at school we had a very close-knit group of friends who were always there for each other. However, at the tender age of thirteen, one of the group was taken from us – Stephen. His Mum sent him to a school that put more emphasis on religion and so we generally lost touch. Therefore, imagine my shock when I received a phone call on my Australian mobile only to hear his voice on the other end.
'Hello buddy, long time no see, I hear you're in Australia' he said with a distinct Aussie twang.
'Stephen! Well I never. Yes I am as it happens, so this phone bill must be costing you a fortune!'.
'No you flamin' galah (I'm not sure if these were his exact words), I'm in OZ too. I've just finished doing the east coast and now I'm chilling in Sydney. Just wondering if you're going to be around these parts anytime soon?'.
'Mate, I'm in Sydney right now, as we speak – I'm in the Footprints hostel, where are you?'.
'You're in Footprints? What room?'.
'Um, I think it's called the church – why?'.
'Open your door…'.
And when I eventually opened my door what did I see? That's right - a galah boxing a wombat. No only joking, it was, as you had probably guessed, my good friend Stephen.

I can't explain to you how good it was, after all this time away, to finally see a familiar face – one that I recognised and associated with home. 'Gosh! It's a small world' I thought.

That was one of my favourite nights in Australia, just because it made me feel at home again, if only for an evening. Emma joined us as we sampled some of the bars serving genuine German lager in big jugs, delivered to your table by waitresses with long blonde plats, wearing stylish dungarees. It was a really good night. At the end, we walked back to the hostel as he offered advice on the best peep shows to visit along the east coast and then we said our goodbyes. Looks like the teachings at the Christian school had really paid off.

Waking early the next morning, I took advantage of the free breakfast for the first time, stocked my bag with more free fruit than Grant had tacky t-shirts, threw Emma over my shoulder and ran all the way to the airport (at least, that's how I remember it) for we had a plane to catch. All aboard for Cairns.

CHAPTER 17

I

Our flight was with the budget airline *Virgin Blue* and so I was anticipating less leg room than when I sat behind my 6'5" friend in his *Mini*, however to my pleasant surprise the plane was actually quite comfortable. Add to this surprising luxury the fact that there were only ten other passengers and I felt like I could lounge around in my underwear and put my feet on the furniture if I had wanted to. Instead though, I made myself a make-shift bed for the three hour north bound flight to the tropics. The whole idea of flying for three hours and being in the *same* country when you land is an experience not many Europeans can understand, which made this event even more exciting. But believe me, on this May evening, Cairns and Sydney seemed a million countries apart.

The flight landed just after 10pm, yet the stifling humidity was unbelievable, especially in comparison to the relatively chilly weather we had left behind. As we walked across the runway to the terminal, I could immediately feel the sweat beads dripping down my back. I didn't really mind, in fact I liked to describe it as 'positively sweating' – a kind of self induced perspiration incurred when you've finally arrived at dream holiday destination. I'm not saying that I was enjoying the sweating, only that it served to illustrate the fact that I had arrived in an extremely hot destination and for that, I was grateful.

Thankfully, we had booked our room a few days previously, and just as promised an old rickety mini-bus was waiting for our custom. It drove us through the deserted suburbs of this famous town and along the promenade which was lined with the little cafés and restaurants you find scattered through the Mediterranean, bustling with life even at this time of night.

I was anxious to get some sleep and so I was relieved when we arrived at our hostel, *'Caravella 149'*. We were greeted at the front desk by, what I can only assume was the proprietor (I have no evidence for this claim) - a sweet but absurdly eccentric lady named Gloria. The Queensland folk are famed for their bluntness of speech and unconventional ways, so I was rather looking forward to this conversation. She presented herself in front of us in a long, baggy dress – perhaps to keep her cool on this incredibly humid evening, or maybe just to add to her crazy persona – and checked us in. Using the computer was her sidekick – a strange man who continually cracked those awful jokes everyone thinks of, but nobody wants to embarrass themselves enough to say. She presented us with our keys, but before we could escape, relax and get some sleep after our incredibly long flight she proceeded to explain 'how things worked' at *Caravella 149*. It was said, in no uncertain terms, that our co-operation would be wonderfully appreciated, otherwise we would find ourselves out on the streets eating from a dustbin (or something along those lines). Don't get me wrong, she was incredibly friendly, but you just couldn't tell if she was emphasising a point for your benefit or merely finding an excuse to destroy any self-confidence you had. Nevertheless I was grateful to know how the washing machines, driers, cookers, microwaves, fridges, freezers, showers, taps, hair dryers, windows and door knobs all operated. She also explained how to use the combination lock on the gate and informed us that, if the numbers weren't punched in correctly and in a certain time period then a fog horn would explode with life, a raw steak would be strapped to our groins and the pet crocodile released in our vicinity. It was a wonderfully friendly place.

The room was clean, fresh and didn't smell like hippies, so I was relatively happy with it. However, the air-conditioning was on the blink and even after a bashing from my shoe, refused to become operational. In keeping with the traditional Australian hostel, the top bunks didn't have any type of safety railing to prevent an unfortunate late night toss being closely followed by a long fall and severe concussion. I therefore did the gentlemanly thing by tripping Emma up and grabbing the bottom bunk before she had the chance.

As she complained, we decided to take a stroll around the town while I explained how the 'survival of the fittest' worked. Initially, as we set out on our walk, the town appeared to offer very little in way of entertainment which was worrying since we had scheduled a huge chunk of our time to this place. However, as we continued to walk it became clear that our hostel was quite far away from the action. The promenade, lined with cafés and bars, was an epicentre of activity with many people eating late whilst enjoying lots of musical entertainment. We entered a couple of tacky gift shops all selling masses of *'Finding Nemo'* merchandise but then decided our purchasing judgement may be affected by the lack of sleep and so made the long journey back to the hostel with our wallets still intact.

The next day, we met the rest of our roomies. They had arrived late that night and woken us up by turning the light on and off continuously, thus creating a strobe-light effect. I have no idea why they did this, but in order to show my annoyance, my singing in the shower the next morning wasn't what you would call quiet or in-tune. To my dismay, one of them was actually a rather pleasant German girl – I would at this point inform you of her name, however having asked her to repeat herself three times and still not understanding, I just gave up. Instead Emma and I referred to her as 'Friend 1'.

We talked for a while about the places we had visited, where we were going and the things we both missed from home. I found it incredibly easy talking to her as she shared my sentiments exactly
'I can feel my mind being broadened, but still, I can't wait to get home and stop living out of a suitcase' she said, and even laughed at my jokes which was a pleasant surprise as it doesn't happen with genuine sincerity very often. Leaving her to unpack, we went off to explore the town with the added advantage of daylight. Having heard a lot about Cairns, I must say I was shocked at the size of the town. I was expecting it to be full of large skyscrapers, long shopping parades and numerous lush parks. However, it was similar in size to a small country town. In addition, I was always under the impression that one of the appeals of living in a seaside residence was

the opportunity to use a beach of some description. I therefore went into a nearby shop and enquired as to where this huge stretch of sand might be found.

'Excuse me, where's the beach?' I enquired with a certain sense of normality.

'The what?' was the confused response from the middle-aged woman behind the desk.

'The beach – you know, an area of sand bordered on one edge by the sea and usually populated by fat, tattooed Englishmen?'.

'Ah there's no beach round here, can't use it anyway most year round because of the stingers you see' replied the lady sympathetically.

Well there you have it. I know, I was just as shocked as you – a beach resort, located in the tropics in one of the most beautiful and spectacular spots in the whole world, and it doesn't have a beach. Still, I was kind of grateful since I had done my research and didn't really fancy a run-in with a jellyfish. In addition, the town incorporated a beautiful artificial lagoon at its centre which was more than an adequate substitute, providing crystal clear, unsalted water to bathe in. Located along the seafront, it was basically a large, outdoor swimming pool and attracted the attention of many types of people. Surrounding it on all sides were beautiful turf areas with numerous benches and free public barbeques. The architecture and design of the town was built in much the same way as all the others, but since Australia is just a baby in terms of age, this was expected as it has had very little time to evolve.

But I wasn't in Cairns to study the buildings, I was here to get back to my caveman routes and find that inner survival instinct. I was here to (hopefully) wrestle a crocodile. However, please be aware that whenever the word 'wrestle' is used, you should replace it with 'watched from a large distance'.

  Many places in towns offered crocodile extravaganza tours, but we settled on one in particular because it incorporated a trip along the Daintree River, a 'local fruit' lunch (which intrigued me) and began in the very early hours thus annoying our new roommates. It cost the best part of $120 but did seem to offer a lot for the money, so I was pleasantly chuffed with our decision.

Unfortunately, on our return to the hostel, Gloria seized me as I walked past reception like a lion on its prey. There was no escape, believe me, I tried, I tried god damn it! But she had me in her grasp as the spotlight was shone into my eyes and I was bullied (yes bullied!) into revealing the details of my day. It was all going smoothly until I mentioned we'd booked a tour, then her jaw dropped to the floor (not literally, that would be hideous).

Apparently, amongst the previous evening's numerous warnings and instructions, she had informed me that if we wanted to book a tour we should do it through her. Personally, I thought this was purely because she wanted the commission, but evidentially it seems that hostels pass their commission onto their customers thus saving you buckets full of cash.

'I want you to ring them right now John and cancel your booking, then we can re-book it right here' she said impatiently, although it was making me laugh.

'Well Gloria, I would but I don't have my phone, I'll just go to my room and do it' I replied with a slight chuckle in my voice. Believe me, it was hilarious seeing her get so worked up over something so trivial.

'Okay, well you make sure you're back here in ten minutes. I'm watching you'.

Well, the cheek of her – trying to save *me* money, honestly! Seriously though, I never did go back – not because I didn't want the money, but because I was willing to *pay* twelve dollars not to see her again that evening. It was a mistake though, because for the rest of our stay I had to do an *Indiana Jones* style roll just to get out of the hostel undetected.

The following morning we arose too late for a shower and went straight out onto the street to wait for the tour bus. It pulled up right on time and we jumped up the steps in anticipation. The youngest other person on the bus was about 85 years old. Emma and I looked at each other and immediately burst into laughter. It was slightly strange to be surrounded by so many oxygen-thieves and I'd be lying if I said I wasn't embarrassed, but they all seemed quite jolly and willing to share war-stories, so we didn't let it get us down.

We continued through the northern suburbs of this small town, collecting a few other younger crocodile hunters along the way, until we finally made it onto the winding road towards the Daintree River. The tour guide was a friendly fellow, but reminded me far too much of one of my science teacher at school and even cracked the same bad jokes, so I found it difficult to relax. Instead, I found myself constantly checking to make sure my shirt was tucked in.

However, I was soon distracted by the stunning view along the coastal road. It hogged a small piece of land tucked closely between a steep cliff face and the incredible sight of the bright blue pacific. I had never been anywhere tropical in my life, but for the first time I felt like I was truly experiencing those magical views seen in so many glorious holiday brochures. The sun was out, the sand was golden, the sea was inviting and we were on our way to wrestle some crocs – it truly was perfect.

Then I looked over at Emma and by her expression, I could tell she wasn't finding the situation quite as mesmeric. Instead, she was staring straight forward looking like she was going to puke all over the granny in front. I enquired if she was okay.
'I'm going to be sick, get him to stop the bus' she suddenly blurted out.
Well, that was all I needed - it appeared Emma's sea-sickness had caught up with her along this winding road, each bump being emphasised by the rickety suspension-free bus. I ran to the front to chat with my science teacher and explained the situation. Unfortunately, he also explained back to me that there was no possible way he could stop because if he did, there was a 99.9% chance that another vehicle would come round the corner and crash into us. I told Emma the bad news and then quickly retreated to find a seat as far away from her as possible. Thankfully though, her outrageous ability to fall asleep anywhere at any time had taken over and soon enough she was out like a light.

To keep myself occupied I just peered out of the window and took in some more of the view. My mind kept leaping back to a story I had read in *'Bill Bryson Down Under'* a few months before departure. It was rather long but I shall cut it down slightly - a couple of people were walking along the promenade somewhere in northern Queensland, minding their own business and generally having fun. Then, out of nowhere, a huge crocodile leapt from the sea, grabs them both and gently slides back into the water, never to be seen again. As I peered down at the wheels of the bus, I noticed it was rather close to the sea and doubted whether it would withstand such an attack. God, what had we let ourselves in for?

Upon arrival, we were quickly ushered into a small building where biscuits and tea were provided in a typically English way. As I munched away on a Bourbon, my gaze was stolen by the cabinet located directly next to me. It was stuffed full of huge (but dead) bugs and moths found within the local area. They were all huge – unbelievably huge - and it scared me slightly. If I wasn't aware of it already, I now knew that this was a place full of extreme wildlife.

Soon the boat was ready and we were led to the docking area located at the end of a long wooden walkway that took us through a dense area of rainforest. Marching through the undergrowth along the shoreline of the crocodile infested water was slightly unnerving I must admit. If I saw a log or stick, I would simply stop in my tracks and study it for a pair of sinister eyes and razor sharp teeth. Trying to calm down, I lightened the mood by pretending to push Emma into the overgrown trees, but I'm not sure if she found it quite as funny as I did. We both stopped laughing when we saw the boat. It was small, old and rather rickety. Basically, it didn't portray any confidence whatsoever considering it was a crocodile free-for -all directly beneath us. Our guide wasn't exactly a stature of strength either, in fact he looked just like a walking skeleton. I never caught his name but he was a tall man and incredibly thin, with tight skin that seemed to grip to his bones. With long grey hair platted to his face, I didn't really have much confidence in him and doubted very much whether he'd be capable of wrestling a crocodile. Amazingly the boat started first time and our guide, who was American, began giving us a run-down of the area.

Although visually he wasn't what we were expecting, his skills as a guide and knowledge of the area were first class. The river and the surrounding rainforest were incredibly diverse and a world away from everything I had experienced so far. Even the smells in the air were incredible. However, it soon started to rain. But in the tropics it doesn't rain normal water, it sends down boiling water, which raises the relative humidity and causes your clothes to stick to your body like a leech. When I took a breath, I could feel the steamy air entering my lungs. It was unreal.
'Hope your sea-sickness isn't hitting again' I said to Emma with a smile.
'Shut it Johnny! Just look over there at all those ants, it's amazing' she replied laughing.

As we drew alongside a branch, we thought the branch was moving like an advertising board, but as we looked in detail, it was just thousands of huge ants moving in unison.

Skeleton man continued to talk us through the various vegetation we were witnessing and took us to a few areas predominantly dominated by salt-water crocodiles. His voice was actually quite relaxing and we all began to chill out, forgetting the immediate dangers that were possibly surrounding us. Emma and I decided to move to the front of the boat and take a few photos capturing the diverse atmosphere surrounding us.

'Get one of me hanging out of the boat' I shouted in an unexplainable act of madness 'I'll pretend I've been eaten'.

As I began to hang my arm over the side, in the corner of my eye I caught a large log floating towards the boat. I immediately thought nothing of it. But then it occurred to me that the log was floating *up* stream! By the time I'd realised and looked up, two murderous eyes were staring at me only two metres away. Retracting my arm like a man who'd just received an electric shock, my terrified momentum took me flailing backwards and almost over the opposite side of the boat. Clinging for dear life, I grabbed the railings and sank to the ground in shock.

'CROC! CROC!' came the screams from the people next to me.

'Cheers guys' I thought, 'you could have warned me earlier, it nearly took my bloody arm off'.

Emma was laughing as I cowered in the corner 'Nearly didn't have to fake the photo, hey?'.

It was a funny experience but one that really did go to emphasise the incredible hunting ability of these creatures. Even though I'd read all about them and was searching for one, I had nearly been taken in by it. That's why they are one of the most successful predators on the planet and have been for millions of years. Staring down at its four metre long body, I was suddenly in awe of the animal for it truly was an awesome killing machine and to see one in the flesh was outstanding. It swam alongside the boat for a moment or two, allowing us to examine the solid markings along its armoured skin which seemed impenetrably strong. And then it disappeared into the darkness of the Daintree. It was a brief encounter but one that stuck with me for a long time - to actually witness a crocodile in its own environment was an incredible adrenaline rush, but it also made the creatures real. Before, they were merely animals I had read about in books and that occasionally featured in documentaries. Miles away from my world, I had almost viewed them as somewhat fictional. Not now though, not now.

Having had our adrenalin rush for the day, the organisers thought better than to over-excite our elderly companions and so soon shuffled us onto the bus for a spot of lunch. I can't say I was particularly disappointed as I had been running very low on finances and food had become somewhat of an unaffordable luxury recently.

The restaurant was unique as it opened into the rainforest and with the rain gently falling, it provided an especially tranquil setting. We were treated to barramundi, accompanied by many tropical fruits and six chips. That's right, six. I wasn't complaining though, as we were being cultured and chips didn't really fit into that plan anyway.

The restaurant owner soon joined us and chatted in intimate detail about each fruit, taking all his examples from my plate and holding them up for everyone to see. He was incredibly eccentric, but also very knowledgeable. Added to the fact that he was holding my dinner, I had no choice but to listen to every word he said. In fact, it seemed that whenever I was about to shove anything in my mouth, he would grab it from my fork and explain what it was to the audience. It was fantastic though, I had only been in Queensland for two days but the crazy, eccentric Aussies you come to read about had already materialised in volumes. I just hoped he'd washed his hands.

With my stomach satisfied for the first time in several weeks, Emma and I jumped on the bus with high spirits. Since beginning our travels back in Sydney, we had generally been sharing the costs of meals. I had been feeling really guilty that my poor finances had been bringing down the standard of our diet, so I was pleased even more that we had been fed substantially.

The bus took us through Port Douglas which was nice. It was perfectly kept and had very splendid views from a cliff which looked right across a sandy beach. With very little time to take it all in, we were soon ushered back onto the bus and set sail for Moffman Gorge.

For every one of the twenty minutes we were allotted to explore the gorge, I loved it. We trekked for a while through the rainforest, enjoying the crystal clear water and wonderful rope swing bridges. The views were amazing and the thought of a crocodile free environment was quite pleasing too. Our cameras flashed away as I attempted to get as many photos as possible of this picturesque scene. At one point, our guide Richard said to me 'look over there between the sugar cane and mango tree' - it was brilliant. For this reason, I was fascinated by Moffman Gorge and was subsequently very disappointed when our tiny slot for exploration had expired. Apparently floating about on a crocodile infested river just isn't enough excitement for one day and so we soon found ourselves on the move towards *Hartley's Animal Sanctuary*.

We had been promised a crocodile feeding show, however as the bus turned a corner along the coastal road we came to a sudden halt. There was a line of cars in front of us and evidently a number of red-faced, angry drivers. After a few minutes of stationary confusion, people began emerging from their vehicles. Emma and I asked one bloke what the hell was going on:
'Apparently they carried out a controlled landslide across the road' he said, as if it was the most normal thing in the world.
'But it's 3pm in the afternoon and there are no traffic lights or roadwork signs' I replied in astonishment.
'Yeah, they always seem to pick inconvenient times'.
I turned to Emma and we both burst into laughter. This was fantastic - not only had they decided to carry out a landslide directly across the middle of a main road, they had also done it during rush hour and told precisely zero people about it. This was Queensland. We waited. And waited some more. Eventually the amusement of the situation began to wear off and annoyance just set in to take its place. Thankfully, they finally waved the bus through as we meandered around the debris and came out clean on the other side.

As the bus pulled into the car park we could hear the cheer as the crocodile feeding frenzy began. I shuffled us along at a quick pace (I was quite looking forward to the show but it was mostly to annoy Emma) through the park to the small arena. As we arrived, a man resembling Steve Irwin was in the process of tempting a large salt water crocodile into the small stadium to perform for the numerous tourists. You see, this particular place was not a zoo so to speak - it was a sanctuary for many varieties of animal.

I'm not entirely sure what his name was but I'll just call him Steve for the purposes of this particular anecdote. So Steve, using a large slab of meat, managed to entice the croc from its natural looking enclosure and into the amphitheatre. From there, he told a few close-encounter stories, and, by attaching his large steak to a long piece of rope, managed to get the formidable creature to perform the infamous 'deathroll'. The power it managed to generate from its huge muscular body just went to heighten my concern about ever meeting one along the promenade. It truly was an incredible sight. I also noticed how closely Steve watched the creature as he spoke to the crowd, never blinking for a second and only too aware of terrible pain it could inflict.

The remainder of the day was spent walking through the pleasant gardens of the park. Excitement grew as the cassowary enclosure approached and I got my first sight of these razor sharp killing machines. Alas, I was not disappointed, although I was careful not to get too close. Having read the story concerning them previously, I was well aware of what they were capable of although I was slightly intrigued as to how such a super, multi-coloured chicken had evolved in such a unique way.

Later in the afternoon, we came across the crocodile enclosures. I was slightly concerned with how low many of the fences were and the fact that I could dangle my hands over them was a little irresponsible from the park's point of view. Before departure however, we got the perfect opportunity to see the crocodiles feeding in their natural environment. Like before, a tiny, timid, leaking boat led us into the middle of the lake as numerous yellow eyes began appearing from the murky water around. The driver then pulled out the 'rump-steak-on-a-rope' apparatus yet again and shook it violently in the pond below. The deadly eyes drifted closer to our breaking life-raft. Suddenly, there was a moment of pure silence. BOOM! From the water, only half a metre from my arm, a five metre long crocodile suddenly launched itself vertically from the water, three or four metres into the air. The driver pulled the meat away just in time as the croc landed in the water with a thunderous smash. This continued for about five minutes, as the frustrated crocodiles flew out of the water at lightening speed into the air, chasing the meat prize but subsequently missing. I couldn't help but feel it was a mistake frustrating them like this. We were surrounded by some very angry crocodiles with supreme athletic abilities. It was a worry and a very surreal situation. I was imagining the condolence letter written to my mother; *Dear Mrs Watters, I'm sorry to inform you that your son has had his head bitten off by our circus crocodile. Unfortunately it was a case of mistaken identity. Apparently, his face has an uncanny resemblance to a slab of meat originating from a cow's back-side. Please find two complimentary tickets enclosed as a gesture of goodwill. Yours Sincerely, The Driver.*

II

The following day Emma went off adventuring without me. Not that I didn't want to go with her, I was merely struggling for money and thought that a day on the beach begging might be slightly more productive. Still, I can't say I wasn't jealous as she embarked on a day full of white-water rafting, although I was looking forward to being on my own, if just for a couple of hours.

It was a relatively cloudy day, so I gathered my thoughts and toured the shops of the town. Although much smaller than I had imagined, I decided there and then that I liked it. Although similar to other Australian towns in that it didn't exactly encapsulate its own unique identity, Cairns was pleasant to look at and the people were amusingly helpful. I purchased a beautiful panoramic postcard picturing 'Palm Cove' – a heavenly beach we had briefly visited the previous day and sat by the lagoon to write about my adventures for my family. It had now been over a hundred days since I'd last seen them.

As lunchtime then approached, the sun made its first appearance in the tropics, so I stripped off down to my boardies and began the long and tedious task of catching some rays. Three hours later I woke up. Having not had an accomplice, I had subsequently not sun creamed my back. This, I was to learn (again), is somewhat of a huge miscalculation - one which I would be regretting for a week or so. As I staggered back to the hotel, Emma greeted me in fits of laughter as I explained how I had had a 'minor disagreement' with the sun. In my defence, I had been under the impression that English skin was so white it actually reflected the sun's rays, but apparently this is not entirely accurate.

'Yeah, keep laughing' I said to Emma as she fell over in hysterics 'next time you fall asleep in the sun, I'm going to write something pretty offensive across your back in sun cream, you mark my words'.

'I'm just imagining your screams next time you try and put a t-shirt on!' she said, unable to breathe.

She was right, it was torture. And she didn't help one bit because she was laughing so much. Nevertheless, she gave me a well done pat on the back.

That night we went for our free meal (offered as part of the room fee) at The Woolshed bar and restaurant, before wandering around the streets at night looking for an entertaining venue to waste some money in. The Woolshed was quite a Mecca for travellers, but I was pretty tired of the place and wanted to find something slightly more diverse. Thankfully, we found the casino. I wasn't sure if we were going to be let in, especially wearing Thai fisherman trousers, a scruffy t-shirt and with skin so red I looked like I'd just received five hundred Chinese burns. But apparently our money is just as good as anyone else's, so we found ourselves amongst the thousands of punters wasting their hard earned cash away on slot machines and black jack tables. We sat and watched one of these particular games for a number of minutes, finding it hilarious to see the amounts of money one man was losing. Then, from nowhere, he suddenly won a massive wad of cash. Quite predictably though, just as quickly as he'd won it, he put it straight back on again and lost. Emma suggested that this possibly signified 'life' but I thought it was more like 'stupidity'. Even so, that conversation was far too deep so as we walked I subtly pushed her into a lamp post and ran away.

We left Cairns the following morning, however not before one last encounter with Gloria. As we were departing, I thought I'd escaped her for good but suddenly she grabbed me with the door only inches away.

'So John, where are you off to now?' she demanded.

'Well, we're off to Mission Beach now Gloria, thanks for the hospitality' I replied in a petrified voice.

'Have you been diving on The Barrier Reef yet?' was the enquiry.

'Not yet, we're going to go from Mission Beach' I replied.

'You're *what*?! Are you crazy?' she said startled, as if I'd just announced my desire to fart in her face 'you can't possibly go from Mission Beach, the weather down there is awful and the boat ride takes at least three hours. You better stay another couple of nights and go from here tomorrow. Come on, I'll book you in now. Right I've had a cancellation on this trip, I can fit you in here, it's a little more expensive but that doesn't matter now does it?'.

'Umm, well, you see…' I was searching for an excuse and looked toward Emma for inspiration. She looked at the floor. 'We're booked on this bus today and we can't un-book ourselves'. It was lame, but it was the best excuse I could come up with under such intense pressure.

'Well okay, you'll just have to come back in the next few days then. Shall I book you on anyway?' Gloria replied reluctantly.

'No, don't you worry Gloria, we'll be back in the next few days and we'll sort it out there and then' I said whilst picking up my bags and sprinting for the door. We had escaped finally and definitely had no intention of ever going back. In actual fact, we ended up missing our bus because of that little delay, but I was in good spirits as I had evaded the wrath of Gloria.

CHAPTER 18

I

Mission Beach was a relatively short drive from Cairns, but we were promised a party atmosphere full of adventure. Unfortunately, upon arrival the tropical rain had set in and everything appeared to have a gloomy look surrounding it. I was expecting a dense township with a vibrant centre – instead, it appeared to consist of a number of small hamlets linked together by a long beach. With such urban spatial segregation, I wasn't immediately impressed with Mission Beach and instead got the impression that we were in the middle of nowhere. Nevertheless, I'd heard good reviews and so was determined to experience it first-hand.

As we departed the bus, there were a number of people from all the hostels attempting to get us to go with them. Emma and I had already decided to stay at *'Scotty's Beach House'* as it had been recommended in *Lonely Planet* and, more importantly, they were offering free alcoholic beverages. Well, it's important to have your priorities sorted.

As the mini-bus drove along the front promenade, I looked out to sea and although the rain still fell, couldn't help but feel I had landed in a scene from *'The Beach'*. With many tropical islands covered in luscious green vegetation, located just off the coast and surrounded by clean, white beaches, it seemed just like Thailand. My opinion was beginning to swing.

Scotty's Beach House hostel was nice and reasonably priced at only $18 a night for a twin room. The buildings were set out like a courtyard with a tropical central pool as the centrepiece. Their verandas, hammocks and numerous cushions gave it a very relaxed vibe. However, there was an incredibly interesting piece of architecture to note concerning the rooms. It appeared they had employed some very stupid builders, or run over budget half way through the work, for the walls didn't go all the way to the ceiling. Unbelievably, it was a huge building with a high roof but the walls only went two metres into the air. As a consequence, we could hear everything going on in each room and believe me, some of the noises we heard on that first night were not desirable at all.

The staff were young and incredibly helpful. Thankfully they assured us, as we expected, that Gloria was merely exaggerating the situation and there were in fact a number of boats running short diving excursions out to The Reef. So we booked up immediately. In addition, we also had the most incredible desire to jump out of a moving aircraft at 10,000ft and ultimately both booked in to do a skydive the following day. I'm not sure what was going through my head, but it seemed like a good idea at the time and *Scotty's* offered us an additional night free for the privilege.

That night we headed down to the attaching restaurant and bar, claiming our free drinks and enjoying a couple of games of pool. We chatted for a while with two Irish girls, Rosaria and Katrina, who were staying in the room opposite. As the wine began to flow, they told us comedy stories concerning their travels so far, remarking on all the strange and pointless jobs they had done - none of which I can remember, but I did underline the fact that it was funny in my journal so I thought I'd share it. With their unique Irish enthusiasm, they managed to convince me that it'd be a good idea to enter a pool competition in which a possible $100 could be won. For some reason I agreed and paid the $2 entrance fee. As it happens, I might as well have spent that $2 on another small beer for somewhere amongst the glasses of wine I had somehow completely forgotten how poor my pool skills really were. Oh well, I suppose the competing is the thing that counts. Unfortunately, I didn't even do that. It was a seven ball white wash. Oh well, I had a skydive to prepare for.

We were picked up incredibly early by the *'Jump the Beach'* skydiving bus and shuttled off towards the headquarters. While there, we were forced to sign some forms saying that if anything went wrong, we accepted all responsibility and therefore there was no point in our families seeking any legal advice or attempting to sue for damages.

'So, you've decided to be a little crazy today hey?' one of the admin girls said as I signed away my life.

'You consider jumping out of a plane at 10,000ft above shark-infested waters crazy do you?' I replied.

She smiled - the sort of sympathetic smile I imagine a doctor gives a dying patient just before the words 'don't worry, you've got a good two hours left in you'.

I was then introduced to my 'Tandem Skydive Master' named Col, which I assumed was short for Colin, but who knows. He was a lot older than I was expecting, which was a little disconcerting since he was going to hold my fate in his hand and I didn't fancy a little heart-attack coming between me and a safe, soft landing. He looked very much like John Voight, the Hollywood actor and I was going to mention it, but then, he *was* in control of my life so thought it best not piss him off.

We were given a 1980s tracksuit to put on - I'm not sure if there was a scientific reason for them or whether they just wanted to make us look stupid, but apparently they didn't have any small enough for Emma or large enough for myself. So as Emma trudged along like the Michelin Man, I followed behind impersonating a Victorian school child in short trousers.

As we walked across the runway, a tiny, rickety plane, obviously carrying the burden of age, swooped low across our heads and completed a rather bumpy landing. It had no door which seemed logical since we were going to jump out, however I didn't feel my parachute would help much if I fell out during take-off and was annoyed slightly that I had been chosen to take the seat next to the gaping hole of doom. I say seat – there weren't actually any seats, instead, we squeezed together between each others legs which sounds romantic, but in reality, it only added to the feeling of despair. Perhaps it would have been different if the groin I was sliding into wasn't that of an old man I had only recently met and totally entrusted with my life. But this *was* the east coast of Australia, where excitement and adrenalin were the aim of the game.

With a surge of power, the plane began accelerating along the runway and slowly started building up speed. I looked at Emma whose completely white face suggested she was either being starved of oxygen or was just as scared as I was. To add to our worries, the plane still didn't seem to be off the ground and I suspected – due to the tiny scale of the runway and the fact we had been blazing down it for approximately twenty minutes – it never would. Just as I was about to take a leap of faith from the inviting doorway, there was a brief sense of weightlessness as the wheels left the ground and we gradually ventured into the sky.

As our altitude increased, my nerves seemed to calm and I just took in the magnificent vista below. Far more relaxed than I had been on the ground, I genuinely loved every minute of the flight, even if Colin was scissoring me with his legs. The views across the ocean and Mission Beach were outstanding and grew in beauty as we went higher, revealing even more of the stunning landscape. The golden beach ran for miles, separating the line of green lush palm tress from the endlessly blue ocean. It also revealed many more exotic islands not far from the coast and alive with vegetation that appeared luscious and foreign, even in this diverse landscape.

But just as I was relaxing, peering from the window and admiring the sights like a seventy year old tourist on a coach-tour, they announced it was time for my jump. That's when it hit me. I was about *jump* out of an aeroplane at 10,000ft! I had been so busy enjoying the view that the mere fact that I was just moments away from throwing myself from a tin can, nearly two miles above the Earth's surface had simply slipped my mind. At that moment it just seemed like the most *insane* proposition ever. I felt like saying 'jump from this thing? Are you out of your mind? I'd rather hand wash Anne Widdicombe' but feared it would make *me* seem like the crazy one. We humans are strange creatures it seems.

At that moment, we entered a large cloud, obscuring the ground below and providing the illusion that far from being high in the sky, I was instead on the verge of belly flopping into a massive array of soft cushions. I saw this as my opportunity and, with adrenalin pumping, shuffled along the floor and positioned myself hanging over the edge of the door. If anyone has been on the *'Oblivion'* ride at *'Alton Towers'* they will understand the sensation of hanging on an edge and waiting for the moment in which you will be dropped carelessly towards the unforgiving concrete floor. This was exactly the same feeling, only a couple of miles higher. The wait seemed to last forever with the powerful wind stroking past my face. Finally though, Colin began the countdown, I took one huge last breath, closed my eyes and fell forward elegantly through the clouds.

This is where a skydive is far easier than a bungee jump – during the latter, the jump is purely down to your will-power and sense of faith, whereas during a parachute jump you have no choice and are merely thrown from the plane by the instructor straddling your back. I see this as a positive in my situation as, given the choice, I'm not sure my legs would have allowed me to jump. This also reminds me of a story a friend told me during this tour. During his first (and only) jump, his instructor decided to play a little trick during the countdown. Coming down from five, he stalled just after one, exclaiming *'OH GOD, I FORGOT TO ATTACH THE……'* before throwing the pair of them from the aircraft. Now, he seemed to find this rather funny (as do I!), but for my friend it resulted in a minor heart attack.

It is difficult to describe those first few moments of free-falling. Immediately, for fear of death, my instincts took-over as I attempted to assume the position taught during the two-minute training. But with the air rushing past at such high velocity, I found it difficult to breathe and therefore concentrate. Finally gaining some composure, we emerged from the cloud and the wonderful Australian coastline reappeared. I was speeding through the air, faster than anyone had ever experienced yet the land didn't seem to be getting any closer. It was like being trapped in a gale force wind as my body appeared to believe it was flying at supersonic speed but at the same time felt stationary. The world seemed vast and ultimately endless from that height and as I fell like a stone toward its centre, my existence faded into insignificance. But yet, I had a remarkable feeling of pure and utter freedom. Or perhaps it was the bizarre sensation of weightlessness that made me question my own being. However, these are perhaps after thoughts. Throughout the entire freefall experience I can't entirely remember much. The body is so overwhelmed with the unfamiliar forces, sensations and experience that it is ultimately unable to comprehend the moment. I do recall the instant the parachute cord was pulled some twenty seconds later. There was a giant tug and I was suddenly thrown back without warning. Now this seems quite logical but at the time, whilst freefalling towards the ground at some forty metres per second, you tend to panic ever so slightly when such events occur. I did for a second believe Col had become detached along with my parachute and lifeline. Soon though, we were gliding smoothly back toward the beach, my feet hanging freely in the crisp air. It was simply amazing, finally experiencing the true sensation of flying – a feeling I have always craved and was not disappointed by. Landing softly on the picturesque beach moments later, I was too overwhelmed to really speak. The rest of the day was somewhat more subdued – after all, what do you do with yourself after a skydive? I just sat in quiet contemplation and downed a couple of beers. It was pure and utter bliss.

II

Now, I don't normally like to pack too many adrenalin based activities into such a small space, but since time was limited, two days later I found myself heading out into the ocean in search of the largest living organism on the planet – The Great Barrier Reef. Although Gloria had insisted it could not be easily accessed from Mission Beach, she was (as expected) 100% wrong. There were quite a number of boat trips the lady in the information centre had assured us the day before. She then proceeded to rip $123 from my hand followed by another $299 for an all-inclusive Whitsunday's and Fraser Island extravaganza. To be honest, it all seemed like a reasonably good deal and since she was willing to throw in a free underwater camera, I was pretty chuffed.

So too was Emma and so that's how we found ourselves sailing out into the beautifully blue, Pacific waters. At least that's how I had imagined it, but the reality was grey doomsday clouds, heavy rain and intimidating, monstrous waves. Our boat – *Blue Thunder* - was being bombarded and struck from every side by huge walls of water. On deck, I clung to one of the seats bolted to one side and prayed. Emma did the same next to me, swallowing seasickness pills as quickly as possible. But no speed was quick enough. Her face suddenly went the palest form of white before she dragged herself up to the side of the boat and gracefully emptied the contents of her stomach into the sea below. As if on cue, the man next to me did exactly the same, although not quite as gracefully as Emma I must say. You see, most people have a wonderful, idyllic view of The Great Barrier Reef, but believe me, the pain you go through to get there is horrible. I must say though that sitting there watching this farce got me into somewhat of a confused state – why is it that the body's reaction to being thrown backwards and forwards is to regurgitate everywhere? Surely that's just going to make things even more difficult – not only are you being tossed about, you've then got to do it with sick all down your front. It makes little sense to me.

Anyway, I'm digressing from the situation in hand. The journey lasted for two hours, all of which I spent sitting between two people simultaneously puking over the side. All of a sudden though, without warning, we arrived. And, at the very moment of our arrival the skies cleared, the sea calmed and the sun revealed itself, illuminating the turquoise ocean below. This sudden transition was extraordinary and quite unexpected. It was like lying distressed and thirsty in the desert before being presented with the most perfect mirage ever seen. The sea had suddenly transformed from a dark, destructive demon into an inviting pool of luxurious, warm water. I was in awe. Speaking to one of the aboriginal crew members concerning this, he explained that no matter what the weather throughout the journey was like, the sun always shone true on this area of sea.

'You look well rough' I said, turning to Emma.
'You bastard!' she chuckled 'I'll be fine once I'm in the water'.
'Good, wouldn't want you being sick in your mask. That would be messy' I added.

This was my first ever scuba diving experience (and what a place to have it!) and I was slightly apprehensive concerning the whole thing. For starters, I looked like a complete idiot in my wetsuit, but the thought of being able to breathe underwater and experience another world so different from my own was worrying, although intriguing. I was also the only beginner on the course as Emma had already completed her PADI in a deserted quarry near her home in Windsor. Our instructor Matty was very patient – he needed to be – and helped explain everything to me as well as conducting a few safety tests which resulted in me flailing about gasping for air. However, I soon picked up the basics (the *very* basics) and found myself sinking through the perfectly clear water until the reef itself was in sight. Oh and what a sight it was. The sun pierced through water above, highlighting every last detail of our new environment.

I followed Emma's lead as she took us through shoals of fish gliding amongst the unimaginably diverse and colourful coral. Occasionally I would sense a shadow over my shoulder and panic believing it to be a shark homing in on me, but once I calmed down I could again enjoy the fantastic experience. As a clown fish swam across in front of me, its orange and white body gliding gently through the water no more than a metre out of grasp, I wondered if there was a more peaceful and perfect place on Earth? I suspect not.

I am now going to provide you with a perfect example of something known as 'Sod's Law'; imagine, if you will, two travellers. Full of pride, they aim to provide for themselves throughout their epic adventure. However, their ambitions are high with a list of truly remarkable things they wish to achieve. They have therefore cut-back on less essential things such as food, water and clothing. I think you can envisage how happy these starving campers would be when presented with an 'all you eat buffet' consisting of incredibly succulent meats, salads, sandwiches, crisps, chocolates and carbonated soft drinks. The first, named John, with a watering mouth, fills his plate to the brim and returns to his seat anticipating his first real meal in a number of weeks. It is then he remembers he is on a boat in the middle of the Pacific Ocean. Why does he remember? Because a huge wave has struck the side of the boat covering him (and his beautifully prepared rump steak) in sea water! The waves continue to build in size until standing becomes impossible and the thought of any type of food induces vomiting almost immediately. To cut a long story short, everyone was ill, the food was left untouched and we departed the boat wondering when our next meal would come. It was probably a mere trick, created by the crew of *Blue Thunder* so they didn't have to give any of their food away. In fact, if you go on this trip I want you to be absolutely sure that the waves aren't being produced by a couple of the crew kicking enthusiastically with their flippers on the other side of the boat.

CHAPTER 19

A few hours later, we checked out of the beach house and were on our way to Townsville. It was quite late at night but this particular driver was surprisingly enthusiastic and helpful. Once we had arrived at our destination, he continued chatting on the microphone as he had done a majority of the way.

'Now, before you leave the bus, please check you've got all your belongings' he said 'for example, try not to leave behind any CD players, MP3 players, mobile phones, wallets, keys, t-shirts, scarves, gloves, bags, rings, necklaces, bracelets, anklets, earrings, shoes, envelopes, pocket watches, books, hole punches, wooden legs or straw hats'

So, with all wooden legs and straw hats in order, we made our way off the bus and into *'Base for Backpackers'*. I was sceptical about using such a large hostel, suspecting it may lack character and style. However, this was a pleasant surprise. It was rather sparsely populated, but it was so clean and the staff were fantastically helpful. They needed to be for this hostel was *huge* and built with the most confusing layout known to man. It truly did feel as if you were bang in the middle of one of the most elaborate mazes ever conceived.

Thankfully though, well stocked with rations, we managed to find our way out of the building and down to explore the town. Running from the centre were a number of quaint little promenades and with numerous white-wash houses with terracotta roofs poking out from the hillside, it had the feel of a lovely town on the Mediterranean. Oddly though, there didn't appear to be anyone around at all, and in terms of entertainment I couldn't see that it offered much really. But then, its beautiful setting and lovely architecture was rather pleasing on the eye, so I couldn't exactly resent the town for its lack of life. It just seemed like a shame that there was no one else around to appreciate it.

Having had an hour looking around, we felt we'd experienced all it had to offer and swiftly booked a ferry crossing to the nearby Magnetic Island. Emma wasn't impressed that, once again, I was late and caused us to miss the shuttle bus from the hostel to the ferry port. So, being the gentleman I am, I led the way as she struggled behind with her huge bag.
'Slow down Johnny' she would shout, struggling for breath (as is normal for a girl sprinting with a 25kg bag in 33-degree heat) 'we don't all have go-go gadget legs!'.

It was a bit harsh of me to make us run, but I did *think* we were going to miss the ferry. In hindsight, I should really have checked the scale on the map because in reality we arrived with about forty-five minutes to spare and could have easily strolled down at a leisurely pace or, better still, got the next shuttle bus.

On the plus side, it gave us a chance to really appreciate the pure heat of the sun's rays, beaming down from the bright blue sky above. This was the first true day of exceptional weather on our east coast tour and it was excruciatingly hot. Nevertheless, the scenery was magnificently spectacular in this beautiful weather and heightened my spirits dramatically.

Magnetic Island looked incredibly appealing from the photos I'd seen from other travellers. Many recommended it as their favourite destination along the east coast so my expectations were rather high. I must say, it didn't disappoint. Immediately upon arrival, I was in heaven. The roads were in an awful state, the landscape was quite rocky and the vegetation was sparse. I know this may sound like a rather bleak picture, but I absolutely loved the island. With the sun beating down so powerfully, it took me back to the summer previously where I'd enjoyed a wonderful sailing trip in Kefalonia. Yes, this was just like a Greek island. And as if to reinforce the point, just at that moment, two young kids without helmets drove past us, incredibly erratically on mopeds.

As we left the ferry, I threw our bags onto the nearest bus that looked like it might have air-conditioning. I was cruelly disappointed. However, not to be disgruntled by our sweaty state, we instead looked at it as a wonderful sign of the fabulous weather we were so lucky to be enduring. The bus engine then began and we started off along the twirling road around the cliff-tops, watching the amazing scenery and blue sea pass by below.

The transfer was only five minutes and then we arrived at out base for the next couple of days – *'Magnetic Island Backpackers'*. Ten points for originality on the name. Upon entering the hostel, I was immediately struck by the calmness of the place. Even the vast array of tropical birds seemed to sing quietly so as not to disturb the peace. The hostel was no different and had a chilled vibe surrounding it. Positioned just across the road from a glorious beach, it was clean and friendly with an open plan layout. Oh and it had its own huge pet crocodile – seriously. Surprisingly though, I hadn't noticed it even though it was sitting in a cage just metres from reception. Leaning my bag against the bars, imagine me dismay when I came to retrieve it, only for my gaze to be met with the sight of huge crocodile sitting only a metre away. Obviously I was not really expecting this, so, like a man who's just urinated on an electric fence, I leapt back in shock.
'What the hell's the matter with you' Emma asked puzzlingly, obviously surprised I could move so fast.
'There's a bloody massive crocodile!' I shouted back in disbelief.
'Oh yeah, so there is. Good luck getting your bag back' Emma chuckled as she wandered across the lawn toward our dorm.

Thankfully, having consulted one of the members of staff they re-assured me that the cage was impenetrable and that the crocodile was quite friendly anyway. Although I found this difficult to believe, I did finally pluck up the courage to get my bag. Then I sat and watched the croc for a little and was overcome with a deep sense of sadness. Crocodiles in general have quite moody looking faces, but this one in particular looked incredibly depressed. It was as if it had just watched an *'Eastenders'* omnibus and was being pushed to the point of suicide. I'm sure as a youngster the cage was substantial in size, but now at three or four metres long, I suspected he'd have difficulty moving around. No wonder he was depressed. It was like having a battery-hen without the benefit of any eggs whatsoever. Mind you, it was nice to know there was one fewer deadly creature roaming the place to worry about.

The next day I woke early because of the blazing sunlight passing through the curtains. It promised to be an excellent day so I was determined to make the most of it and top up my tan for the ladies. A short walk from the hostel I found myself on the glorious beach, applying layers of sun cream and taking refuge under two palm trees. My book of choice at the time was Mary Shelley's *'Frankenstein'* and this kept me entertained for hours. The lobster-like back I had acquired in Cairns had just about recovered and resorted back to its natural, bright white colour. I therefore decided it needed a little attention and so alternated between lying on my front and back in order to gain a nice, even glow. Deciding when to turn over was literally the hardest decision I had to make on that afternoon. You see, on Magnetic Island there isn't much to do - but that is the charm of the place. It truly is the perfect location to unwind, relax and just let the day slip by. It was as if this land had a magical quality about it where all other worries and stresses would gently fade away into insignificance. This was serenity at its most greatest. As I sat on the white sandy beach beneath the dreamlike palms, I found myself completely at ease with the world and decided if I were to die at that moment, I would die a happy man. This was a remarkably powerful place and one I adored wholeheartedly.

As evening came, Emma and I decided to make our way back to the hostel for some food and drink. However, as I sat up, Emma fell back down to the sand in fits of laughter.
'What??' I chuckled back 'is my hair looking bad?'.
'Look at your chest!' she eventually managed to muster between breaths.
As I looked down I saw exactly what she was hysterically laughing at. It appears that lightening really does strike twice. Apparently my application of sun cream hadn't quite been as even as anticipated and instead of a nice brown tan, I had a giant, red, sunburn handprint right across my left pectoral.

'For God's sake! I finally shed my back skin and look what happens to me! Shit! I look like an idiot, don't I?'.

She didn't answer because of the laughter, but I took that as a yes and smiled. Nothing could get me depressed on Magnetic Island. Not even my departure from the weekly Pool competition in the first round later that evening. As we had sat eating our dinner of incredibly cheap breaded fish fingers and mash potato with mayonnaise, we got chatting to our roommates Fergus and Ellen. Having just finished their university degree, they were now embarking on one last adventure before the depression and responsibility associated with a real job could take them captive. They were obviously well educated and spoke fondly of the exciting things facing us during our first year in higher education. Not that they discussed the education part much, more the late nights, heavy drinking sessions and their vast collection of stolen signposts. But it sounded exciting and I loved listening to all their stories.

Emma and I therefore decided to join them in the bar for a bottle of wine. This was the third leg of their round the world tour and they recalled tales long into the night about various other exotic locations they had visited. I listened with intrigue as they told us of the hundreds of cockroaches and spiders they found in a dorm room in Thailand, but explained that for 20p a night, they couldn't really complain. I suggested sleeping out on the street would probably have been better and saved them their money. We then chatted about our time on camp and relived exciting stories of kids falling off rock-climbing walls and drowning in mountainous rivers as they listened with mirrored enthusiasm. It may have been the wine affecting me, but I found this situation gave me great hope for humanity- the thought that four people from different backgrounds, who had been brought together in this tiny corner of the world through chance, could simply enjoy each other's company so much, was just stunning. Fergus and Ellen soon went to bed, but Emma and I sat recounting funny stories from the past few months whilst watching one of the tame hostel possums attempt to propel itself from a nearby wall into a tree. It missed. And that added yet another humorous tale to our ever-growing list.

We nearly missed our bus again the next morning. However, having just made it in time I realised I had left a sentimental piece of jewellery back in the room. I therefore rushed back, leaving Emma confused and alone on the bus. This was like mission impossible. When I returned, the bus had gone – along with Emma and all my bags. The boat was in twenty minutes and with our booked *Greyhound* coach waiting for us back at Townsville, I had no option but to make it. I started running - well jogging - as fast as I could along the mountain road in the draining heat.

With only moments left, I still had a couple of miles to go and so resorted to hitchhiking. Luckily, a newly married couple driving past in a 'pimped-up' golf-buggy stopped, threw me in the back and sped towards the ferry port. I made it with a minute to spare, wished them a happy honeymoon, thanked my lucky stars and boarded the boat. Unfortunately, I had assumed Emma would be on deck, but she wasn't – she was waiting for me in the terminal building. Thankfully though, through some frantic waving I managed to get her attention and she scurried aboard, the whole of her 5'5" frame struggling under the weight of four bags.

'Well, nothing like a bit of drama in the mornings' I said calmly as she dumped herself into a seat, red faced and out of breath.

CHAPTER 20

The countryside between Townsville and Airlie Beach was stupendous. Throughout the three hour and twenty minute journey, I marvelled at the huge fields of tall sugarcane plantations before they faded into vast plains with distant mountains lining the horizon. This Martian landscape was one of the great appeals of Australia – the diversity of the land in such a short space of time is truly unique.

I had been looking forward to arriving at Airlie Beach – 'The Gateway to The Whitsundays' – since hearing a number of stories from fellow travellers about the great parties. Having recharged quite convincingly on Magnetic Island, I was ready for some clubbing action and was not disappointed. Having arrived and seen a couple of bars and cafés, we were soon whipped away by the mini-bus to our hostel for the evening called *'Reefos'*. Although it promoted itself as being only a 'short walk' from town, it was actually a 'long walk' as I found out later that night. The hostel itself was quite nice and consisted of many self-contained cabins built on a large complex. They were based in a small woodland area, with each containing a number of incredibly uncomfortable bunk-beds, a small kitchen and a bathroom. Upon arrival, we found we had an extremely strange and possibly psychotic room mate who was rambling like a madman in his sleep.

Mind you, he was probably equally scared of me when he discovered my face pressed up against the window trying to spy on what he was doing.

Considering we had just left all our worldly possessions in a room with a possible mentalist, we were in relatively good spirits as we caught the bus into town just as the sun's final rays of the day scattered across the ocean, illuminating it like the surface of a beautifully sculpted crystal. I soon discovered that the vicious rumour told to me by the drunk man at the bar on *Neighbours Night* was in fact true – Airlie Beach did not have a beach. Just like Cairns there was an elegant public lagoon located in between the sea and the town which was very nice, but I couldn't help feel slightly conned by the name. The main street was full of tacky souvenir shops just like the ones lining the streets of Blackpool and Skegness, but that is where the similarities ended. There were also a number of travel agents offering numerous boat trips to the hundreds of exotic islands, and a small second-hand book store.

At this time of night though, these were all closed and the resort was dominated by lively bars and open plan restaurants. It was getting rather late into the evening, but the town was only just coming to life as people wandered along the street in shorts and flip-flops looking for a bite to eat. I looked into one of the bars and saw a group of girls, each holding some of the most extravagant cocktails I have ever seen. It was still hot – the sort of warm evening heat that convinces you that you're on holiday and that late-night skinny dipping is a good idea.

Dominating the centre of the town was a large hostel with an adjoining bar, however there were rumours going round the town suggesting it was suffering from a recent bed-bug outbreak. For some reason though, we still decided to go to the bar, where I waited for a reunion with my Kiwi friend Mel. We found her enjoying a cranberry juice on a bench outside with a huge smile on her face.

'How's it going?' she said 'ah, it's so great to see you guys, here I made you a bracelet'. Her dreadlocks were longer and thicker than ever. The bracelet she had made me was constructed of a number of strange looking beads and only went to add to her hippy stereotype. I didn't think I'd ever wear it, but the thought was fantastic and seeing a familiar face was even better.

'So Mel, shall we go get some 'fish and chups'?' I said to her, laughing at my quick witted piss-take of the New Zealand accent. She laughed for old-times sake.

Mel was always a very resourceful person, so it didn't surprise me to find out that she'd been surviving on a very small budget throughout her tour of the east coast. Always chatty and with a welcoming smile, she made friends more quickly than a *Lotto* winner suffering from Alzheimer's. As a consequence, people constantly seemed to be throwing accommodation her way and saying 'sure, come in and eat all the food you can and, when you've finished, feel free to sleep with my husband and borrow our new car'. However, she wasn't afraid of confrontation and told us a story about how she'd confronted a couple who were getting jiggy in one of the hostels she had stayed in. Apparently, she had got out of bed and shouted at the naked, embarrassed couple. When Emma and I had encountered a similar situation, we had just attempted to keep in our chuckles.

At this current time, she was camping just outside the town and told us about a couple she had met with a fishing boat.
'I've never really been fishing before, but they've invited me out tomorrow to try and catch some Spanish mackerel' she said really excitedly 'do you guys wanna come over tomorrow for a barbie? Well, if we don't catch anything it might not be much of a feast, but there are some good guys to chat to and we could always go and get some fish and chups'.
The thought of having a large fish feast was amazing, especially considering I had only eaten crisps and cheese for the past few days. We finished our drinks and agreed to meet the following evening when Mel returned from her hunting and gathering. That night I slept dreaming of the meal to come.

The sun was shining the next morning as it always seemed to in The Whitsundays. And I was even happier when I realised our possibly psychotic roommate had departed. My towel hadn't been washed for about three weeks and so I invested three dollars in some washing powder and gave it some much needed attention. Later that day, I came out of a shop having been for a swim in the lagoon, turning to Emma I said
'Hey, pass me my towel will ya?'.
'Well I would if I'd got your towel, but since I don't, no, I won't' she replied.

'Bollocks'.

Having retraced my steps throughout the entire day and not finding my soggy, old (but newly washed) towel anywhere, I concluded that some incredibly scummy person had stolen it.

'Brilliant, not only have I just wasted three dollars on washing my towel, but I didn't get to appreciate the lavender aromas and now I have to splash out on a new one' I complained to Emma in pure annoyance and disbelief that someone would want to steal such a rubbish item.

'What is the world coming to?' That's about all the comfort Emma could muster.

Now, I feel I'm painting a slightly negative picture of The Whitsundays with towel thieves lurking around every corner, waiting for the best opportunity to take advantage of the seasoned traveller and stripping them of all dignity and drying apparatus. This is not realistic. In contrast, Airlie Beach was a fantastic place and I was more impressed with it now than the previous night. The souvenir shops were open and as we toured the shelves I contemplated buying a 'Kangaroo Scrotum Purse'. If the title wasn't appealing enough, the packaging portrayed a kangaroo with a bandage covering his groin and shouting 'I'M ROO—IND!!' Brilliant! Australia is probably the only country in the world where they shoot and devour their national animal and then sell off its genitalia for profit. So, I bought three – after all, you can never have too many scrotum purses. Okay, this probably isn't helping to paint a better picture of Airlie Beach. But it really was a beautiful place. The town was clean and quaint, the people were happy, the weather was perfect, the sea was a warm, inviting blue and there was a bar on every corner. What's not to love?

The remainder of the afternoon was spent lounging around the lagoon which was large, beautiful and surrounded by neatly landscaped gardens. Just beyond them was the picturesque ocean, lying subdued beneath hundreds of luxurious yachts. Hugging the shoreline of the main bay was a raised stone walkway which I decided to follow through no reason other than curiosity. As it curled up toward the headland, I marvelled back at this superb secluded little town and the numerous glorious islands protecting it from the giant Pacific. The path led past a number of small restaurants and cafés where families were enjoying the final specks of evening sun with lattés and extravagantly constructed ice creams. As I rounded the headland, the main dock of the port presented itself with hundreds of huge yachts and boats moored in a sun-trapped little bay. Well I say boats, but some of them were the size of luxurious cruise liners. My curiosity got the better of me so I clambered down the pathway and walked amongst the vessels bobbing elegantly in the water, wondering if I would catch a glimpse of anyone famous. My mind filled with dreams as I, well, spied on all the families enjoying champagne and relaxing in their private spas. This was the life for me. However, I think all my staring may have made some of the families uncomfortable and so I scurried back off towards the town. After all, I knew my place.

Since the weather was so glorious, Emma and I foolishly decided to walk into town from *Reefos*. The vistas along the way were glorious, revealing the fantastic hilltop views of the bay in closer intricate detail. However, it was much longer than we had anticipated and Emma got increasingly frustrated as her unfavourably proportioned legs attempted to keep stride with mine.

Eventually, with a sigh of relief, we arrived in town victorious and with a (albeit short-lived) sense of athletic pride. That was until we realised that the campsite was even further away, on the opposite side of town. Not to be disheartened, we popped into the High Street supermarket, purchased a perfectly round onion and began our second march of the evening towards the grand banquet.

The campsite was set in luscious green fields, divided into sections by a number of different varieties of Eucalyptus. This was surprising since all the previous campsites I had visited in Australia had been constructed on the most uncomfortable, rocky ground, covered by a thin layer of dirty sand. In contrast, this was actually rather pleasant. We followed Mel's directions down to a tee and, as ever, got lost. Eventually though, we heard some commotion occurring on the other side of a hedge and, through pure inquisitiveness, decided to investigate. We were faced by a banquet. In the middle stood Mel, looking deservedly pleased and holding a large Spanish mackerel in her hands to show the group. And it was a large group. It seems the three successful fishermen had gathered quite a crowd around the kitchen area with many people coming to examine the feast being prepared. The funny thing is that, until that point, I really didn't like eating fish or, come to think about it, any type of seafood. However, it just looked so appetising and fresh.

'I think that'll just about do me' I said strolling towards Mel surrounded by her adoring fans 'but where's the fish for the rest of you?'.

'Ha-ha, you wish. Look at this – me risking my life out at sea, providing food for you all and what do you turn up with – an onion!' she replied with a sly smile.

'A perfectly spherical onion I'll have you know' I said, correcting her clumsy oversight 'in terms of roundness, perhaps the greatest onion in all of Australia'.

'Well, I couldn't disagree with that! Let's eat'.

  The campsite had a number of wooden shelters, within which were a series of 'pay-as-you-go' barbeques, a sink, a fridge and some wooden picnic benches. Emma and I grabbed a knife and quite reluctantly began chopping our onion. It was then that Mel introduced us to the couple who had owned the boat and taken her on the great hunting adventure. In their mid-thirties, they were just as agreeable as Mel in terms of joyfulness and welcomed us with open arms. Having chatted to them for a while, it appeared they spent most of their weekends relaxing on their boat, which they drove to different towns along the east coast, making new friends in the process. In a way, I suppose they epitomised the Australian culture – 'work hard, play harder'. They looked at each other with pure happiness and an affection which showed that their lives had turned out perfectly as imagined without complication. Coming from England where work dominates people's lives, this is a rare thing to see and it gave me hope knowing that the dream can actually become a reality.

  It appeared Mel had made a number of friends on the site who, one by one, arrived for the party and contributed food as they did. One of them was a young farmer from England named Zach. Although, he wasn't a typical farmer – for starters he was travelling around Australia instead of getting up at 5am to tend to his cattle, and a cloud of cannabis smoke appeared to follow him wherever he went. He was quite chubby with a few days worth of stubble growing across his chin and had one of those strange ear rings that extended your earlobe and made the hole about 2cm in diameter. I've never understood them – honestly, what man wants a 2cm hole in his ear? Unless of course you were going to hang things from it, like a wind-chime or birdfeeder, it seems remarkably useless and looks simply awful. Anyway, he was an incredibly pleasant fellow and spoke adoringly of the way of life he had encountered in Australia. But mostly, he was in awe of the whole travelling experience.

'I was sitting in a pub the other day and just went up to a guy at the bar and started chatting. After a few more stubbies he offered me his house to stay in – I mean, how fantastic is that? In England, if you go and chat to a bloke at the bar, he thinks you're either a psycho or a homosexual. Here, in Australia, everyone wants to help everyone else out whether a friend or a stranger. It's just a far superior way of life and one that I prefer' he explained when asked why he loved Australia so much 'I don't want to live in a society where you're frowned upon for merely chatting to someone you don't know. Plus, the weather's bloody amazing over here' he added.

It made a lot of sense, and Emma and I, indeed the rest of the group, found ourselves listening intently to his opinion. He had an air of wisdom that was far beyond his years. However, I was curious to know if he had anything negative to say about the experience.

'Don't you hate asking the same old questions all the time – 'where do you come from?' and 'where are you going next?' for example?'.

'No I don't, because the great thing about travelling is that, although *your* answers are always the same, everyone else has a completely different story to tell. And that doesn't get boring at all. When I meet someone new, they may have already been to a place I have visited but their perception and experiences of the place will be completely different. It's so fascinating'.

I had to agree with him on that one and he had summed up the travelling experience perfectly – it was not a simple case of moving from place to place, the real experience was the characters you met along the way. And he certainly was a good one.

Mel finished cooking the mackerel and presented it with a full spread of vegetables, jacket potatoes and salads. The fish was superb and quickly satisfied my cravings for a proper meal. I don't think I'll ever forget that first taste as it melted in my mouth. The rest of the camp goers forced wine and beer down our throats as we chatted into the early hours, like a group of friends who had known each other for years. They do say that alcohol is a social lubricant, but I like to think that it was the coming together of so many different people, all with the same goal of enjoying life, that allowed the conversation to flow so easily.

The next day, Emma and I checked out of *Reefos* and made our way to the marina as we had booked a boat cruise of The Whitsundays for two days. I was quite optimistic because, although we had not seen our luxurious vessel, it was situated at Abel Marina which I had toured the previous day. We were however, in for a disappointing shock. There was perhaps an element of warning in the price tag attached to this tour but, nevertheless it was still surprisingly bad. Not the catamaran itself you understand – named *Jade*, it was 55ft long and rode the waves gloriously as it came into dock and collected its most recent guests. There were thirty-six of us. That's right – *thirty-six* guests and four crew members on a 55ft yacht. It was chaos to say the least.

Realising the potential problems that could arise from the situation, Emma and I ran straight to the front of the boat and got ourselves a fantastic seat near the jib, lying across the trampoline-like material which was holding *Jade* together. Inevitably, and before much time had passed, my view was ruined by the numerous other bodies being packed onto the boat. At one point, I doubted whether *Jade* could take the weight and was convinced I could feel her sinking. I joked and told Emma it was probably due to her arse. Her facial expression suggested she did find it that funny.

Before long though, we were motoring out into the open ocean and away from Airlie Beach. Our destination for the next two nights was a little hotel on Long Island, but our days would be filled with exhilarating diving and swimming experiences amongst some of the most beautiful scenery in the world. As the invitingly warm, light blue glow of the shallows was replaced by darker, more sinister waters, the captain killed the engine and engaged the sales. A true Queenslander, his name was John and he proceeded to describe the itinerary for the next few days in a bluntness I had become accustomed to.

'You get what you pay for people. Look at this boat, it's got over four times the amount of guests it should. But you should have known that when you booked. Don't be expecting any luxury accommodation either – this is the cheapest tour in The Whitsundays and there's a reason for that. But I'm sure if you listen to me and have a good attitude, we'll have an okay time.'

Wow! Where do I sign up?! The sad fact was that I already had and we were only being told the truth whilst about a mile off shore. There was no escape. However, I am a great believer in making the most of a bad situation. When John had finished his depressingly truthful description of the trip, he stopped talking and so did everyone else. The silence was wonderful as we gently rocked over the forthcoming waves as if trying to send a baby to sleep.

I climbed over a number of bodies to the front of the boat, put my feet over the edge and let the waves lick at my feet as we continued towards Long Island at a soothing, leisurely pace. We were travelling west just as the sun was setting and Southern Cross began to glimmer in the indigo sky above. I just sat in quiet contemplation as more stars revealed themselves and day turned to night before my eyes. I wasn't thinking about anything in particular, just taking in the beautiful scene revealing itself and thanking god that I was able to experience it.

By the time we arrived at Long Island, it was dark. We were informed that it was a 4* resort only accessible by boat, however our accommodation was definitely not 4*. 'Incredibly basic' would be a far more accurate description. The resort itself though was beautiful – incorporating its own personal beach, it housed a number of stunning buildings, bars and hot-tubs. It was all linked together with a series of walkways throughout luscious, tropical vegetation adding exquisitely to the tranquil setting.

Emma and I shared our room with a woman named Cory. At twenty-eight years old she was a seasoned pro at travelling and explained how she was a professional marine biologist but had fallen out with her boss and simply left. That was two years ago and she still had no intention of returning in the near future. For me, this added to the diversity of long distance travelling and showed once again what an enriching experience it can be. In bleak contrast, our room was not enriching - it was soul destroying. The cupboards were broken and falling to pieces and the roof fan was on its last legs. The lock didn't lock either. But who cares? I didn't really have that much worth stealing apart from my towel and that had already been taken.

So we made our way, the happy threesome, towards the beach and spa. I'm sure the guests paying thousands of dollars for their 4* accommodation weren't that impressed when thirty-six young scallies turned up on their beach and raided the sauna, but it wasn't really my concern. Having had a couple of cocktails with Cory, we soon found ourselves taking advantage of the facilities being offered. A large group of young Irish lads were – having drunk an astonishing amount – playing volleyball on the beach in the pitch black. Along with four young girls from Brighton and a South Korean American named Jimmy, I decided to experiment with the Turkish steam room. It truly was a multicultural experience. But after thirty seconds of not being able to breathe, I found myself retreating back to the hot tub on the beach. There I found Emma and Cory attempting to make conversation with four Israeli men who had a limited grasp of English. Well, I say make conversation, this really included a lot of slow and loud talking followed by some elaborate hand gestures that didn't really appear to mean much at all.

  The girls from Brighton soon followed having been shrivelled as much as is humanly possible, but Jimmy stayed in there for hours. After about thirty minutes we began getting worried that he had maybe slipped over, knocked himself out and was slowly being steam-cooked like an unfortunate vegetable. But, to our relief he soon re-appeared, apparently refreshed and ready to entertain. As the warm bubbles surrounded us under a blanket of stars with the gentle waves breaking majestically on the tropical shoreline just metres away, I suddenly realised I was in paradise. This was pure tranquillity and a moment never to be forgotten. As I reached across for my Pina Colada, Jimmy returned with a guitar in his hand and gave us a rather elaborate rendition of *'Brown Eyed Girl'* by Van Morrison. Even the Israeli guys knew the words as we all sang along through the night.

We were woken the next morning by one of the crew banging our door backwards and forwards on its hinges. It was 6.30am, but apparently there was a big day ahead. I left Emma and Cory in bed and decided to take a small walk. It was early, but the hot sun was already beating down on the beach and a number of Irish bodies who had passed out in the early hours. They looked rough - very rough. Definitely not the sort of rough you want to feel when being faced with a day at sea.

  When I returned to the room, Emma and Cory had fallen asleep so I jumped on them in order to provoke a reaction. This didn't quite go down as well as I was expecting, but nevertheless we soon found ourselves taking prime position on the trampolines at the front of *Jade*. With most people on board – many with hangovers, including our captain – we made our way out to begin the tour. As the sun rose higher, I remember watching the colour of the sky alter until it matched the sea like an iguana adjusting to the surroundings. It was at this point that we suddenly met a patch of water so calm and still it appeared motionless, causing the horizon to become indistinguishable. I'm not sure if it was to do with the currents, but the wind seemed to cease and we became motionless. The whole world stopped around us as we slowed to a halt out in the Pacific. I dipped my feet into the water below and it felt warm – warmer than it should it be. Then, after a couple more minutes, the wind blew and we once again moved through the calm waves. It was bizarre and unexplainable.

Apart from Jimmy, everyone was quite tired at this point, but he seemed to be plagued with energy. Unlike most Americans, he had actually left his country so I had a lot of time for him and listened intently as he explained his family history. I suppose the knowledge that the roots of his family lay elsewhere had given him an inquisitive nature towards travelling. Although many people found his loud, outspoken opinions slightly irritating, I admired Jimmy as we shared many of the same beliefs. Back home, he was a computer programmer but was concerned and could feel himself slipping into an inescapable rut. Like I, he strongly believed that life should not simply pan out in a job, wife and 2.4 children and so left to find an adventure. It was only a temporary measure, but Jimmy had left America alone on a personal journey of self discovery. Like Cory, I admired this quality they both possessed – being able to drop a job, a house and a life in search of a better existence.

Having sailed for a number of hours we soon approached Whitehaven Beach. Having been voted in the top-ten beaches in the world for tranquillity and cleanliness, I was certainly looking forward to it. The island it is situated on is a protected site and so no buildings are located on it. Only nature determines how things occur on Whitehaven Beach. However, it does get a number of visitors per day from the numerous tour operations running from Airlie Beach. Thankfully, we had arrived early and were the first to experience the pure white sands hugging the coastline. Having recovered from a hangover, our captain John dropped anchor about thirty metres from the shore and proceeded to explain the dangers of jellyfish.

'Now, you all know the dangers of box jellyfish but you've gotta really watch out for small bastards in these waters. There's loads of tiny little bastards in here. They're invisible too so you're never gonna see them. So make sure you wear your stinger suits at all times'.

And with that, he turned and jumped straight off the side of the boat with only a little pair of shorts on.

'You see, I'm an experienced Queenslander and can see these little bastards coming' he shouted from the water.

'I thought you said they were invisible?' I shouted down at him.

'But you guys? You'll be in trouble if any of them get you without a stinger suit on' he said, totally dismissing my comment.

    The stinger suits would have been slightly more comforting had they not been riddled with holes. In addition, the flippers only seemed to come in one size too, but I didn't let it bother me. Instead, Emma and I, dressed like flamboyant 1980s super heroes, climbed onto the roof of the catamaran and leapt into the warm, tropical (and jellyfish inhabited) crystal water below. The clarity of the sea made it almost drinkable, apart from the whole salt thing. With the flippers digging into my feet, we paddled towards heaven, or haven if you will.

    The first noticeable quality of the beach was the cleanliness and striking white colour of the sand. It was as if someone had walked along the shore delicately sieving flour onto the floor. I couldn't believe how fine and smooth the grains were. Just at that moment, as if to emphasise the point, three seagulls flew from under my feet into the sky – I hadn't noticed them simply because their heads were camouflaged against the beach. Due to the nature of the island and the protected environment, the air was swarming with hundreds of different varieties of tropical butterflies and moths. It was a spectacular place and well worthy of its top ten finish. The sea water was so clear that it appeared completely white around the shore, revealing the sand along the bed below. Gradually, this thinned out transforming into a very light, diluted sky blue beneath the hull of *Jade*. You see, the beach at Whitehaven doesn't just end at the sea's edge - it extends and reaches out beneath the water for miles. Throughout the rest of the morning we enjoyed the stunning setting and had a giant game of football on the beach. The Irish didn't seem too keen as their stomachs were obviously still delicate. Having participated in a little scuba-diving along the shoreline, we were soon shepherded back to the boat for lunch and then motored our way out of the bay just as all the other day trippers were arriving. John steered our vessel around various other islands, pointing out a number of large villas owned by Hollywood's elite before stopping near a little coral reef. It turned out that local knowledge did have quite a few positives. Although visibility was low and the flippers were ripping my feet to shreds, I soon found myself swimming amongst shoals of elaborately decorated fish only normally seen in a tropical fish tank. With more confidence and not feeling sea-sick as I had at The Great Barrier Reef, I could really appreciate this underwater world for all its mysterious and unseen beauty. Jimmy had purchased a whole range of gadgets including a waterproof box for his extravagantly overpriced digital camera. It weighed a tonne and unfortunately, he wasn't the greatest swimmer in the world. We had a great laugh watching him attempting to keep his head above the water as he doggy paddled with a massive camera around his neck towards the reef. Imagine how much we laughed when he came back up to the surface revealing that he'd forgotten to put the batteries in.

As we slowly sailed back toward Long Island repeating the journey from the night before, I sat and spoke to Jimmy. He had been travelling up the east coast so I wanted his opinion on great places to visit.
'Fraser Island is completely unreal' he said enthusiastically, obviously happy that someone had asked his opinion. I got the impression he was slightly bored of travelling alone. 'Lake Mackenzie is the most beautiful place I've ever visited man – it's the only water I've ever dived into and wanted to drink at the same time'.
Lake Mackenzie was a fresh water lake on a Fraser island – a sand island just off the east coast at Hervey Bay. This was our next destination and the way Jimmy spoke about it with such genuine enthusiasm and admiration got me excited. But for now, I just wanted to enjoy the scene in front of me.

      As the sun set, it illuminated the clouds making them appear like an array of bright sand dunes reflected endlessly on the surface of the millpond beneath. As I watched the colours develop through different shades of orange and red, I felt ultimately peaceful with the world and wanted so much to share this moment with those whom I cared for, as it was one of those perfect moments in which no photo can ever do justice.

As Venus appeared in the sky, Jimmy pulled out his guitar. And this is how it came that a computer programmer from Massachusetts, a marine biologist from Canada, a drunken Irish man, four girls from Brighton, Emma and I, ended up singing *'Wonderwall'* and *'I'm a Believer'* beneath the stars on a yacht in The Whitsundays.

CHAPTER 21

As our boat pulled away from the harbour, I looked down at all the 4x4s on the deck and wondered just what was in store. We could see Fraser Island from the shoreline, but even so, it still portrayed a sense of remoteness – remoteness intertwined with adventure. I felt like an alpine pioneer, battling my wits against the vicious wrath of nature and hoping to make discoveries which would change all perceptions of the Earth. Behind us, Hervey Bay faded into the distance and almost immediately out of memory.

We had arrived a couple of days earlier, having completed a thirteen hour overnight trip from Airlie Beach. This seemed logical as it saved money on an extra night accommodation and meant we could afford to participate in the 'all-you-can-eat' pizza challenge at the *'Palace Hostel'*. Having arrived early that morning I was exhausted and in need of a power-nap. Emma on the other hand – a girl who could sleep through a *'Stomp'* concert, was positively glowing at the thought of exploring a new town. The hostel was lovely - probably the nicest so far - and set out much like a mini-hotel you would find along the Spanish coast. With pure white-wash walls on every side, it was divided into a number of quaint flats each containing a couple of bathrooms, lounge and kitchen. The rooms were kept immaculately clean, even incorporating a lovely little balcony to enjoy the evening sun.

After a quick energizing sleep, I took to the street to find Emma and explore the town myself. What I found was a rather disappointing, quiet seaside resort, hiding in the shadow of the famous island just a short boat ride away. Don't get me wrong, it was clean and tidy but seemed to lack any kind of personality. There were advertising hoardings everywhere, but instead of boasting about the town itself, they all focused on the attractions of Fraser Island. It seemed strange to me that a place would focus *all* their attention trying to get tourists to go *somewhere else*. The bungalows lining the street were all similar in style, each surrounded by its own pristine garden and competing with each other to see who could fit the most garden gnomes onto their small patch of suburban land. I caught up with Emma.

'God, this place is a little dire isn't it? Can't imagine there's much to do at night around these parts' I said. Looking around at the small esplanade, it seemed strange that almost all the shops appeared to be closed. 'Or during the day, it seems' I added.

'I've just been down to the beach' replied Emma 'it's got that horrible sticky sand on it. It's all over my feet and I can't get it off'.

Well, this really did put the nail in the coffin as far as Hervey Bay was concerned – not only was there nothing to do, but its beach was also smothered in 'sticky' sand, whatever that is. There was no way back I'm afraid.

So we filtered away the next few days visiting the shopping mall and as it was 'tight-arse Tuesday', watching cheap films at the local cinema. As we strolled back through the dark, lifeless streets having just seen a particularly gory war film (my choice surprisingly!), we discussed the sportsmanship associated with war

'I don't think they could have done that in real life, I mean, it would have breached the Geneva Convention' I said sarcastically, referring to a particularly horrible part of the film in which someone was tortured brutally.

'The what?' Emma replied.

'Didn't you know? Apparently prisoners of war have rights – you can't treat them too badly at all, otherwise you'll be in trouble. I mean, it is a war so you can go around dropping bombs wherever you like, but god, if you don't provide a prisoner with a cup of tea and a Bakewell Tart every afternoon then you better watch out'.

We had laughed about how ludicrously pointless these laws were all the way home before getting our heads down and preparing for the next few days of camping.

I went back to our truck on the deck of the ferry and started chatting to the group we had been put with. There were seven of us in total – five Irish and then Emma and I. Much to my disappointment, the older two – a couple named Eva and Tom (who oddly enough shared their names with the two survivors of the Loch Ard Gorge disaster along The Great Ocean Road) – had been designated as the drivers due to their maturity. Not that I was jealous you understand. The other three Irish girls were from Kilkenny and to this day I'm still not sure exactly what their names were. It wasn't because we didn't talk, in fact we talked quite a lot, it was simply because when they spoke I couldn't understand a single word coming from their mouths. It was like having a conversation with someone who spoke Hungarian and as a result, I found myself using the exaggerated hand gestures I had perfected whilst talking to the Israelis in order to communicate.

    With map in hand, I jumped into the passenger seat and helped Tom plan a route around the island. In our particular tour, there were two other 4x4s travelling, carrying groups of young English lads, a few mildly eccentric Germans, some Canadians and a Norwegian. Having consulted with them and shown Tom the route they were taking, we decided it would be sensible if we all stuck together, at least for the first day. I took out the safety guide book we had been given and decided to read a little about Fraser Island and the general etiquette expected on it.

    The first interesting fact of any note is that it was originally named K'gari by the Butchulla people, which actually means 'paradise'. According to legend, the island was formed from the goddess K'gari - a messenger from God - who had fallen in love with the beauty of Earth. In order to allow her to stay, she was transformed into a heavenly island of pure beauty. However, since the westernisation of Australia, many original Aboriginal names have been changed into more practical but slightly less imaginative ones. Captain Cook initially noted the island in 1770, giving it the name

'Indian Head' having spotted a number of natives inhabiting the land. In 1836 this was changed to 'Fraser Island' following the extraordinary survival of Eliza Fraser who lived on the island having been shipwrecked for about six months.

Following this, attention grew towards the island and it soon built itself up as an incredible tourist attraction due to its wondrous natural beauty, emphasised by the numerous fresh water lakes and exceptional forest. Stretching over 123kms in length and covering a staggering 184, 000 hectares, it is the largest sand island in the world and the only one in which rainforest vegetation reaches over two hundred metres high. Within the majestically sweeping sand dunes, the island hides away over one hundred fresh water lakes each enclosed by beautiful white sand and numerous crystal clear creeks that run throughout the dense vegetation. According to this safety guide, the immense sand-blows *'act as fossilized secrets from the past'*, providing the oldest age sequence of any dunes throughout the world. It was therefore declared as a World Heritage site in 1992, thus explaining the vast numbers of pedantic laws being quoted throughout the guide I was reading.

Two arrestable offences that captured my attention in particular were 'burning wood from the ground' and 'interacting with dingoes'. However, it wasn't so much the laws themselves that intrigued me, but the wording used. For example, 'interacting' seems like a very interesting word to use when talking about a human and a wild animal. I mean, for me the word 'interacting' sparks up images of some sort of conversation - are there humans and wild dogs out there having fierce political debates? Or does it just mean 'heavy petting'? Either way, I couldn't see any of these situations arising. At least, I severely hoped not. Also, why couldn't we burn wood from the ground? I'm sorry, but surely phrasing something like that is only encouraging deforestation:
'Shall we burn this old, rotten driftwood I've found on the ground Bill?'.
'Are you absolutely crazy Jim?! Have you not read the Fraser Island environmental guide?'.
'No sorry Bill, what does it say?'.
'You can't burn wood from the ground you crazy boy. Here's a chainsaw, go chop down that tree instead'.

I couldn't really make much sense of this, but I put it down to the eccentricity of the Queenslanders and concentrated on the adventure ahead.

Having arrived on the island, we made our way in convoy into the dense forest. After a few hundred metres, we came across a little shop with all the essentials you could ever need. The roads were smothered in tarmac and, to be honest, it all seemed pretty easy going. I think god was reading my mind however, as when we turned the next corner, we were faced with the road ahead. I say road but really it was a deep sand track, hugged on either side by thick vegetation which stooped across, blocking our field of view. The main highway was on the opposite side of the island and this was the only route to it, so we had little choice. Besides, this was the name of the game and the whole reason you embark on a 4x4 safari. Isn't it?

Tom looked worried, so we pulled over and released some air from the tyres in order to increase their surface area and provide some much needed grip on the difficult sand track. Approaching slowly, we entered the dark tunnel and left all signs of daylight behind. The track was littered with deep potholes, causing the truck to oscillate vertically in a sporadic fashion. This was worse - far worse - than being back on *Blue Thunder* and heading out into the stormy Pacific. I could see Emma's face changing to a pale shade of green. With each bump being exaggerated by the seemingly non-existent suspension, I wasn't feeling too great either and neither were the girls from Kilkenny.

Then all of a sudden, we stopped. It was relieving to have a break from the never-ending rollercoaster but worrying as to why we had come to such an abrupt halt. I jumped out the back and ran round to the front of the truck to join Tom who was looking concerned.
'What's up mate? You look worried' I said noticing his confused gaze.
'The road seems to have stopped. There's nothing up ahead at all' he replied, pointing to a huge shrub which was standing in our way. He was right - the road seemed to have come to a sudden end. As the other drivers from the two trucks following came to join us, I suddenly heard a massive roar coming from the other side of the thick shrubbery. But it was not from an animal. It was an ongoing destructive noise – one that gave an impression of sheer power and force. It was the sound of millions of gallons of water falling through the sky and crushing the ground below into oblivion. The

others hadn't seemed to notice as they retrieved the maps, discussing whether we should turn around and take another route. Instead, I began walking towards the shrub, approaching the noise as it grew louder and more prominent. I reached out, grabbing the braches and to my shock it moved aside. Old and rotten, it had simply fallen across the track blocking the view in front. As it moved from my view, the vegetation cleared on either side of the track to reveal the source of the noise. In front of me was the sandy beach and bombarding it were some of the most gigantic waves I have ever seen. Natures symbol of pure explosive brilliance, they broke on the beach with such power it caused the ground to shudder slightly.

    The beach was wide and there was still about fifty or sixty metres between myself and the waves so I decided to try and get closer to investigate. But as I walked out from in between two sand dunes I got a shock. ZZHUMMMMM! That was the sound they made as the Doppler Effect kicked in and the first of many trucks sped past my position at high speed. I had completely forgotten, but during our briefing we had had the beach explained to us. We were looking for the highway and here it was. You see, on Fraser Island the beach *is* the main road. I had completely forgotten and nearly got myself a face full of truck because of it. I looked left to the north and saw a seemingly endless beach reaching the horizon, about fifty metres in width and with hundreds of 4x4s zooming along it at high speed. It was a fascinating sight. I suppose it's only logical if you have a seventy-five mile stretch of beach to use it wisely – I mean, why waste the natural habitat, time and money building a motorway when there is a perfectly good, natural one already in place? Well, I say 'perfectly good' but it didn't exactly have any road markings, speed limits and periodically disappeared completely with the tide, but apart from that it was great. Anyway, those things only go to hinder the fun possibilities we could have on major roads in the western world, so I was rather chuffed. I could never see this concept ever being envisaged in England, but that was the point, this wasn't England, it was a country that knew how to use its natural resources to its advantage. Or maybe it's just a country full of nutters, either way I was looking forward to getting on the open road. Sorry, I mean beach.

    With the tide dictating our plans, we decided to use the time available and head north up the beach towards The Champagne Pools on the north east part of the island. It was a strange sensation speeding along the beach, watching the waves break perpendicularly to our motion. Occasionally we would pass the odd fisherman casting in from the sand. I always thought fishing was supposed to be a relaxing sport but I can't imagine it was very stress-free doing it in the middle of a freeway. The beach was also littered with mini-streams running from the dense forest down into the ocean, some of which had caused quite deep erosion through the sand. This somewhat hindered our progress and made for a rather frustrating journey which was constantly stopping and starting. In that respect, it was like driving in London. But that is where the similarities end. The sense of freedom was overwhelming. Looking at the open beach ahead and the powerful blue sea on our right, I knew I was part of something unique. After about thirty minutes of this stop-start routine, a large, dark object gradually revealed itself on the horizon. As we drew closer, we began to slow down as the object in question was obstructing a large portion of the beach.

'What the hell is that?' I said leaning forward to ask Tom and Eva in the front.

'No idea, I think it might be that shipwreck though' Tom replied.

'Shipwreck? In the middle of the road? This place just gets more unique by the second' I said reaching for the guide book. If there was a large shipwreck, I was sure it would be in there.

And it was. Approaching the wreck with half its massive hull buried and half sticking out into the air, the sheer size soon became apparent. At 400ft long, *The Maheno* was a luxury liner completed in 1905 for fast travel between Wellington and Sydney. Having recorded the fastest crossing between the two, it was given prestigious status and treated as a national treasure. It then went on to complete a stint of national service during the First World War. However, failing to keep up with technology, the vessel was replaced by some far superior ships. In 1935 she was decommissioned and sold to a Japanese firm to be used as scrap metal. Ironically though, it would be the *journey* to Japan that would see *The Maheno* scrapped. Perhaps destined for a noble death, the vessel ran into trouble during the final voyage en route to face the firing squad. In cyclone-like conditions, the tug rope broke and she was washed ashore on the east beach of Fraser Island. By looking at the crowd of tourists surrounding the ship however, it appeared her popularity has increased dramatically in death. By inadvertently avoiding such an undignified end in such dramatic circumstances, the ship had cemented its name throughout history. And here we were, enjoying that splendid piece of history in front of our very eyes. As we walked around the huge wreck, watching the sea and beach slowly chip away at its foundations, I felt emotional. To think that this ship had achieved so many great feats and had played a part in winning the First World War was incredible. Although it was a wreck, its glorious past somehow shone through as it sat in front of me with a strange sense of pride. For me, it simply symbolized the indestructible nature of the human spirit in the fight against evil. Even now, one hundred years on since its construction and sixty since it was sentenced to death, *The Maheno* still survived, more prominent than ever.

Having completed our photo session, we jumped straight back into the truck and continued north along the beach. The traffic was getting far more busy and we found ourselves swerving in and out of slower vehicles at high speed. There didn't appear to be any kind of rules on which side you should pass or any visible lanes – it was like the start of *Whacky Races* with every vehicle doing whatever the hell it wanted. As we ate up the miles, I continued to read on through my fascinating guidebook discovering the wonderful secrets this island had to offer. Eventually though I started to feel a little ill from reading and travelling so put the book away.

Everyone seemed quite tired now so conversation was down to a minimum. Instead, I put my face up against the window and peered aimlessly into the breaking waves. It then struck me that I had seen no bathers or surfers in the ocean which seemed strange, especially with brilliant high waves like the ones I was staring at. Yet again, I found myself clawing for my guidebook which was now lying on the floor having been shaken from my bag during a particularly large bump. However, I couldn't really find much information about the beach and was just about to give up searching when my eyes were drawn towards the nature section. Suddenly everything became clear – the reason no one was even going anywhere near the sea was because that this particular section of ocean was a *huge* tiger shark breeding area. So, the ferocious nature of Australia's wildlife had struck again. It was slightly gutting as I was imagining myself waking up by the campfire and running down to the beach for a picturesque and refreshing morning swim. I was just thankful I had read this information before embarking on such a trip as it may have been my last.

By the time we arrived at the headland protecting The Champagne Pools, the sun was beginning its descent. The sand beneath the car was also beginning to get a lot deeper and dry, making driving conditions very difficult. As we pulled in to park, we saw a number of people having to dig themselves out of deep sand bunkers.

There was a small track going inland connecting this north part of the east beach with the northern beach, effectively cutting down walking distance to The Champagne Pools by quite a substantial amount. However, we had been severely warned against attempting to drive it during the briefing due to pockets of sinking sand. Following this advice, we parked up and decided to walk the extra distance. Within minutes we were incredibly glad that we had. The track was quite wide and had enough space to fit two or three vehicles at a time. With steep sand hills lining the path on either side, the sun illuminated it like a bright, golden corridor. Ironically, this beautiful setting made for a complete massacre of 4x4 trucks. They were littered throughout the entire path, half submerged with their inexperienced drivers flooring the accelerators in an attempt to get out of the dire situation. I ran over to help a German couple and beckoned Emma to give me a hand pulling the vehicle out of its grave along with ten or so other volunteers.
'What possible difference will I make?' she said.
'Come on, you can anchor us at the back' I said making a little joke.
'Oh, that's a bit harsh' came the reply, but not from Emma - it was a little guy standing just in front of me tugging the rope as well. I quickly noticed him as one of the drivers from a truck in our convoy 'you wanna give him a slap for that luv. No sex for you tonight hey mate?' he said laughing to himself
'Nah, we're not going out mate. She's all yours' I replied and we both laughed. Emma punched me on the arm and looked only mildly impressed.
He told us his name was Tim and he was on a month holiday from England with a number of his friends. Emma and I both liked him straight away as his quick wittedness and natural humour caught our imagination. As we continued to try and pull this German couple out of the sand, there was a great sense of community and team building within the group – after all, we didn't even know this couple and here we were using all our energy to help them. If we had been driving along the motorway in Britain, would we have stopped to help them? I doubt it. But this was Australia, where everyone

goes that extra step to help those in need. I suppose we had all been captured by the situation.

Having helped the Germans out, we continued to walk along the track and up a small hill towards The Champagne Pools. It was pure pain. You see, although sand dunes are idyllic to look at, to climb up them is exhausting beyond belief. It takes the will power and strength of an Olympic athlete, as the ground seems to constantly be giving way beneath your feet. My calves felt like they were going to burst. By this point, we had been joined by one of Tim's friends, Ryan. He was tall, stocky and with short dark black hair, although he always wore a baseball cap, and spoke with a thick Canadian accent. It amazed me just how many Canadians I had already met during my Australian adventure, yet only one American.

Anyway, as the sand dunes ground away our energy, Tim continued to keep our spirits high by telling some amusing anecdotes concerning his travels so far and how he'd been frustrated following our 4x4 for most of the day

'That bloody Tom is a shit driver. Did you see him coming across the island? Might as well have been stationary he was going that slowly. I was like 'mate, get the hell out of the way and let me lead'. It was so frustrating. Bet you were frustrated sitting in the back?' he said ranting to himself in his strong north London accent.

'Listen to him – he's been going on like this for the past five hours' Ryan quickly jumped in apologising, but obviously seeing the funny side too.

'He seemed to be going quite quick to me. Mind you, I've got a one litre, 4four gears, 1989 Peugeot 205 at home, so a sit-on-lawnmower seems fast to me' I said, laughing at myself in the unique way English people do.

'Ha-ha really?!' said Tim 'you must be looking forward to going for a bit of a razz in these 4x4s tomorrow then?'.

'Can't. I couldn't get insurance because I'm under twenty-one'.

'Yeah, but surely Tom'll let you have a sly drive?'.

'Nah, he said I couldn't apparently'.

'Are you joking? Who cares if you're not insured? There's not exactly much to crash into around here! I tell you what, come with us tomorrow and I'll let you take it for a little spin'.

'Cheers mate, that'd be sweet" I said as we finally turned onto the northern beach.

As soon as we did, my theory that driving across this particular bit of beach would be suicidal, was confirmed. Unfortunately, one group of Irish lads had evidently learned this the hard way. Their truck was upside-down in the sand, wheels spinning like the legs of a capsized tortoise and debris scattered across the surrounding area. Seemingly oblivious to the dire situation they were in, the owners of the smashed up vehicle were sitting around the car playing a guitar, each with a can of *XXXX* gripped in their palms.

'What happened boy? You guys okay?' I asked approaching them just as one of them cracked a particularly humorous joke, resulting in a burst of laughter.

'Wha's tha' boy? Ah thee truck – jus a spot ah bad luck. Nothin ta worry yaself about' one of them said reaching for another a beer from the cool box they had managed to retrieve from the rubble. Examining the situation, I noticed that, along with the guitar, this was the only thing they had retrieved! Well, I suppose it was important to get the essentials sorted.

The Champagne Rock Pools were rather enjoyable with some spectacular views across the ocean, but it was something I felt I could experience at most English seaside towns. In contrast, there was a rumour that whales and dolphins were usually visible from the top of the headland, but having hiked across the deep sand, Emma and I were rather tired and decided to enjoy the final piece of sun at sea level.

When the others returned, we decided to head back down the east coast and find a nice spot on the beach to set up camp for the evening. After a little while, Tim went past us at unbelievable speed, obviously frustrated by Tom's lack of adventurous driving. I was just happy not to be upside down like the Irish. About thirty minutes later we saw him take a sharp, erratic right turn in between two sand dunes, covered with marram grass blowing in the wind. We followed suit and found the others unpacking their camping gear in a lovely little circular camping spot, protected from the fierce coastal winds by dunes on one side and dense forest on the other.

With daylight reducing quickly and having no experience of how our tents were constructed, I quickly jumped out and began assembling them in the most illogical way known to man.

'Umm I'm not sure it's supposed to look like that' Emma said watching me struggle, stuck in the canvas.

'I don't know - it looks okay to me. Maybe you could lend a hand?' I said through gritted teeth.
'I'm okay actually - I'm quite enjoying watching your attempt! You carry on'.
I did and a mere one hour later, the tent was constructed and as sturdy as ever – a fine place to reside indeed. Apart from the drooping roof of course.
'Finished!' I shouted emerging from the tent and standing back to admire the handy work 'let's just hope it doesn't rain'.

Whilst I had been constructing our shelters for the evening, the others had been assembling the barbeques and preparing generous portions of meat for everyone. In addition, the beers had been cooling nicely and were now ice cold. As Tom, Eva, Emma and the other three took care of our cooking needs, I put my scouting skills into operation and started collecting fire-wood. I have to say, not using timber from the ground was quite a challenge! Luckily though, we had stopped off at one the assigned collection points to gather some earlier during the day. As I began to assemble the fire surrounded by smoke from the sizzling barbeques, Ryan came over to give me a hand.
'I can see you've had fire-building experience' he said remarking on the textbook scout fire I had built.
'Well I should, it's all I've been doing for the past few months on camp. God, I've just put a bit of pressure on myself to perform haven't I?'.
'Yes, I believe you have!'.
The western part of the sky had now turned a deep shade of red which slowly faded into indigo, navy and finally black the further east you looked. A few stars were scattered across the darker regions with The Southern Cross again posing brightly, even at this early stage of the evening. I gathered a few more pieces of damp wood and continued to build up the fire as I remarked on the view to Ryan.
'That sky looks absolutely amazing doesn't it?' I said, as Ryan began to strike a match.
'Yeah man, it's fantastic and so beautiful. I tell you, when I get all my travel photos developed I'm going to have enough incredible sunset shots for an entire album' he replied looking up at the beautiful colours above our heads.
'I know, it's superb isn't it? I just hope I don't start taking it for granted'.

'No way man. I've been travelling for nearly a year and I love it every time I see a sight like that. Even if you lived around here, you'd never ever get bored of seeing that at night. God I love it here'.

I agreed - it was a truly incredible sky and probably the most perfect setting for a camping trip. Yet again I wished my friends and family were here, experiencing it with me, as I knew no words or photos would ever portray the incredible feeling of freedom and happiness sights like this could provide.

The fire flared up on the first attempt and went someway to restoring my pride that had been unquestionably damaged during the tent construction. Ryan threw me an ice cold beer as we fashioned a number of seats from the surrounding sand and sat back admiring the glorious scene in front of our eyes. We didn't say much in those few minutes, instead we stared into the mesmerizing fire watching the blanket of diamond stars reveal itself above our heads. A few moments later, Emma came to join us with a plate full of cooked cow and a mountain of baked potatoes. There were many varieties of steak, burgers and even beef sausages which I felt obliged to sample along with another chilled stubby of *XXXX*. As I munched through my steak, drank my beer and stared into the fire I had just built, I felt like a man. A *real* man! On a negative note, most of the food seemed to have a large sand content but I think that is one of the things you have to expect on an island constructed from the stuff. Apart from that, the food was gorgeous and left me feeling positively stuffed at the end.

Having completed my best attempt at washing up, I returned to the fire area and took my seat next to the warming flames as night started to close in and the temperature dropped. Ryan and I threw on the rest of the wood to create a furnace as all the other members of the camp came across to socialise and enjoy the security of the fire. In the third 4x4 there was an incredibly eccentric German lady on a honeymoon with her husband who seemed quiet and conservative. They had been arguing for the entire day in German making it quite clear that she wasn't satisfied with camping on their honeymoon, and as a result was refusing now to leave her tent. I couldn't imagine the tent was much comfort, but I think secretly he was relieved to have escaped her childish screaming, so made little attempt to persuade her out and instead came to join us for a drink. He had short dark hair, glasses and a suede coloured shirt which was tucked into matching shorts. In true stereotypical style, he was wearing lovely sandals over a pair of bright white socks. All of this meant that he wouldn't have looked out of place working as an archaeologist in Egypt. We handed him some food and gave a sympathetic look towards the tent. He didn't speak much English, but he made hand gestures which seemed to say 'Women – who needs them?'.

The tide continued to come in as the roar of the sea increased a few more decibels making the ground shake beneath us. By this point, everyone was huddled around the flames, wrapped in blankets and enjoying conversation. Tim, having taken an obvious liking to Emma, came and sat next to us and proposed a game where we all introduced ourselves and explained where we were from. It felt kind of childish, but was certainly interesting to see the variety of cultures on our trip. As we all talked amongst ourselves, I heard Tim lean over to Emma
'You know what luv, I really miss just having a cuddle. I love cuddling' he whispered.
I burst out laughing, unable to contain myself. With no embarrassment at all, Tim stood up and announced to the group his desire to have a cuddle with someone. Thankfully, with rejection looming, Ryan stepped up and took one for the team, grabbing Tim in a tight bear hug much to the amusement of the audience.
'Guess how old I am' Tim said addressing the group.
'Thirty-eight' I shouted as my response.
'Cheeky bastard. Nah, I'm twenty-four. But, I am proud to announce, I am the most immature twenty-four year old you'll *ever* meet'.
'Ha-ha, well that's good to hear' I said 'what's the most immature thing you've done?'.
'Well, now that you ask, there was this one time when I was drunk that I really wanted to meet Pete Waterman. You know – the geezer from *Pop Idol*. I thought I'd ask him to give me a job. So, in order to meet him, I went down to the auditions. Unfortunately, they stood me there for a preliminary round before I could meet him and asked me to sing'.
'Really?' Emma said laughing 'what did you do then?'.
'Sang the first thing that came into my head - the '*Only Fools and Horses'* theme tune'.
'Brilliant! Ha-ha – so what happened?" I asked.

'They threw me out actually. Never did get to meet him. Ah well, it's quite a funny story I suppose'.

'So is that why you came travelling – because you didn't make it as a Will Young look-a-like?'.

'You know what – I just wanted to experience the world. I was sitting in a rubbish job and one day mentioned to my mate that I might want to do a bit of travelling and he looked at me and said 'are you stupid? Why would you want to go and waste your money on that – you'll end up driving a *Corsa* for the rest of your life?!' and that sealed it for me really. I was surrounded by people with such a lack of ambition – people who measured life on what car they drove. I didn't want that, so I got out as soon as possible'.

'Fair play mate' I said 'I think most people here have a similar outlook'.

It was true and that's why you get on with most people you meet travelling. Although you all come from different backgrounds and cultures, the overall beliefs you possess are the same. Sensing the conversation was getting a little too heavy, Tim then broke into song and gave us his appalling rendition of '*Only Fools and Horses*', only to stop half way through as one of the Danish guys gave a massive, highly pitched scream. I looked up to see what was going on and there, about ten centimetres from his face was a dingo. Its face was half illuminated in the fire light, as it sat there staring into his eyes. Because of the singing, we hadn't heard it sneak into the camp and, looking at its dirty face, go through our bin. We all sat in complete silence, staring back and wondering what it would do. Then, as quickly as it had appeared, it turned and vanished into the night. Nervously laughing about the situation, we all returned to our tents quite quickly and zipped them firmly shut.

Throughout the night we were kept awake by savaging dingoes surrounding our camp. It sounded like there were hundreds of them and at one point I was convinced they had developed the dexterity to open the zip and so grasped my pocket knife ready for a fight.

As the sun breached the horizon, the noises ceased allowing me to venture out and inspect the damage. The camp was a mess as all the bins had been ripped to shreds by the wild dogs, allowing the rubbish to flutter into the surrounding forest. In addition, the humidity had increased dramatically leaving me feeling sweaty. Nobody else was awake at this point so I grabbed my towel and ventured across the beach to the water for a little wash.

Luckily, there was no traffic on the road and I was able to cross without any problems before stripping off completely and diving into the refreshing water. This may seem like a slightly crazy idea, indeed you may be asking yourself why the men in white coats hadn't arrived to take me away before this point, but I just wanted to embrace this moment in touch with nature. So far I had camped, eaten lots of meat and built a fire – the next logical step was to go skinny-dipping. Plus, I calculated that if a shark was going to be big enough to take me, it would need water deeper than a metre to swim in, so I didn't venture too far out from shore. As I had imagined, the feeling was completely liberating and separated me totally from the stresses encountered in the modern world. I say - forget about going to university, earning money and getting a mortgage – just strip off and go jump in the sea! Thankfully the waves had lost a lot of their enthusiasm, becoming relatively gentle and allowing me to swim parallel to the shore without much hassle.

Unfortunately though, the moment must have grabbed me slightly too much as I heard the imminent roar produced by a 4x4 convoy motoring in my direction. Suddenly very aware of my naked state, I frantically clawed my way to the beach looking for my towel. It then became apparent that the moment had *really* taken me and I had in fact swum quite a distance along the beach. In doing so, I had lost my towel and, with it, my dignity. It was too late now though, the chance to save myself had passed – I was now merely an incredibly white naked man, covered in goose pimples, parading naked in front of a mass of traffic. They beeped a lot. One person may have even shouted 'it must be quite cold mate'. Either way, my embarrassment had been sealed.

Upon returning to the camp, most of the other guys had risen and were beginning to pack the kit away. 'You look really tired mate. Dingoes keep you awake?' I said noticing Tim's drained look.
'No they bloody didn't – it was this idiot' he said pointing to his close friend Dave. 'He was so scared they were going to break into the tent that he lay hugging me for the entire night'.
'Well you did say you liked a little cuddle' I remarked.

'True, but not from him. Plus I was bursting for the toilet this morning because this git wouldn't let me go in the night – he said the dogs might 'get him'. What a woman'.
'They might've though' Dave said in defence.
'Sure mate, and then what would they have done?'.
'Don't know…licked my face or something I suppose'.
So you didn't let me go for a piss because you were scared a dog was going to lick your face? Fan bloody tastic'.
Tim, Ryan and Dave decided to go off and explore the island on their own during the day, although we all agreed to meet up again for camp in the evening. Having spoken to Jimmy in The Whitsundays, I was anxious to venture inland and explore the fresh water lakes dotted across the island. By far the most notorious is Lake Mackenzie, but we had been assured that the adrenaline junkies amongst us would really thrive at Lake Wabby. So that's where we went first of all, with the intention of enjoying Lake Mackenzie on the return journey. However, upon arrival we realised our day was going to be filled simply by getting to Lake Wabby.

    Having parked the car we wandered into the wilderness, following the signpost which stated the lake was a mere 1.8kms away. Now you must understand that, under normal conditions and on a tarmac road, this would not be an issue. Indeed, for the first few hundred metres, we walked on solid ground through the vegetation, and covering the distance seemed like a relatively straight forward task. However, this feeling was short-lived, and as we emerged from the rainforest, I saw one of the most beautiful sights known to man – and one of the most demoralising. Stretching out in front of us were hills and valleys of beautiful rolling sand dunes. Illuminated in the strong midday sun, with the wind causing a gentle shiver across their surface, it looked like an infinite field of golden corn moving gracefully in the breeze. But the thought of having to cross it with the sun beating down from the zenith was one of utter despair.

    However, chatting to the others, we agreed that Lake Wabby (from all the anecdotes we had heard) would be worth the effort and so set off on foot to cross The Sahara. After approximately thirty seconds I had enough sand in my shoes to build a beach in Dubai, so I took them off and threw them into the paralysing bag upon my shoulder. The sand was scorching on my feet but this only made me walk faster thankfully.

A long time seemed to pass in those dunes, but eventually the lake came into view submerged at the bottom of a huge hillside. You see, this was the appeal of Lake Wabby – it was surrounded by some of the steepest dunes on Fraser Island, making it incredibly fun. Immediately, through a combination of relief and exhaustion, I collapsed at the top of the largest dune, turned onto my side and let gravity do its job as I rolled down the slope. The thrill was incredible and as I gained momentum, my turns increased in frequency as the water at the bottom got closer and closer. By the time I reached it, I had lost all sense of spatial awareness – I may have been half way down the slope, or still near the top, I simply had no idea. But then the spinning stopped and my body was engulfed by clear, fresh water all around. It was cold - *really* cold. As I scrabbled around to the surface in order to gain my balance, my dizziness set in causing me to tumble backwards into the icy lake again. Eventually I managed to gain my footing and emerged from the water. It was then that I realised, for the second time that day, I had been caught with my shorts down – quite literally. Still, we all had a good laugh.

    Lake Wabby was a sublime place to have fun. Throughout the entire afternoon we devised different games to play in and around the water. Obviously most (if not all), involved some kind of rolling, running or sliding down the huge slopes into the beautiful water below. Someone even managed to successfully ride the dunes on a surf board – unfortunately the front of the board dug into the dune at the bottom and sent him belly flopping into the lake. Everything followed the same pattern of gaining great speed down the slope before launching one's body into the water. But this giant sandpit was bloody brilliant and the perfect way to release your inner child who had been suppressed for years under the immense strain of the western world.

Forgetting about the monstrous trek back, we thoroughly exhausted all our energy. Consequently, the hike to the truck was even more daunting. When we eventually made it, the day was coming to a premature close, leaving no time to explore Lake Mackenzie. Instead, we headed inland towards the central station campsite. Having had our night in the extreme wilderness, it was a relief to see a shower and toilet block, alongside some gas barbeques. Luckily, we met the other two 4x4s by chance and followed them to our designated plot of land. I found the tent much easier to construct on this occasion and even had time to laugh at the German Princess who was shouting with frustration at her new spouse as he struggled to peg down their guide-ropes.

It was difficult to tell how long it had been since the toilet block was last cleaned, but needless to say it wasn't during this century. Nevertheless, it was nice to finally have some warm, running water and even more satisfying to get rid of the sand between my toes.

The 9pm curfew on the campsite made for quite a peaceful setting as darkness set in and Ryan got another blazing fire going. Compared to the previous night, this one was rather subdued as we sat around discussing favourite childhood TV programs and commenting on the unnaturally large size of the steroid loving ants dashing around our fire. Two German girls from the camp next door came and sat with us, bringing beer as a present as we gave them a jacket potato in return. Although nothing really eventful occurred, it was just nice to be a part of this somewhat old-fashioned but ultimately superior society.

There were no dingoes that night, but the ground was so uncomfortable I failed to sleep once again. My frustration and anger soon evaporated though when I got out of the tent and saw that Eva had risen early and bought Emma and me an ice cream. She was so lovely and quickly becoming a very dependent mother figure. Emma, not surprisingly, was fast asleep in the tent. She didn't appreciate me jumping on her at all, but soon changed her mind when she spied an ice cream coming her way.

Our craving for sugar satisfied, we packed up camp in super quick time in order to make the most of our time at Lake Mackenzie before catching the ferry back to Hervey Bay. I felt sorry for Tom as the inland driving was proving very challenging along the tracks leading to the lakes, causing stress levels to rise slightly. It was times like these that I was actually relieved *not* to be insured. At one point, the track simply fizzled out eventually to the point where it simply ceased to exist. Not to be outdone though, we grabbed the cricket stuff and marched purposely through the wilderness towards the lake. And there it was. Through a gap in the trees, there was a sudden sparkle like a diamond glistening in the sun light. As we drew closer, I realised that it was the crystal smooth water of Lake Mackenzie lying flat on a bed of pure white sand. Having seen Jimmy's photos in The Whitsundays, I recognised the unique lake but was not prepared for its sheer extravagance. The elegant sand was reminiscent of that at Whitehaven and created a beach about twenty metres in width. Enclosing the entire space was dense vegetation consisting of gum trees and encapsulating the scene in a landscape of its own. In doing so, it ensured that nothing escaped the eye and all the intricate details remained captured in this small space. The most dominating feature however was the lake itself and the mixture of colours it incorporated into the inviting waters. With a clear, turquoise blue surrounding the shore, the water suddenly dissolves into a dark navy about ten metres out, with the border between the two so sharp, it gives the lake the appearance of an exotic cocktail.

       Standing at the beach's edge, the others walked on to set up the cricket whereas I just stared in amazement – this scene was a defining moment for my year abroad and truly signified the unique diversity Australia has to offer. Just as Jimmy had said, I dived straight into the water and felt like I could drink every drop. It was pure and free from salt so there were no extreme bouts of choking or intense eye irritation. It was simply clean, fresh and exhilarating.

       We continued the theme from Lake Wabby, jumping around like children, splashing each other and occasionally dunking our heads under the water. Thankfully I didn't expose myself this time. Having such a large height and weight advantage, I ran across to Emma and, with the help of Tim, threw her elegantly through the sky, landing in the lake with massive splash of water. Looking back, I suppose this was the great appeal of Fraser Island – its detachment from the mainland meant a subconscious extrication from the mental responsibilities associated with it. On the island, the mask of maturity could be taken off without critical peer judgement and life could simply be enjoyed. This was of course a unique place because of its special, natural beauty, but its spiritual effect on individuals was even more powerful.

       We spent the remainder of the day playing cricket on the beach, involving everyone we could find. It was a truly fantastic experience, one which I didn't want to end. As I approached a group of young women to invite them to join in with the game, I noticed that one of them was Cory – the Canadian marine biologist Emma and I had met in The Whitsundays. This only went to increase the pleasure of this wonderful day as we caught up and shared stories concerning the island. Apparently she had been lucky enough to see some dolphins off the coast early the previous morning – right about the time that I was running along the beach naked frantically searching for my towel. I'm not sure my story was quite as impressive.

Then, without warning, the sun went below the tree-line and departed, taking with it our last few remaining moments on K'gari. The others returned to the 4x4s but I stayed behind, just for a few seconds, to take in the wonderful scene for a few more moments. But no time was long enough. Back in Hervey Bay that evening, all the group got together for one last drink before it was time to depart. We had all shared such an enlightening and enjoyable experience together and now it was time to go our separate ways.

CHAPTER 22

To try and compare Hervey Bay with the town of Noosa is unfair. It would be like having a match-up between AC Milan and Bournemouth. You see, as I stood in Noosa town centre peering in the windows of the boutiques, they portrayed an image of elegance, of class. Whereas Hervey Bay was a retirement home for the oxygen thieves clinging onto life, Noosa was a cultural venue for the country's stylish. Night was just drawing in, but the town's cosmopolitan vibe was coming into its element. Emma and I walked through the main paved centre, watching wealthy people dine in the numerous fancy restaurants that lined the main square. They were the sort of people who live in ultra-modern apartments constructed entirely out of glass and own a collection of *Brita Water Filters*. I watched in envy as the perfectly groomed waiters arrived at their tables with portions of succulently cooked salmon, beef and lobster.

As we reached the end of the square, there was a fantastic looking bar where many important looking people were ordering bottles of champagne and fruit packed, sparkler decorated cocktails. The men wore nice designer suits with the odd tuxedo here and there and the women a variety of extravagant dresses you might see on ladies' day at the races.

'Shall we go in and get a drink? Couple of bottles of champagne would be nice hey?' I said sarcastically to Emma 'my treat, don't you worry'.

'You know what? I have a feeling they might, *might* not let us in'.

'Really? What makes you say that? I mean, I can see why they wouldn't let you in, but *me*? I'm on their social and intellectual level'.

'Well, it might just be me, but it looks as if you might have fallen in the sea with all your clothes on. At least, that's what the litres of water seeping from your rotten trainers would suggest'.

'I thank you for your honesty. Shall we retire to the hostel?'.

'We shall'.

She then linked my arm in an eccentric 'we're just off to the opera don't you know?' sort of way and we headed back to *'Noosa Backpackers'* hostel. As we did though, I caught a glimpse of my reflection in a little boutique window and witnessed the extent of the rain on my fragile appearance. In my soaking, white t-shirt, I looked like a drunken, young slapper just fresh from a wet t-shirt competition. Only a few hours previously, I was smartly dressed to the extent that I may have even managed to get into one of the bars without drawing too much attention to myself. That is of course if they hadn't noticed my overused trainers whose white surface was now a kind of pale brown having been worn every day for the past four months. I dare say they were beginning to 'pong' a little too. But apart from that, I must say I looked rather dashing and was keen to explore all that this lovely town had to offer. Then I felt the full fury and unpredictable nature of, well, nature.

Named after the Aboriginal word for 'shade', Noosa was a relatively late developer in terms of tourism, surviving for most of the 20th century as a small, local fishing town. It appears that, like many Australian towns, it first sprang to life as a logging community with the population booming throughout the gold rush. Surrounded by beautiful sea and glorious mountains, it is easy to see why its popularity grew. In the 1920s, its famous 'Noosa Surf Life Saving Club' was developed and remains an integral part of the town to this day. As Emma and I walked along the coastal path on this first day, the waterfront appeared to be a bubbly and exciting place with many surfers and sea-kayakers enjoying the secluded and protected bay.

In any other town, this would have been the main attraction and selling point, but not Noosa for it is surrounded by acres of sublime national park. Springing up from the volcanic mountains, the park covers the rocky headland with a blend of dense rainforest and native Australian bush scrub, just metres away from the town itself. Having read about this previously, I was concerned that the town may intrude upon these natural delights. However, I was pleasantly surprised.

Thankfully, the unique landscape has been recognised for its natural beauty and was declared a town reserve as early as 1879 before becoming an official National Park in 1930. How lucky is that?! In 1879 the town's folk were so forward in their thinking that, instead of indulging naively in its splendour; they decided to protect it from the concrete chain of destruction we now refer to as development. If they hadn't been innovative, would the park exist today? I doubt it.

As Emma and I continued along the coastal path towards the park entrance, I turned and looked back at the town admiring the modest, simplicity it exuded. Just like the first settlers, it appeared that the modern council were determined to promote the harmonious existence of a thriving cosmopolitan town alongside the park. I read later that, in order to achieve this they have introduced a population cap of just 50,000 and some incredibly strict height and design restrictions for proposed building work. With an emphasis on conservation, self-sustaining and recycling, the town is simply angelic in modern terms.

Five minutes later and we were entering the mouth of the deep bush and anticipating the delights that lay ahead. Unfortunately, the past couple of months had seen us develop the undesirable talent for getting lost rather easily. Of course, the blame was mostly put on my head and so on this occasion I relieved myself of the responsibility and handed the map to Emma.

'Okay Ems, lets see you put the lady stereotype to shame and navigate us somewhere exciting' I said.

'Fine Johnny, I will. Let's see' she said taking the map from my grasp and looking confusedly at what it had to offer. 'According to this there's a place called 'Dolphin Point' –as we were too lazy at Fraser Island, perhaps we should go investigate?'.

'Ah yes, but is it called Dolphin Point because there's loads of dolphins? Or is it just that the cliff is in the shape of a giant dolphin?'.

'I don't know but it kinda makes me want to investigate more'.

I thought about this statement for a while to work out whether it was genius or merely idiotic. Then with a shrug I said 'let's go for it'.

So setting off in a nice, freshly ironed white t-shirt and a pair of shorts, I started marching behind Emma and into the depths of the wilderness ahead. After a couple of early wrong turns (which I mocked to a huge extent) we finally reached the coastal path and decided to follow it all the way to Dolphin Point. Although the bush was thick, the pristine sea was still visible crashing into the cliff below our feet as sparkles of sunlight flickered through the canopy. About twenty minutes passed of fierce uphill climbing to a peak, leaving me so breathless that I was relatively unresponsive when spotting the spider. It is strange – upon arrival in Australia, my obsession of checking for spiders and snakes under the toilet seat was stringent, but by now it had completely fizzled out. Encounters with these animals had been so rare that I had simply forgotten that they were there at all. But not now. At this point, the memories and stories I had read pre-departure were now all coming back to haunt me. Across the path there was a web. A web that I had almost inadvertently head-butted just like on that first night at Lady Northcote camp. With a startled look I jumped back into Emma who was now following.

'What the hell are you doing?!' she shouted as I stood all over her feet.
'Don't be alarmed now Emma, please be very calm.' I replied in a whisper.
'Be calm about what?'.
'About fifty centimetres in front of us is the largest spider in the history of the world. It makes that one at your camp look like a midget's offspring'.
Emma reacted well to this news and after a brief spell of hyperventilating we plucked up the courage to inspect the oversized arachnid. The web was huge, covering the entire width of the three metre path with its owner sitting proudly in the centre seemingly unbothered by our close examination. Realising the spider was not going to move, we ventured into the bush so as not to disturb it anymore and continued on our route.

Happy that we had survived that obstacle and adamant there would be a group of dolphins performing tricks for our amusement at our destination, we continued to climb the path towards the headland. At one point, to our surprise, a couple of wild turkeys ran out in front of us – well, I did say Australia was diverse didn't I?

On our right we then passed a small wooden shelter in which about ten other ramblers were huddling beneath the roofed porch. This seemed rather strange to me since the weather seemed to be quite agreeable and so, instead of questioning their behaviour, I simply choose to ignore it. This was a decision I would live to regret. Unfortunately for us, the others seemed to have consulted the weather forecast but Emma and I continued into the wilderness with an air of ignorant bliss.

And then the heavens opened. Really – it was just like that. The weather had been fabulous up to this point – with clear blue skies dominating the horizon. But now, with no sign of warning, this had been replaced by thick, demonic clouds. As if to add insult to injury the rain was the heaviest, thickest and wettest I had ever experienced. It was as if the entire Earth had been turned upside down and the full weight of the ocean was falling down from the sky. Within ten seconds my white t-shirt was completely see-through (Emma was thankful she had worn a blue one) as I stood with my arms out-stretched peering into the clouds above. I bet God was having a right good laugh at me – along with all the guys who had taken shelter and conveniently forgotten to inform us. By this point, the water was now streaming through my hair and following the grooves down my face and into my eyes. The rain was coming down with such force it actually started to hurt. I looked at Emma and she looked back at me – we had said nothing so far, just simply stopped in disbelief at our bad luck. Her hair was stuck to her face, her clothes clinging to the outline of her body as I imagined mine were too – then, without any warning we both started laughing, although it was difficult to hear over the monstrous noise caused by the falling rain.

'Shall we go back to the shelter?' I shouted once the laughing had subsided.

'I'm not sure there's much point – we can't possibly get any wetter, can we?' she replied.

'Ha-ha, I don't think we could! To Dolphin Point!'.

With that, we continued on our quest with water squelching in our shoes but adventure and intrigue in our (damp) hearts. It was not in vain however as we finally reached Dolphin Point with a satisfying feeling of success – we had taken on nature and conquered it! While the other walkers remained huddled and beaten in warmth, we were here, we had succeeded, we were the elite! Not that there was that much to take in – the sheets of rain were so incredibly thick that visibility was reduced to a mere few metres and besides, my eyes were blurred from all the water anyway. We couldn't even see the ocean below, let alone any dolphins. Everything around me had been reduced to a grey smudge. I tried getting closer to the edge but, fearing the fierce wind would throw me off the cliff like a leaf in the way of a freight train, I withdrew. But it didn't really matter. We had overcome fierce creatures, the overgrown wilderness and the torrid weather to reach our destination just like the earliest explorers in Australia. Even in the pouring rain, this gave me a warm feeling inside as I got a tiny of glimpse of the mountain task they had faced in this incredible land.

Noosa had provided the perfect gateway for such an experience. Walking back through the park towards the town soaking wet, I really did get the feeling that the two worked perfectly in unison. They complemented each other – here on the doorstep of this glorious, untouched national park was a town that mirrored its elegance and symbolized the magnificence of human ambition. Then, as we left the park and entered the town, the rain stopped as abruptly as it had begun. I attempted to dry my eyes with my soaking t-shirt. Failing badly, I looked at the glamorous bar in front of us with envy, turned to Emma and said
'Shall we go in and get a drink? Couple of bottles of champagne would be nice hey?'.

CHAPTER 23

Two hours after leaving Noosa, our Greyhound bus sped along The Bruce Highway and my eyes caught a sudden startling glare in the distance. It had been over a month since I'd last seen a major city, so the sudden dominance of the mirrored skyscrapers on the horizon was somewhat overwhelming. It filled my heart with excitement as it had on that first daunting night in Sydney. That was nearly five months ago now but still the thought of city living appealed to me greatly.

Compared with our other Australian journeys, this one between Brisbane and Noosa was so short I can't really remember it. If I were in England, I could have travelled from London to Birmingham in such a time, but in this enormous country the distance seemed minuscule. But that is the Australian way and I found myself being taken in by it. The thought of driving three thousand miles in order to get a pint of milk, a can of *7-Up* and a packet of chocolate covered *Hobnobs*, no longer seemed like a daunting one. You see, they don't think anything of driving such great distances because, well, they have to in order to get anywhere. It is a necessity and one I was beginning to adapt to. I thought to myself 'when I get home, I'm going to do a day trip to John O'Groats. No problem. I might even pop to Landsend on the way home'. Seriously though, this type of thinking would never faze or seem even relatively abnormal to an Australian as most of them travel that sort of distance just driving to work in the morning. Still, it was nice to have such a short journey but one which resulted in a vastly contrasting environment.

So far as a backpacker I had learned never to pass the chance of a free meal. Eat as much as you possibly can because you never know how long it'll be before your next feeding. This was rule number one in my handbook. The second thing I had learned was that a friend of a friend's parent's, great uncle's, daughter's, half-brother's, step-father's niece could provide essential accommodation in certain situations. Mel had taught me that when she had gone to stay with LJ's grandparents. I on the other hand was not quite that extreme, but still decided to delve into the family tree and search for a long lost relative. In reality however, my first cousin Frances was now residing in Brisbane and so I decided to give her a call. She wasn't a distant relative and although I hadn't seen her for a while (well, she had been living on the other side of the world!) our families were generally quite close so I didn't feel awkward asking her for help. Besides, I knew from chatting to her mum that she had been a keen backpacker, so would be sympathetic towards our needs.

Thankfully I was right. Having not seen her since I was fifteen, I was slightly concerned that recognising her would prove slightly tricky but luckily the uncanny resemblance between her and her mother was still very apparent and we spotted each other immediately. Having exchanged pleasantries and many thanks for letting us stay, we jumped into her car and she whisked us off to her lovely apartment over-looking the river. We had our own bedroom, bathroom and even washing machine.
'From my experience of travelling, the thing you miss most is just having the chance to relax in a bit of privacy and not being woken up by loads of people in the morning' she said handing over a set of keys 'so I want you guys to feel right at home – come and go as you please and just chill out'.

For the first time since leaving camp, I was able to unpack my backpack. This may sound like a rather mundane thing to do but the idea of not living out of a bag was pure bliss. Plus, if you are like me, you will have packed far too much stuff. Thus, not wanting to repack your bag too often, you will have made use of the 5 or so things located towards the top of the bag. Emptying it into a wardrobe did not just relieve the mental strain the bag had put on my life but also allowed me to discover hundreds of items of clothing I had simply forgotten about. It was like unwrapping hundreds of presents at Christmas and being momentarily ecstatic before realising it was the pair of socks your gran had knitted last year that you'd worked so hard to conveniently lose.

Having emptied that burden, I then jumped into my own private shower – complete with cleaning products – before retiring back to my room and jumping excitedly onto my own, personal, comfortable mattress and double bed. Ahhh, it was amazing. But even more amazing is how small trivial things - such as a mattress not filled with jagged shaped rocks - could boost morale. Having given all my clothes (including my trainers) a good clean in the washing machine, I grabbed a glass of wine and went and sat on the balcony for dinner.

This was the first time in ages that I'd had a real meal cooked in a lovely, backpacker and bacteria-free kitchen. But being able to enjoy eating it in privacy was the main luxury. Emma and I must have looked like starving children as our thin hands stretched across the spread and we stuffed food down our throats like there was no tomorrow. I ate until I couldn't physically fit anymore food inside my mouth, then sat back, grabbed my wine and admired the view across the city. The sun was moving down behind the skyline, silhouetting the buildings against the horizon. Frances was very relaxed and appeared genuinely happy to have us here as guests as we discussed encounters from our travels so far. She had loved the backpacker experience, and in essence still experienced it by moving from place to place throughout the country on a regular basis. Like the rest of my father's family, she was originally from Ireland – a tiny little, country town (although it still managed to fit in fourteen pubs!) called Ballybay in County Monaghan. This lovely apartment overlooking Brisbane seemed like a world away from that of rural Eire.

'So, how come you decided to move away from Ireland?' I asked.

'Ah well you know, there's only so much of it you can take. I never really planned to stay away that long' she said thoughtfully. Her accent, although still detectable had faded with a touch of Aussie twang coming through 'I just wanted to go and try something different. But I fell in love with this country. There's so much diversity and I suppose I just wanted to experience it all'.

'I can appreciate that – we've been here for nearly half a year now and I only feel like we've touched the surface'.

'The weather's a little better than Ireland too. So where are you guys heading next?'.

'Well, we've got a night booked at Surfers Paradise and then on to Byron Bay for a few days'.

'Byron Bay is lovely but you've got to be very careful. There's lots of drugs and some dangerous stuff going on'.

'Really? Like what?'.

'Well, I was down there for New Year and I got my drink spiked. There are lots of drug dealers on the streets too'.

Many people we had met along the way had explained about all the cannabis going around at Byron Bay – they called it a 'mini-Amsterdam'. But it all seemed to be treated rather lightly. However, listening to Frances' story about it did make me slightly more wary.

After dinner, Frances gave us a guided tour of the neighbourhood. The gardens nearby were all perfectly manicured and streets completely litter-free. As we walked along the riverside we encountered a number of beautifully-kept parks intertwined between the buildings. It was a Sunday evening and loads of families were enjoying the last weekend sun by using the public barbeques and playing cricket. As we went further along, a large group of teenagers were having a game of touch rugby on a small patch of grass. This was the idyllic picture I had had of Australia before I'd left England – one of enjoying the outdoors. Here I was, in a city, which seemed to gleam with a real sense of community. Not that all Australia is filled with this, but I was happy I'd found it somewhere. This was a place where, in my eyes, nobody even knew what a television or *Playstation* was, and *that* was a lovely thought.

As I stared enviously at this perfect way of life, Frances announced that she was heading home as she had a very early start in the morning. Emma and I however had nothing to get up for – we could sleep for as long as we desired. For this reason, we decided to make our way into the city and work out what Brisbane really had to offer. Just a few metres from the apartment block was a taxi ferry stop, so we made our way there in the hope of hitching a boat ride into the city itself. However, upon arrival we noticed there was a pontoon walkway floating on the river and leading the entire way to the city. It was fantastic, purely for the reason that it meant getting lost would prove absolutely impossible – even for us!

'Forget maps, compasses and St Christopher medals! This is the greatest navigational invention of *all time*. A heavenly floating path taking us *exactly* where we want to go - superb!' I said in admiration of the bridge that had so conveniently helped our depleting navigational skills.

Perhaps it wasn't exactly heavenly, but it was an enjoyable walk into the city on top of the rocking waves, which we shared with numerous joggers and people on rollerblades. Although the evening was getting quite late, I was still keen to explore the city and found that it gave off a rather European feel. Smaller than Melbourne and Sydney, it wasn't built in the standard grid formation and in contrast was rather sporadic. Still, there were some similarities with the unoriginal street names making an appearance. Walking along 'George Street' I even spotted a 'Little George Street'. God, their creativity knows no bounds! But that's where the comparisons end. Indeed, the random distribution of the city was rather pleasant and made me feel much more at home, if not a little more vulnerable to getting lost.

Along the main shopping precinct, there were a number of people all making their way towards a 'traditional English pub'. It seemed rather lively in there but the rest of the city was surprisingly subdued. In fact, once away from the main centre there weren't many people around at all which seemed strange. Following the curvature of the river, we came to a number of futuristic, high-rise buildings all housing some spectacularly rich businesses. At the base there were a few restaurants which were being enjoyed by a number of locals, but that was about it for life. To say a city is quiet and peaceful is rather unexpected to say the least, however this only added to the great appeal of it. This was a real place – a cultural city for normal people to *live* in. Not a holiday resort or entertainment capital. Everything in it had been done for the benefit of its residents and not for tourist appeal. It was not covered in glossy paper or flashing lights and because of this, it was oozing with charm and character. Having grabbed a quick drink, we wandered back to our home and I was happy in the knowledge that I was experiencing the true Australia as one of its own.

The next morning I woke naturally of my own accord. I was not disturbed by anyone snoring, blowing their nose or doing yoga. That, I tell you, was a bloody brilliant feeling. Emma said she had slept well too and so, full of energy, we grabbed a load of fliers and assessed what we could do that day. One thing in particular stuck out – Australia Zoo – a must-do by all accounts. During their time on camp, Sian had told Emma that it was one of the best days out she had experienced. Although I doubted this somewhat, I was still intrigued to get close to a Tasmanian Devil and stroke a Kangaroo, so duly agreed to sample its cultural offerings.

Having had such a great sleep however, it was disappointing to see that our timekeeping was just as poor as ever – a point I reiterated to Emma as we sprinted through the streets of Brisbane towards the train station. Exhausted and sweaty but ultimately relieved, we stumbled into the station just in time to buy our tickets and jump on the train. But it wasn't on the departures board. This seemed a little peculiar, so I approached the desk in order to investigate why I had just run like a lunatic for a non-existent train.
'Umm, excuse me, I just wanted to enquire as to the whereabouts of the ten twenty-three train to Australia Zoo' I said politely approaching the enquiries window.
'What's that mate?'.
'The ten twenty-three to Australia Zoo, it seems to be invisible'.
'There's no ten twenty-three on a Monday – you must be wanting the eleven thirty-one'.
'No no, there's definitely a ten twenty-three – look' I said holding my timetable up to the window and consulting my watch 'although, if it does in fact exist, it'll be gone by now'.
'Yeah, but having last year's timetable doesn't really help, does it you silly POM?' he said laughing his head off at what an idiot *I'd* been. Apparently the tourist board of Brisbane don't see it as necessary to put an up-to-date timetable into their fliers – instead they just pick one at random from the past couple of years and hope that'll do.

As you can imagine, Emma's face had a slightly annoyed look to it when I explained she had just sprinted an incredibly long distance, with a backpack on, for no reason whatsoever. Well it would have if it hadn't been so red and sweaty. But, just in case she felt the need to snap, I decided to remind her of the hundreds of children in the less economically developed world who have to run hundreds of miles each day *just* for water, which *my* cousin was supplying *her* with, free of charge. The guilt trip worked perfectly! Besides, I had managed to find us a good $35 ticket deal which seemed rather reasonable in comparison to the others that were being touted around.

Originally opened by the passionate reptile scientist and enthusiast Bob Irwin in 1970, the park solely focused on the care and rehabilitation of unwell or injured animals around the surrounding area. However, as the park's popularity grew throughout the years, it subsequently expanded dramatically allowing it to encompass many different species from all parts of the world. Bob named the park 'Beerwah Reptile Park' but in 1991, under the ownership of his son and equally enthusiastic enthusiast Steve Irwin, it became known as 'Australia Zoo'. Now there's patriotism for you. It has seen a rapid expansion throughout the years going from a mere four acres to an area now covering over seventy-five, incorporating large roaming areas for animals, as well as a stadium aptly named the 'Crocoseum'.

So there you have it – Australia Zoo in a nutshell, but standing outside the modest entrance I couldn't help feel slightly let-down by its modesty. To be honest, for something that had been named 'Australia Tourist Attraction of the Year 2003-04' by the Australian tourist board, it just seemed, well, a little like a wooden shed. Behind these doors, could there *really* be that much wonder and excitement? Upon walking through the turnstiles I was happy to discover that, despite its shabby entrance, the park *is* indeed a TARDIS. In fact, the amount of stuff they managed to stuff in was somewhat overwhelming.

Looking at the huge, fold-out map our $35 had provided us, we decided to make our way immediately to the Crocoseum as there was a show which had just begun. Approaching the massive 5000 capacity arena, I was full of anticipation and excited to see another saltwater crocodile on this antipodean tour. The man conducting the spectacle that day was very enthusiastic and issued strict warnings on the severity of interacting with such monstrous creatures, saying things like 'now listen here goys. Don't get yourself anywhere near a croc, because if it grabs you and starts a wrestling match, you'll lose'. Sound advice I thought, but not the sort I suspected was particularly necessary. The only thing was, he then backed up this story by telling a graphic tale about how a particularly large crocodile had gone for a bite at his wedding tackle and he had wrestled it to the ground, tied it up and then shouted 'who's the daddy?!' at the top of his voice. There seemed to be a bit of contradiction there. Apart from that, the show was pretty similar to the one we had witnessed in Cairns, so we slipped out quietly so as not to cause offence.

Instead of following the map, we decided instead to simply follow our instincts. However, it was impossible to escape the cheap (but actually incredibly expensive) merchandise. Everywhere we went, there were tacky talking dolls of Steve Irwin, his wife Terri and their daughter Bindi. But even worse was the department store which had every conceivable item known to man with Steve Irwin's face printed on it. Grant would have been in heaven. Having said that, the park did have an underlying educational theme and a good moral message. Not forgetting its origins, there was a strong emphasis on conservation and respect for nature, but I couldn't help feel that they could have achieved this in a somewhat more dignified manner.

Trying to escape the plague of commercialism, we went indoors to examine all the different varieties of poisonous snakes I had studied before departing England, which seemed to make them even more lethal in my mind. Having then calmed the afternoon down by watching a mother wombat wander around its pen at an incredibly leisurely pace, we came across the much talked-about Tasmanian Devil. Peering into its enclosure I witnessed what can only be described as a small, black piglet running frantically around in circles. It was possibly the most bizarre thing I'd ever seen, but then, aren't most creatures in Australia?

Having scanned over the dingoes and camels, we walked amongst the tame and somewhat nosey kangaroos, before heading towards the elephants for feeding time. This was a classic example of how this park had developed from a small reptile reserve into a miniature Noah's Ark. Even more surprising than the sheer size (and greediness) of the elephants, was whom we bumped into in the queue. Surrounded by children, we were slightly embarrassed lining up just to hand an elephant half an apple, but thankfully we had spotted another group of young adults and made our way towards them. Strength in numbers! But to my shock, I recognised one of their faces – it was Rich. We hadn't seen him since The Grand Prix in Melbourne, but here we were on The Sunshine Coast, feeding the same elephant. It amazed me that, in such a large country in which I knew only a handful of people I could see a familiar face – 'Gosh, it's a small world isn't it?!'. As per normal, we exchanged stories and asked about the rest of the *World Challenge* crew. He informed us that Harry had flown home and a number of others had remained at camp having been offered paid positions. Since he was travelling north, I was anxious to see what was in store for us down the coast.

'What's Byron like mate, we've heard there are loads of drugs?'.

'Yeah there is – I was there for about thirty seconds before being offered pot. There's a great bar there though called 'Cheeky Monkeys' so check it out.'.

'Fantastic stuff, that's what I like to hear. How about Surfers Paradise though?'.

'Hmmm, well there's two good things about Surfers – the first is getting yourself a nice hotel room in one of the skyscrapers and watching the sun rise across the pacific. It's the most incredible view ever'.

'Wow, it does sound amazing – but a little out of our budget. What's the second great thing?'.

'Leaving'.

This had generally been the vibe most travellers had given, but I was keen to pass judgement myself and go there with an open-mind. Besides, we still had to navigate our way back to Brisbane. Having left the park and arrived at the train station, I looked at Emma and she looked back, nervously.

'Look, it can't be *that* difficult. We'll just have to listen to every announcement really carefully' I said.

'Okay, if we both listen, we can't possibly go wrong' she said, trying to convince herself.

Twenty minutes later we found ourselves sprinting off that train and over a footbridge at the next station. My back arched under the weight of my Terri-Irwin-doll-filled backpack as I ran in what seemed like a straight line, taking poor Emma with me. Confused and disorientated, we ran through some kind of tunnel and were presented with another train. But with no time to gauge its destination, I took a leap of faith, grabbed Emma and pulled us both aboard seconds before the doors shut. It was like a scene from *Indiana Jones*. Relieved we had made the connecting train but completely breathless,

I slumped down against the carriage doors. It was then, looking around at the surroundings, everything began to seem rather too familiar. I watched Emma for a second and caught the exact second this realisation dawned upon her. We were on the same train as before. In the confusion, we must have doubled back on ourselves and ended up in exactly the same seats we were in only moments previously. The rest of the commuters must have thought we were absolutely off our minds or just training for some sort of mad fun run. Out of pure frustration, we both laughed. But such a story wouldn't be complete without a subtle touch of irony. As we gathered at the door of the train, preparing to run for another connection at the next station, a voice came over the loudspeaker and announced in a voice tinged with constipation 'passengers, the next stop is Brisbane. Brisbane the next stop. Please alight here for Brisbane'. We hadn't needed to change trains at all. This, yet again, resulted in an even bigger bout of laughter and summed up our navigational skills perfectly.

Frances' oven had broken throughout the day – nothing to do with me you understand – so we grabbed a Greek take-away and ate it on the balcony once again. It was pretty good living this high life. Out of the blue, I then received a phone call from Grant saying that he was currently in Brisbane. Keen to catch up with my old pal and looking for an excuse to sample the delights of Brisbane's finest nightlife, I got into my newly ironed clothes, jumped on the pontoon and walked into town. Although Emma wasn't too keen, I had convinced her to come along as well and listen to all of our reminiscent camp stories.

Since leaving him two months previously, Grant had participated in a five-day surf tour of the east coast just north of Sydney and if he hadn't told us, his clothes certainly did. His hair was now long and deep blonde in colour as he stood in front of me sporting a 'Byron Bay' vest, long board shorts and a pair of flip-flops. He had been completely 'Australianised', but I have to admit, it suited him and he looked very happy.
'Bloody hell, long time no see, how's it going mate?' he said in a thick Aussie accent.
'Yeah not bad mate, just went to the zoo today, it was pretty good. You're looking, well, very Australian to say the least'.

'Really? Ah jeez, thanks mate! Surf tour was awesome! Let's go for a walk and I'll tell you about it'.

Since the night was young, it seemed logical to take a little stroll before having a couple of beverages, plus Frances had recommended some really exciting parts of the city to check out. We walked towards 'Southbank' which I had been reliably informed was the entertainment centre. However, before getting there I was shocked when turning a corner to discover the 'city beach'. No prizes for working out what it was. Seriously, it was a beach, with a large swimming pool (lagoon), right in the middle of the city. It was a vibrant oasis giving life to the concrete desert around us. I had never seen anything like it – the way the energetic colours contrasted against the dull grey buildings surrounding it was superb and only went to increase my affection for the city.

Southbank, as I was expecting, was a lovely place full of lively fountains and extravagant walkways, but was far more low-key than its Sydney and Melbourne counterparts. Besides, there are only so many fountains you can take so, stopping Grant in mid-sentence I said 'beer time I think'. Emma agreed rather enthusiastically as we turned on our heels, picked up the pace and ended up at *'The Pig and Whistle'* - the traditional English pub we had seen the previous evening. Now, I have been to a few English pubs in my time, a number of which I would describe as 'traditional' and this did not fit the bill. As I sat drinking my *VB*, I looked around and wondered which part of this pub made it traditionally English. Ahhh, there it was - a Union Jack flag. It was British, not English, but I supposed it'd do.
'So tell me more about this Surfing Safari Grant, where did you start from again?'.
'Just north of Sydney mate, then it was five days on a bus up to Byron Bay. We stopped off at loads of little beaches and slept on the sand, it was awesome!'.
'Really, I imagine you're an expert surfer now then 'dude'?'.
'Yeah, can just about stand up on the board which isn't too bad I suppose. I was even trying some turns by the end'.
'Did you see about that guy who got eaten by a great white just off the coast of Perth the other day?' I said, just to scare him a little.
'Really? Ah well, looks like I got away lucky then! How's your trip been?'.

'Yeah pretty good, Fraser Island and The Whitsundays were as amazing as ever. Emma's been getting us lost loads though, haven't you Ems?' I said looking at her with a grin 'she even made us run in circles around a train today'.

'Ha-ha, you two are a bit mental, I don't know how you manage to get anywhere'.

'Me neither mate, me neither. But, we always seem to, which is nice and somewhat relieving'.

'Any word from Sian?' Grant said causally to Emma. I think he still had a little thing for her as she was the girl that got away.

'I spoke to her the other day, she went home a few weeks ago and is getting herself a job' she replied.

'A job?! Jeez, kinda makes you realise how lucky we are out here' Grant said.

'Yeah, but we've worked for it guys, remember the hours of minimal wage labourer we put in to pay for this trip?' I chipped in 'I propose a toast – 'to making the most of the time we have left''.

And to that, we banged our glasses of Australian lager together in true, traditional English style.

The next morning we rose early to pack and say goodbye to Frances. It had been so wonderful just living a normal life, if only for a couple of days. I had wanted to invite Grant to stay, but not wanting to burden Frances with the pressure of three dirty backpackers, he had stayed in a hostel.

Our bus to Surfers Paradise was leaving in the afternoon, but it still left us a few hours to sample our final Brisbane delight. Resentfully, Emma and I heaved our backpacks on, walked down to the ferry port and caught a boat ride into the city. Finding Grant tucking into his morning bagel, I suddenly realised that this was the last time I was going to get to see him in Australia so we decided to cap it with the crème de la crème of tours and sample the very thing that puts Brisbane on the world map – *Castlemaine Beer*.

Since I was a child I can remember seeing bottles of *XXXX*, which says a lot for its worldwide stature but probably more about my upbringing. The credit however, has to go not to an Australian but to two Irish immigrant brothers named Nicholas and Edward Fitzgerald. Being stereotypically Irish, they were both fond of sampling an alcoholic beverage now and again and were reportedly shocked by the lack of quality and depth in the Australian beer trade. Being the sons of an experienced brewer, they combined their expertise and alcoholic desires (what greater incentive could there be?) in creating this unique recipe and introduced the natives to the delights of the Irish culture. After years of travelling, they finally settled in Brisbane, built the brewery and named their new beer 'Castlemaine' after their home town in Ireland. I like to imagine that, after this, they sat in a couple of rocking chairs on a veranda, looked out across the beautiful pacific and had a bloody good piss-up. Even so, I'm sure in their beer-induced optimistic state, they still couldn't imagine the huge global success their company was going to eventually have. But here it was, over one hundred years later and still dominating the world market.

So for me it was not just a case of getting to sample some free beer, it was about being able to sample a tiny slice of Australian economic history. It was a symbol of two brothers who immigrated to an unknown, hostile land and made a success out of their lives. Okay, it was because I heard they gave you free beer at the end of the tour, but the other things sounded impressive didn't they?

I was mightily impressed by the visitor centre which was modern, sleek and full of some very insightful information and more facts than you could ever wish to know about beer. The tour itself was incredibly lively - full of movies and mechanical statues that moved backwards and forwards, performing the same motion endlessly. I felt like saying 'come on, you've been hammering the same spot for the past five years. No wonder that barrel's nowhere near getting finished' but sadly I refrained, concerned that if caught chatting to a moving manikin, questions might get asked. Our tour guide Paul (or Mr Castlemaine as we liked to call him) was very interesting too, managing to answer all my questions concerning hops flawlessly. Then, having been to the factory floor and witnessed more alcohol per square metre than an alcoholic's glove compartment, we went to the bar. Included in the price were four free drinks, which was incredibly reasonable since the ticket only cost $16. However, it being only 11am and having had very little breakfast (not that I'm making excuses) those four (premium) pints rather caught me off guard and the rest of the morning was a slight blur.

According to Emma, I had a great time and was rather emotional when it came time to say farewell to Grant. This was our final goodbye and it was conducted with a strong (but manly) hug. Our buses left at the same time and followed each other out of the city, then, coming to a crossroad, his turned north and we went south. Next stop - Surfers Paradise.

CHAPTER 24

I looked at Emma in despair, the weight of my backpack preventing me from getting up off the ground.
'Can you stand up and look over this fence? Please tell me there's not a lake there' I said to her, gripping our map tightly in my hand.
'Why? Oh my god, yes there is' she replied taking a look. 'What does that mean then?'.
'Well Emma, remember thirty minutes ago when I said 'I think the hostel's up this street'?'.
'Why do I have a feeling I know what's coming next?'.
'Well, it means I was wrong. Wrong on a remarkable scale as it happens. Which is really annoying, but not in the least bit surprising. You probably don't want to be bored with the details and the severity of the situation might just depress you, so just follow me and I'm sure we'll be there before nightfall'.

Arriving about an hour before this point, the tourist information had reliably informed us that our hostel *'Backpackers in Paradise'* was within walking distance and even drew it on a map. For the first fifteen minutes, I had set off confidently with Emma marching behind, until we went round a corner and I announced in arrogant confidence 'and if we turn this corner, I think you'll find our hostel right in front of us'. The only thing in front of us was the bus station again. I had taken us round in a circle. Mind you, that seemed a minimal inconvenience compared to the massive detour I had taken us on this time. Nevertheless, my sense of direction had abandoned me yet again and I found myself swallowing my pride and asking for directions. Eventually we arrived at the hostel and settled into the dorm we were sharing with six others.

Approaching Surfers Paradise on the bus had been a strange experience as it looked just like Brisbane had on the journey from Noosa. With the sun reflecting off the great, mirrored towers, I had been given the most remarkable sense of déjà vu. Chatting to the bus driver about this, he reliably informed me that many people say the same thing and some even come off the highway thinking that it is in fact Brisbane. But once you get into the town, it has a completely different feel.

Whereas Brisbane was a city built for real life, Surfers Paradise was the exact opposite. Yes, it looked like a city from afar, but once up close the skyscrapers all reveal themselves as a series of characterless hotels. Located along the seafront, they even block out the afternoon sun, bathing the beach in cold darkness and leaving it empty. Oh the irony.

It is a manufactured holiday resort, built purely for the tourist industry - catering for women in pink limousines and men with 'L' plates strapped round their genitals. In the town, there is a *Hard Rock Café*, a *McDonalds* and a shop called *'Condom Kingdom'*. But, the most amazing thing is that it's completely unique. This is why everyone talks about it. Throughout all other countries in the world, especially ones with such a great climate, there are large towns like this dotted all along the coast. But Australia has managed to pack it all into one large resort, thus allowing the rest of the country to live relatively tacky-free. It acts as a giant sponge, absorbing all the bar crawls, stag do's and topless women for miles. For this reason, Surfers Paradise should be embraced by all Australians! It takes the pressure off all other towns by acting as the sole distributor of cheap cocktails and vulgar merchandise. In other words, Surfers is the 'one night stand' of towns – people get obscenely drunk and think it's the most beautiful place on Earth, but ultimately by morning they realise it was nothing more than an alcohol-induced illusion and so leave as quickly as possible. Needless to say, I was eager to give it a go.

Our hostel was called *Backpackers in Paradise* – I think it must have been a sarcastic title. In comparison to other hostels, it was incredibly dirty, old and rundown. Even the bathroom sink didn't really work and, as we soon discovered, anything being 'cooked' in the kitchen needed to be microwaveable or fit into a shabby toaster. But, in the spirit of things we got on with it, showered under a dribbling tap and made our way downstairs for the 'club crawl' – well, if you're going to hit Surfers Paradise at night, you've got to do it in style, haven't you?

It wasn't quite as cringing as a pink limo, but the double-decker open-top bus did have a certain amount of 'Benidorm panache' about it. The next three minutes were spent dodging various drunken bodies obstructing the road before arriving at the main part of town. Since we were only staying for one night, it seemed silly to try and explore the whole town by ourselves, so we had opted for the organised tour as a way to maximise our fun. Plus, for our twenty dollars we were offered a free photo and 'key-chain' making refusal impossible.

It was quite early on, but the town was already alive with over-enthusiastic Brits, all wanting to be my friend. I couldn't help thinking that they'd peaked a little too soon. In terms of cleanliness the town kept to traditional Australian style and was immaculate. But apart from that, there was nothing incredibly special about it and it may just have been a typical English town centre on a Friday night. The weather was much warmer though and, because of the lovely paved, clean streets, I felt I could have wandered around barefoot. However, for a number of obvious reasons, I opted not to.

There were loads of bars in this part of town, each with their own unique theme and trying to pull you in with tempting drinks offers – as the great Oscar Wilde once said *'I can resist everything, except temptation'*. I believe he said that with me in mind. Anyway, we first of all found ourselves in a bar harnessing an American West theme, with swinging saloon doors and even a few old drunk men propping up the bar seemingly oblivious to the world around them. I pulled the free drinks vouchers from the bar crawl out of my pocket, leaned over the bar and order a bottle of *Tooheys*.

'What's that you're drinking there boy?' someone said in a strong Irish accent from behind me.

'Tooheys mate, you in?' I replied hoping to make some new friends for the night.

'Too right I am! Get this man another' he shouted over to the barman 'don't want you going thirsty now. I'm Reggie and this is my friend Simon' he pointed to a shy looking guy standing behind him.

'Nice to meet you lads, so where are you from?'.

'I'm from Ireland; I thought the accent might give me a way!' Reggie shouted over the cheers that had just arisen from a group watching the rugby in the corner 'Simon's absolutely mental – I met him along the way, he's from Denmark. I think'.

They both seemed interesting so we grabbed a few more beers and continued to chat over the very loud music. It turned out that Reggie was actually called 'DJ Reggie'. He was a wedding DJ from somewhere in Ireland. Oh and I also discovered towards the end of the night that his name wasn't Reggie at all. That one was never explained to me properly though. Simon was indeed Danish and indeed crazy. Not in an axe-wielding maniac sort of way, but a kind of eccentric way – the best type of crazy if you ask me. I got the feeling he just wanted to make friends as he was travelling alone and Emma and I were happy to oblige.

    As the social lubricant within our blood started to thicken, the flow of conversation got much easier. Before long, our group had grown as more people came to join the festivities until I heard someone shout those dreaded words – 'Tequila anyone?'. I don't really remember much else from the night, although the snippets of memory I have managed to retrieve are particularly amusing ones. For example, I recall Reggie stripping to his underpants and running through the streets. I loved it, for in that one moment, we had managed to capture the true essence of Surfers Paradise. Later, I'm pretty sure we went onto a club and I fear my drunken dancing may have made an appearance – an expected event for most men on a night out, but a shocking one to think back on nonetheless. I also remember Simon claiming that every single band on the sound system were Danish.

'You hear this?' he would say.

'Yeah, it's quite loud. Quite difficult to miss it really'.
'They are from Denmark, we are very proud of them'.
'It's Oasis. They're from Manchester!'.
'No, no. They started off in Denmark though'.
'I'm pretty sure the Gallagher brothers aren't in the slightest bit Danish, Simon'.

After this point he chose to ignore me, but then every time a new song came on this conversation would be repeated. It was good fun though and thankfully stopped me dancing, if only for a short time.

    The next morning, I was rudely awoken by some loud snoring. As I sat up in bed trying to take in my surroundings and compute my exact location, I realised the snoring was actually mine. By some sort of drunken miracle, it appeared that I had somehow managed to get back to my dorm room. God knows how. The stale beer and tequila flavour combination was sickening, so I got up to fetch a drink of water. Thankfully I still had all my clothes on, including my shoes, so I ventured down the stairs to claim my free breakfast bap. Emma came down moments later as we tried to recall the humorous events of the previous night. As we chatted, I looked over towards a sun-lounger and noticed DJ Reggie asleep and, against all odds, fully clothed.

'How are you feeling mate?' I said walking past, not sure if I would get a response.

'....who's....idea was tequila?' came a groan from beneath the sun hat covering his face.

    I laughed and carried on up to the room to pack my stuff. I certainly hadn't got myself undressed, but for some reason I had pulled all my clothes out of my backpack in some mad act of random drunkenness, which was annoying. However, thirty minutes later, I was packed and ready to leave. Emma was ready too, so jolly and surprisingly hangover free, we walked into town for one last look around.

    It was a wonderfully hot day meaning the town was alive with activity. We bumped into Simon who, like us, was surprisingly sprightly after such a heavy night. He accompanied us as we explored *Condom Kingdom* and even purchased a mug with some obscene sexual innuendoes printed across it. With our energy drained from the lack of sleep and intense heat, we found ourselves a spot on the beach and relaxed for an hour or two.

The surf wasn't brilliant on this particular day so the sea was dominated by swimmers and water-sports enthusiasts. I looked around at the scene and was incredibly glad we had scheduled this stop. Although the town lacks any class and draws in some rather undesirable characters, the beach itself is gloriously beautiful and stretches endlessly in either direction. As a result, there is so much room you feel like you could be on a secluded beach in the middle of nowhere. But Australia has hundreds of these beaches and most of them *are* secluded and not thrown into darkness during the afternoon. I had a little chuckle to myself as I peered into the sky focusing on the monstrous hotels all contributing to their own downfall. It had been a great night out, but after twenty-four hours I was ready to leave, happy in the knowledge that my one night stand with Surfers Paradise was complete.

CHAPTER 25

An hour and a half down the coast and we were greeted with the normal array of hostel representatives trying to trick us into their individual minibuses. As Byron Bay was such a popular destination, they tried all sorts of new tricks such as free drinks, breakfast and internet. Not to be fooled however, I led Emma over to the rep offering the cheapest accommodation and happily jumped into his bus. Like most of these reps, he was a fellow British backpacker just trying to pay his way along the coast, so I was happy to oblige. Ten minutes later however, having driven quite a distance out of the town, I was beginning to regret my decision immensely. Turning to Emma for some support, she merely looked back as if to say 'well, you can pay for the taxi'.

The Rainforest Hostel was well worth it though. Clean, fresh and literally built amongst tropical plants, it was a pleasant break from the disease infested accommodation of Surfers Paradise. Marching across the raised walkways amongst the oversized leaves and flowers, we were shown to our six bed dorm and pleasantly surprised that we were sharing with four Irish 'lasses' we had met on the bar crawl in Surfers. However, just like us, their hangovers were just about kicking in so the conversation was extremely limited as we all lay on our beds wondering why the hell alcohol comes with such harsh repercussions. As had become customary since my near death experience in Sydney where I had rolled off the top-bunk, I lay on the bottom bed and lapped up the comfort given by a mattress more than a centimetre thick. Then, before I knew it, I had slipped into a deep sleep.

I woke suddenly not knowing how much time had passed. The noise of the crickets and exotic birds outside was overwhelming and I suppose that's what had sparked my attention. Daylight was fading quickly, but I was still keen to have a little explore of the town and beach. Grabbing a pair of shorts, I sneaked to the door and eased it open slowly, hoping not to wake the others. However, it was all in vain as when the cold air hit me, I let out a loud scream of shock. The drop in temperature had been inevitable, but the degree of change was somewhat larger than I had expected. Only a week ago I could have been strolling around Brisbane in just a loin cloth – now I found myself reaching to the bottom of my bag for jeans and a woolly hat. My girlish shriek had disturbed Emma so, determined not to waste the remainder of the day, she grabbed a scarf and joined me for a walk. She too was shocked by how cold the evening was
'Never let an Aussie tell you how hot their country is ever again!' she said wrapped up in a scarf.
'I know - I've got goose pimples all over me. I'm beginning to think we're travelling in the wrong direction Ems' I replied 'if only we were travelling north the weather would be getting warmer and warmer'.

Looking at my map, I happened to notice that there was a little detour we could take through an area of park to a beach.
'Okay Johnny, but are you absolutely sure this is the turning?' Emma said responding tentatively to my suggestion.
'Seriously, look at the map - it's just a short walk down this path' I said.
'I don't exactly trust you with directions, but I suppose a walk will do us some good anyway'.
Although my directions weren't wrong this time, the scale on the map must've got slightly blurred because after thirty minutes of walking, the beach was still nowhere to be seen. Surrounded by overgrown vegetation, the night was drawing in quickly making the area rather spooky.
'I'm not going to accept defeat Emma – I know the beach is down here. I haven't gone the wrong way. But….'.

'But what?'.

'It is getting rather dark, we're in the middle of nowhere and it's freezing cold. Shall we give up on this adventure?'.

'Good idea' she said smugly.

'But before we do, let's just confirm that the beach *is* this way and the reason we're giving up is because we're scared and *not* because I got us lost, agreed?'.

'So you'd rather be known as a scaredy-cat?'.

'Yes, yes I would'.

For the rest of the journey, convinced we were on the verge of becoming the next victims of a gruesome backpacker murder, we used the only defence we could think of and sang. To be honest, I thought my rendition of *Bryan Adam's 'Summer of 69'* was rather impressive but Emma's expression suggested otherwise.

When we eventually arrived, the town was submerged in the full darkness of night. Based around a long main street, it had quite a linear feel to it with loads of bars, restaurants and shops. So many people we had spoken to along the way described the 'spirit' of Byron as if it were some sort of mythical, care-free dream world where everyone lived in peace. The image that had been painted for me was one of 'Hippy Heaven' where everyone drove battered VW Beetles with flowers painted on the side, never got a haircut and smoked so much marijuana they turned themselves schizophrenic and believed that their pitiful life was somehow saving the world. But, as we walked down the main street, I felt none of that. The place was more like a ghost town where no one dared venture outside after dark for fear of the ghostly souls inhabiting the settlement. Perhaps they had smoked so much pot they *had* been turned insane and this idea wasn't too far from the truth.

Failing to find any shops open and disappointed by our failed attempt to reach the beach earlier, we decided to follow the flashing lighthouse and head for the promenade. It wasn't so much that we wanted to find a patch of sand, it was more in a desperate attempt to discover a bit of life and perhaps another human or two. Disciplined as ever and with the lighthouse as our guide, we made our way along various residential streets for several minutes in pursuit. The problem was that the light didn't appear to be getting any closer at all. I suppose a flashing light in the dead of night does not give a very good indication of distance. This was a lesson we were learning quickly.

However, determined to complete our journey we finally turned onto the street running parallel to the shore line. And then I saw a fire. It was about a hundred metres ahead I estimated – situated on a cliff just overlooking the beach. I could hear the crashing waves from here. Approaching through the darkness like a lion hunting its prey, Emma and I edged towards the fire eager to see what was happening. As we did, I suddenly heard laughter and then, to my utter amazement and sheer delight, there was the plucking of guitar strings. We were so close now that the fire illuminated their faces and revealed a large amount of dreadlocked hair. To my disappointment, there didn't appear to be an old VW van, but their long flowing clothes certainly suggested there was an element of hippy in them. I couldn't quite hear what they were discussing, but it seemed to be quite engaging and philosophical. The guitarist then began playing a new tune – I didn't know what it was, but the others certainly did and all joined in unison. Thinking back to my time on Fraser Island and The Whitsundays I actually felt quite envious of them. However, this was overcome by a great sense of satisfaction - not only had we found other people in Byron Bay, we had found its spirit too.

The next day I strolled around the town like a satisfied man. You see, Byron had nothing left to prove to me – I could now simply enjoy it for what it had to offer. It was like I had finally met Father Christmas, Jesus Christ or Frodo Baggins – these things were no longer distant, mythical legends to me – they were the truth. I had experienced them first hand. So often on this trip the stories of passing travellers had built up expectations to an unachievable level. But, by seeing those hippies, Byron Bay had delivered perfectly and I could happily pass on the knowledge to my fellow man.

So, without a care in the world or a judgemental bone in my body, I set off towards the beach. Emma had been shopping for kangaroo scrotum purses and I had agreed to meet her for some lunch and a swim. With the sun out, the weather was back to its incredibly warm self which put me in an even better mood. After all, I hadn't travelled to the other side of the world to suffer rain, wind and snow now had I? Following the crowds and with the assistance of daylight, I soon discovered that the beach was far closer than the detour I had taken us on the previous night suggested. My only hope was that Emma, having completed her shopping, would not notice and instead follow those tracks, thus saving my manly pride.

The beach yet again was an absolutely amazing sight. If this had been England, I imagine people would flock for miles around to see it. But this was a common scene in Australia and one I wished I could experience on a much more permanent scale. If you lived there, would you take it for granted and soon be blinded to the unique beauty in front of your eyes? I'm not sure, but if the Australian's I had met testaments were representative of the nation, I think they really do appreciate the gifted landscape they possess.

I had initially found us a picnic spot on the grass before the beach, but having been attacked yet again by those incredibly persistent and giant Australian ants, I had moved down onto the beach itself. I lay on my towel, looked up into the clear blue sky and reflected on the past few months. This was Emma's last full day in Australia but it was the first time this realisation had hit me. The journey was nearly at a close. We hadn't known each other beforehand and were forced together through chance. Thankfully though, we had developed a wonderful friendship not to mention a unique sense of humour. It always seems strange to me how circumstances beyond our control often bring two people together – I mean, why us two? Out of all the people in the world, why did our lives end up crossing? It is a mystery, far greater than the appeal of *Busted*. We weren't a couple, we were just great friends and I couldn't think of anyone I would have rather shared the adventure with. It suddenly occurred to me that in fact, the development of this friendship and the relationships with fellow travellers *was* the adventure. The whole travelling experience is not about seeing new places at all – these merely provide a stage or scene – it is to interact and develop friendships with people you normally would not. By taking yourself away from your comfort zone and steady life, you are suddenly forced into a position where you must socialise with many different characters in order to gain a little human interaction and acceptance. The discovery is not about going to new places - it is about experiencing a little piece of culture you were once ignorant about and embracing it. But better still, I had come to Australia alone, developed a lifelong friendship and we had embraced it together.

'I got you some noodles, do you like chou mien?' a voice came from behind me. It was Emma, walking across the beach with two steaming take-away pots.
'No. You're the worst friend ever, go get me something decent' I said with a smile before grabbing the noodles from her hand and tucking in.
'Hungry are we?' she said watching me stuff my greedy little mouth.
'Can't talk. Eating' I replied.

When we finished, we played around on the beach a little and topped up our tans. I got Emma to take a photo of the tan lines around my waist and ankles for all my friends to see. After her departure, I was planning on travelling into The Blue Mountains for a few days before catching my flight home a week later and was sure that in those seven days my body would quickly get back to its normal, dazzling white colour. We then sat and merely contemplated life, sharing un-awkward silences as only good friends can. The birds were singing quite loud in the trees now as the sun began its descent towards the ocean below.
'So, Ems, what's been your favourite part of the trip so far?' I asked.
'Oh Johnny, there's just been too many to pick out one, although Fraser Island and The Whitsundays were both crackers. Of course, making our friends list was quite good fun as well'.
It was true, ever since Cairns we had kept a list of all our friends – it was quite an honour to be added and people often ended up fighting merely for the privilege.
'I know, it's difficult to sum it all up' I said, trying to think of the right words 'shall we write a poem to commemorate it?'.
'Ha-ha, why not? Why not indeed?!'
So that is how Emma and I came to write our travel poem on the beach at Byron Bay. It's called 'Following the Sun':

We came all the way from England,
It was a long, long flight,
But the land Down Under,
Was such a great sight.

We saw The Harbour Bridge,
And The Opera House too,

*But something was missing,
There was no Kangaroo.*

*That night, we went to Scruffy's,
And drank a little beer,
But there was still no kangaroo,
And we felt a little queer.*

*On the train to Melbourne we saw one,
Our hearts started thumping,
Oh no wait a minute,
It's just a cow jumping.*

*So, we arrived at camp,
And helped children aspire,
To the dreams that they wanted,
And really desire.*

*And this is where,
Our story begins,
Our tales of travels,
And naughty little sins.*

*We're cool and fun,
And good looking as well,
We're Johnny and Emma,
You'll love us, we're swell!*

*So we left our friends,
For some fun in the sun,
We took a flight to Cairns,
But the rain made us run.*

*And so we embarked,
On our journey down the coast,
Our epic adventure,*

Although we don't like to boast.

Dicing with death,
We leapt out of a plane,
Rafted down rivers,
We must be insane.

We travelled together,
To every little bay,
We made twenty-five friends,
Along the way.

Our sense of direction
Is bad, it's true,
But we didn't have a map,
Or even a clue.

However, where we want to go,
We always arrive,
We have a sense of adventure,
And a will to survive.

We've seen beaches a plenty,
High rise buildings and shops,
We toured the 4 X brewery,
And smelt the fresh hops.

So here we sit in Byron,
Where the birds are humming,
It's been thirty-one days,
But the jokes keep on coming.

And there you have it,
The end of our tour,
There's been so many laughs,
But it's left us quite poor.

However, hear a final word,
About our day in the Zoo,
We didn't see Steve Irwin,
But there's the damn kangaroo!

We then wrote a series of stupid letters just for a laugh. For example, we wrote to *Nestle* and asked 'just how does the chocolate on Maltesers solidify in a perfectly round shape? Does it dry floating in mid-air Mr Nestle?' It's a valid point but we never did get an answer leaving my life feeling strangely empty still to this day.

Walking back along the sandy shoreline, we bumped into Ellen and Fergus - our friends from Magnetic Island. It had been a long time since we had seen them last so we stopped for a conversation. It is funny how the travelling situation kind of forces friendships to be developed at a far quicker pace than they normally would. We had only really spoken to these two for a few hours, but here we were gossiping away like life-time friends. I think it is perhaps a direct consequence representing the lack of familiarity in ones life at the time, so when someone appears that you do recognise, the immediate reaction is to embrace the situation.

As it was Emma's final evening in Australia, I thought I should send her off in true style so, on Fergus' advice I made my way to a nice butchers and spent a fortune on barbeque delights. The meal could not however be that simple. As if to bring us back down to Earth, the harsh realisation that we had no way of cooking the before mentioned food soon hit home. As a result, 'The Last Supper' proceeded to become a highly dangerous task involving us jumping over the fence into the caravan park next door to our hostel. Taking with us utensils we had stolen (on a temporary basis) from the kitchen, we jumped through a bush, over a fence and finally into the park where we proceeded to pay for the use of their gas barbeque facilities. So, not quite as dangerous as I had originally envisaged, but it still felt like another little adventure.

The food was superb, even if I do say so myself, and to cap it all off we made our way into town for a drink at the infamous *'Cheeky Monkeys'*. Run by the same people as *'The Woolshed'* in Cairns, *Cheeky Monkeys* had a legendary reputation amongst travellers as the scene of some of the wildest nights out on the east coast - *'it is to Byron Bay what Surfers Paradise is to Australia'* someone had once said trying to describe it to me. I think they were right. In the middle of a generally subdued, fresh and clean town stood a bar where all notions of self dignity were left at the door. I have to admit, I was rather looking forward to it, not because I had been promised it was 'wet t-shirt' night, but because it was like finally meeting a famous person. Surfers Paradise aside, these two bars were the most talked about party-places along the east coast, with the huge distance in between forming a superb pilgrimage for their fanatical supporters to follow.

The previous night there hadn't appeared to be much going on, but entering the town on this occasion we could already hear the cheesy music drawing us in like a fog-horn. At the door we stood aside and let two girls dressed in skimpy cowgirl suits squeeze past. From that moment, I knew this was going to be a good night out. Forcing our way into the crowded room, I pushed my way to the bar and ordered us a jug of *Tooheys* before retreating from the hoards and finding Emma at a table. The DJ was playing a series of classic cheesy tunes making this feel like a typical student night back in England. I think it was the *Baywatch* theme song that was playing when Emma grabbed my attention. Pulling me towards her she shouted in my ear: 'Oh my god, look who's up on the stage' she said pointing towards the stage just beyond the dance floor.

I couldn't really see much as there was such a huge crowd of people gathered, so I stood up and made my way forward. It was then that I saw Tim and Dave, our friends from Fraser Island, topless on the stage, swinging their shirts around their heads and trying to sing along to a song. As the crowd started giving quite a good clapping beat, I think Tim may have even tried a little break-dancing. I didn't know what was going on, but they both seemed incredibly smashed. I wanted to go and say hi, but since they were pulling in so much hysterical attention, I decided to wait and declare them my associates at a slightly more low key moment.

'What the hell's going on?' Emma shouted from my side. Due to her unfortunate capabilities in the height department, she couldn't see a thing over the crowd.

'They're absolutely smashed – off their faces, it's hilarious. Do you want me to put you on my shoulders so you can see?' I said. She responded with a punch to my arm which I had been anticipating and accepted honourably.

I then saw Tim running to the bar, order an entire four-pint jug for himself and then start making his way to the stage area. Walking over I tapped him on the shoulder. Well I've never seen anyone so happy in all my life. I felt like a celebrity as he grabbed Emma and me for an enormous hug, sending half the contents of the jug across my newly-cleaned shirt.

'What the hell's happened to you? You're absolutely smashed'.

'We won!' he shouted over the music. It didn't really answer my question though.

'Won what?' I enquired.

'Football competition earlier today. Dave, Ryan and me won it and got a free one hundred dollar bar tab. It's awesome. Here have some beer John'.

Well, I'm not one to turn down a free drink now, am I? So we danced the night away with the rest of the crew, but didn't drink too much as we had an early departure the next morning. It was fantastic and there was not a hint of violence. Everyone was just happy and concentrating on having a good time. There was no hostile behaviour – everyone just wanted to be everyone's friend and that will always be my memory of *Cheeky Monkeys*.

The next morning the bus picked us up from the town centre. Sitting at the bus stop we saw two incredibly drunk Englishmen stumbling down the street towards us. It was Tim and Dave still out from the night before, but I could see that it was no party anymore. In the hot morning sun, their hangovers had obviously begun to kick in. Eager to get back to bed, they said some swift goodbyes before continuing on their staggeringly indirect route.

The bus then arrived to pick us up for the last leg of our incredible journey. It was a long ride down the coast to Newcastle (which is where I was departing – Emma was staying on the bus to Sydney before catching her flight home). We didn't really say much to each other. I suppose there was just nothing left to say. Flying from England alone as a nineteen year old, I was disappointed none of my school friends had decided to come with me as I doubted I could ever develop a close bond in such limited time. But meeting Emma had been a pleasure and a blessing to my journey. Although we knew things would never be the same again, we just hoped we'd see each other once back home in England. As the bus pulled into Newcastle we shared a hug.

'Try not to get lost on your way to the airport, okay?' I said in a pathetic attempt to lighten the mood.

I looked up at the window with a lump in my throat as the bus left the station. Looking around, I realised I was all alone.

CHAPTER 26

It was probably because I was feeling depressed and lonely, but Newcastle really didn't appeal to me. I wasn't sure about the history of the place but suspected it was traditionally a ship-building town. With the industry now in sharp decline, it displayed the telling scars of a town suffering, following a sudden fall from glory.

As I walked through the centre, I noticed a scattering of tasteless, concrete buildings symbolizing a period on the architecture time-line where flare and inspiration were in a distinct short supply. As I came to a corner near the seafront, I was faced with an old, red-brick, Victorian factory. Most of the windows had been boarded up but those that hadn't were smashed anyway. In England, this would be a not too unfamiliar sight, but here in Australia it was. Suspecting my sudden isolation was having a negative effect on my outlook, I made my way down to the seafront for some cheering up. Here at least, the town had begun its recovery from the pits of depression by introducing some nice gardens, sculptures and walkways - the focal point of which is a giant lookout tower which the locals have named *'The Giant Penis'* - the resemblance was uncanny.

I had read in my guidebook that the town had quite a rich military history and was keen to sample the numerous free museums displaying relics from this time. However, they were all closed. As a traveller you tend to lose track of time and I had subsequently not realised it was a Sunday. Stuck with nothing to do and my budget growing worryingly small, I simply continued to walk and ended up back along the seafront where hundreds of youths were gathering. I wasn't sure what was going on but decided to take a seat and simply watch. The crowd soon got larger and my excitement grew. Then, as if from nowhere, loads of thuggish youths turned up in some over-elaborate, pimped up and essentially very cheap cars. The body kits were stunning and probably worth more than the cars themselves. More vehicles with blacked-out windows and pumping sound systems turned up before the road was completely jammed full of them. But they weren't doing anything - they were simply driving incredibly slowly in their manufactured traffic jam up to a roundabout, then turning round and coming back in a long drawn out procession. I felt like I was at a carnival for the working class. It had no appeal whatsoever. I spoke to the guy standing next to me about it.

'So, is this an organised event then?' I asked.

'No way man - everyone just turns up on a Sunday afternoon to show off their cars. It's awesome to watch'.

I didn't think it was very awesome - pointless would be the adjective I'd use. Newcastle really would have to create something very special to turn this around in my eyes. Suspecting it wouldn't, I booked myself on a bus for Sydney and left the next morning.

Throughout this trip I had spent quite a lot of time in Sydney but the sight of Circular Quay as we drove across The Harbour Bridge was still breathtaking. Since this was where I was flying out from, I suppose I saw it as home, providing me with a unique sense of familiarity in an otherwise unfamiliar land. It was a welcome relief from the waves of sadness I associated with Newcastle, lifting my spirits quite substantially.

Rejuvenated after a couple of days of glorious Sydney living (which involved hiking The Harbour Bridge just so I could say I had), I decided to spend my last night in The Blue Mountains. It wasn't a decision I had taken lightly – after all, the train ticket alone had reduced my final week's food budget to just $8. As if that wasn't bad enough, having used all this money to purchase one can of tuna and an enormous bag of economy penne pasta, I then ran into trouble attempting to open the incredibly stubborn packaging the pasta came imprisoned in. Standing in the middle of a dirty kitchen, I proceeded to get my teeth involved in the process. This was ultimately a mistake and one I realised almost instantly as the bag exploded in my face, sending its pasta contents sprawling across the dust covered floor. In one moment of unexplainable cooking naivety, all my food was gone. However, it's amazing what desperation will do to you – after all, is there anything less dignified than a grown man on his knees, desperately collecting pieces of economy pasta from underneath an unwashed, communal cooker? Probably not, and this was something I was very aware of as I crawled along the floor gathering my cobweb-covered food. The Blue Mountains were now under a lot of pressure to deliver a memorable experience.

    I was staying in a hostel called *The Fox and Duck* at the time of my departure. It was very friendly and had some stunning views from the rooftop garden across the city skyline. I had made quite a number of friends and took advantage by convincing them to buy all my old travelling gear such as a pair of portable speakers and a book of stamps. Thankfully, this extra cash came in handy and I was able to buy a can of budget tomato sauce for my tuna pasta. The word 'luxury' now had new meaning.

The first part of the journey went through typical Australian suburbia before a startling and somewhat sudden transition into bush land. Named after their appearance from a distance caused by the volatile oils within the eucalyptus trees, The Blue Mountains aren't actually mountains at all. From a modest view, they only really achieve heights slightly bigger than large hills. But the series of intricate jagged cliff faces, deep gorges and dense forest give them a much more sinister feel. Thought to be impenetrable by early settlers, they were forced to try and cross the mountain range due to the demands on space and resources caused by a rapidly growing population. This is surprising since during the early years there were approximately twenty men to every woman and the country was consequently riddled with homosexuality – a thought I kept in mind when being referred to as an 'English Poofter'. I can visualize the scene when a new ship of convicts was arriving at the docks - a mad dash would arise between the crazy frustrated men in a desperate search to find themselves a mating partner.

    However, after many years the population did begin to rise during the gold rush and as Australia's reputation increased, so did the amount of voluntary migration into the country. So the land and resources available could no longer support the ever growing amount of people. In 1813, there was a bad drought which damaged crops and killed many sheep and cattle, causing a food shortage. So, with no other choice, the settlers made a bold attempt to penetrate the infamous Blue Mountains. The credit goes to three explorers named Gregory Baxland, Lt. William Lawson and William Charles Wentworth who eventually achieved the impossible later that year. Learning from the mistakes of previous expeditions, the three men had the advantage of knowing which routes not to take. Nevertheless, their success was still a great achievement considering the vast numbers that had failed miserably before them. Their journey however, was not entirely straight forward as they suffered from terrible bowel problems whilst following a sharp ridge route. Eventually though, three weeks after their journey began, the group surmounted one final peak as the wonderful grazing land west of The Blue Mountains unfolded before their eyes. In stark contrast, the return journey took a mere five days and subsequently paved the way for the expansion of Australia.

It was early June by this stage and the air had a fresh crispness to it like an autumn morning back at home. I could feel my tan fading away and thanked God I had taken a photo of it for evidence. The hostel was lovely and had the appearance of a wooden mountain lodge. Situated along the main high street in the town of Katoomba, it seemed to double up as a family home giving it an incredibly warming atmosphere. The dorms and lounge were downstairs in what appeared to be a basement, but because it was built on a hill, this was merely a lower floor. The rooms were clean and the lounge was cosy, especially after I got the large fire blazing. It wasn't busy at all, in fact I appeared to be the only guest on this first morning. Not sure if this was a good or bad sign, I decided to forget about it and made myself right at home by putting my weary feet up on the sofa. Enjoying the beautiful warmth of the fire, it felt like a pre-Christmas Sunday afternoon. But that didn't last long. Suddenly aware that my time in Australia was nearly at an end, I jumped from the sofa, threw on my walking boots and went out seeking one last adventure.

Having asked at the front desk, I was assured that the famous 'Three Sisters' rock structure at Echo Point was a highly achievable five minute walk. 'An asthmatic, one-legged granma could make it' I was assured. Twenty minutes later, I found myself still walking up and down numerous town streets, searching for a sign post, or at least a hopping, breathless ninety year old woman to follow. Convinced my sense of direction had deserted me again, I was on the verge of turning round when I suddenly caught a glimpse of a tour coach in the distance. Following its every move I descended down one final hill before finally spying the visitor centre on my right. I was quite excited and hardly noticed the sound of screeching tyres behind me. I certainly heard the sound created as a ford falcon took off over the brow of a hill and landed at 70mph though. Spinning around quickly, I suddenly saw the car swerve uncontrollably onto the other side of the road. Trying to correct the turn with no decrease in speed, the driver overcompensated as the car veered straight towards me. In disbelief, I think I must have stood and watched the scene unfold for a split second before I realised there were two tonnes of metal hurtling in my direction. There was no white light, nor did my life flash before my eyes as I'd been promised. I was quite thankful actually because without any of these inconvenient distractions, I mustered up a sudden burst of adrenalin and dived into a nearby bush in dramatic James Bond style. Then I heard the smash. Suddenly very aware of the seriousness of the whole situation, I leapt to my feet and ran to the car that had smashed into a lamp post just in front of the place I had been standing only seconds before. Smoke was bellowing out of engine, the front bumper was lying on the road and was only attached to the vehicle by one solitary screw and one of the front tyres had completely left its rim. Grabbing the passenger door to try and help the victims out, I was in disbelief when I saw the driver trying to start the engine up. Somehow it started and before I could say anything he threw the car into reverse (nearly running over my foot in the process) and sped off down the hill with a line of metallic sparks from the wheel tracing his path into the distance.

    My heart was thumping hard, but I did have enough time to mark down the registration plate before I heard the sirens. The police whizzed past about five seconds later, following the fire path left by the joy-rider. I didn't think it'd be long before they caught up with him. Granted this was not a 'classic' near death experience, but it was certainly the closest I'd been in a long time. I was just thankful I had studied so many action movies throughout the years, completely unaware that I was absorbing essential information that would someday save my life. To me, Roger Moore now holds a Divine position in my life - all hail Roger Moore, for he is my saviour! A moment or two later, the sirens faded into insignificance and I continued on my walk strangely impressed by the exhilarating thrill one could experience during a walk in Katoomba.

The Three Sisters are a series of sandstone stacks parading from Echo Point into a spectacular valley. Surging from the cliff beneath my feet, the dense forest spread towards the horizon and smothered the distant hill tops. Only the occasional sandstone ridge could be seen with its light colour contrasting dramatically against the surrounding dark green sea. Looking at the mountains now, I could tell why early explorers thought them to be impenetrable.

Along with the elegance of The Three Sisters, it is the sheer magnificence of this setting that makes this such a tourist hotspot. Surviving thousands of years of erosion, these simple stone structures were representing all the changes that had occurred across the planet. Battling against the elements, many had fallen, but these three still stood isolated in the valley and separated from any human interaction with their huge stature promoting a unique sense of permanence.

Their name originates from an interesting Aboriginal legend. According to the fable, the three sisters 'Meehni', 'Wimlah' and 'Gunnedoo' were originally part of the Katoomba tribe living in the Jamison valley. Falling in love with three brothers from the neighbouring Nepean tribe, they were devastated to discover they could not marry them due to tribal law. Unwilling to accept this decision, the three brothers took the law into their own hands by raiding the tribe by force and taking their three-loved ones. As is so often the case in these stories, this apparently launched a massive tribal war throughout The Blue Mountains. In order to protect the sisters from any harm, the tribe's witchdoctor decided to turn them into stone (as you do) for the duration of the battle. If you ask me, I think this was probably the first mistake and if I were one of the sisters, I'd have begun asking questions:
'So I have this idea – in order to keep you from any harm, I'll turn you all into stone. Good hey? Yeah I know I'm a genius' the witchdoctor would say. 'Ummm sorry, did I hear you correctly? You're going to turn us into stone? Look I'm no witchdoctor mate, but I'm sure there's a much better idea out there – perhaps something that doesn't involve us transforming into anything? Run away for example, that works for me. Maybe we could have another brainstorm session?'.

But anyway, apparently the girls quite foolishly agreed to this absurd plan and were subsequently transformed into these giant rock structures. In an unfortunate turn of events, the witchdoctor was then killed during the war, and having failed to pass on the antidote to anyone, the girls were frozen as rocks forever. On a more positive note, they make quite a nice tourist attraction so their death wasn't completely in vain. And maybe someone will find the antidote one day.

Having consulted the map, I decided to hike along The Prince Henry cliff top towards Leura Cascades. Scattered along the way were a series of intricate look-out-points with majestic views across the breathtaking valley. In order to experience the full beauty of the scenery, many of these viewing platforms had been designed to stick right out over the cliff front. The illusion it created was marvellous, if not a little disconcerting, although I did start to feel vertigo setting in on a number of occasions. Apart from that, I couldn't really fault this part of the walk which was a relatively easy- going path integrated with some stunning sights. The sign posts were slightly confusing however, and on a number of occasions I felt like I was going backwards as the distance to Leura appeared to be increasing. I'm not sure if that was a test to check your will power and desire to succeed, but contrary to what the signs had been telling me, I continued following my map and arrived at Leura in rather good time.

As I had expected, there wasn't much there apart from some more great photo opportunities, however that's all I really wanted. This was my last full day in this wonderful land and I was determined to relax and take in all the diverse nature it was offering. So, map in hand, I just continued on my hike, studying the different types of eucalyptus trees lining my path. On the next plateaux I ended up at Bridal Veil View before stumbling across the Federal Pass and descending that to the base of the valley. Peering between the trees, I studied the spectacular landscape hoping to get a glimpse of the blue haze responsible for the name. I couldn't see it at all. Arriving at the bottom of the cliff, I looked back up at the sheer height of it and suddenly realised that I would have to climb back up at some point. It was a depressing thought to say the least.

Not to be put off, I continued along my trek in the wilderness. I was surprised by the lack of people, and combined with the lack of mobile phone coverage and hundreds of deadly creatures lurking in the bushes surrounding me, it made me slightly apprehensive. I could see a *'999'* disaster story developing quite quickly in my head. *'Man Has Left Leg Eaten by Snake – Then Eats His Right Just to Stay Alive'* the headline would read. Granted it's not that catchy, but it gets the point across.

Anyway, an hour or so later I arrived back at the foot of The Three Sisters and tried to find a point where I could ascend back to the real world. I saw on my map there was a 'Giant Staircase' located just to the right of them - however upon arrival it was closed due to a landslide. To be honest, I was quite relieved as the word 'giant' had put me off quite a bit. Night was drawing in quite quickly now causing the temperature to drop rather alarmingly, so I picked up the pace and searched for another way up. A lift would have been nice, but all I found was another staircase which I quickly climbed (at first) before nearly suffering a heart attack half way up. Although many people claim they are merely 'The Blue Hills', when going up those steps, they bloody well felt like mountains.

By the time I reached the summit and escaped the cover of the rainforest, the sun was down and a full moon was just revealing itself across a dark navy sky. Following the road back to Echo Point I had a great sense of achievement – I had explored The Blue Mountains and not really got lost at all. Plus, I was still alive – which was nice if not slightly surprising.

Arriving at the visitor centre, most people had gone but there was still a few keen photographers scattered throughout the area. Walking back to the viewing platform, I collapsed on a bench through exhaustion and listened to the variety of noises coming from the valley below. Again, as had been the case on so many days, there was not a cloud in the perfect sky as the moon grew brighter and illuminated The Three Sisters in front of my eyes. I thought of the thousands of people who had come through time to stand at this point and the thousands of tribesman who had worshipped it before that. All it literally represented was a simple case of erosion over time, but because of its Divine appeal, it holds a place in this country's unique history. I was eternally grateful that I could sit here now and experience it in all its glory. Behind me, a shutter clicked on a photographer's camera, capturing this moment in time forever.

CHAPTER 27

Sitting at Echo Point the previous evening had provided me with one final piece of satisfaction for my trip. Within myself I now felt I had achieved everything I had set out to do. It was time to go home. I found it slightly ironic that one of the great discoveries I had made whilst travelling was how much I really appreciated home. I just hoped it would be the same as in my memories.

That night I carried out the same walk I had made on that first evening to say my goodbye to Sydney. I leave you with my final journal entry:

"I sit here now with the sun setting one last time on this great journey. And I am at the place where it all began - Circular Quay. I owe a lot to The Opera House and Harbour Bridge as they have provided me with a warm sense of familiarity in this somewhat unknown land. Whenever I have felt lonely or down, this view has always restored the dreams of this Australian adventure and for that I am eternally grateful. Perhaps without this, I may have failed on this quest and never touched on the fantastic experiences I feel so lucky to have had. I feel privileged to have done the things I have done, seen the things I have seen and most of all, met the people I have met. Has it changed me as a person? There is no doubt in my mind that this journey has defined who I am and ultimately altered my perception of life. As an old man, I will look back at this adventure as the moment where I left all regrets behind, distant hopes became fantastic opportunities and ambition finally prevailed. I shall live the dream."